Mental Health in the Digital Age

Sheri Bauman • Ian Rivers

Mental Health in the Digital Age

2nd ed. 2023

Sheri Bauman
College of Education
University of Arizona
Tucson, AZ, USA

Ian Rivers
Faculty of Humanities & Social Sciences
University of Strathclyde
Glasgow, UK

ISBN 978-3-031-32121-4 ISBN 978-3-031-32122-1 (eBook)
https://doi.org/10.1007/978-3-031-32122-1

© The Editor(s) (if applicable) and The Author(s) 2015, 2023
This work is subject to copyright. All rights are solely and exclusively licensed by the Publisher, whether the whole or part of the material is concerned, specifically the rights of translation, reprinting, reuse of illustrations, recitation, broadcasting, reproduction on microfilms or in any other physical way, and transmission or information storage and retrieval, electronic adaptation, computer software, or by similar or dissimilar methodology now known or hereafter developed.
The use of general descriptive names, registered names, trademarks, service marks, etc. in this publication does not imply, even in the absence of a specific statement, that such names are exempt from the relevant protective laws and regulations and therefore free for general use.
The publisher, the authors, and the editors are safe to assume that the advice and information in this book are believed to be true and accurate at the date of publication. Neither the publisher nor the authors or the editors give a warranty, expressed or implied, with respect to the material contained herein or for any errors or omissions that may have been made. The publisher remains neutral with regard to jurisdictional claims in published maps and institutional affiliations.

This Palgrave Macmillan imprint is published by the registered company Springer Nature Switzerland AG.
The registered company address is: Gewerbestrasse 11, 6330 Cham, Switzerland

SB: To my loving, patient, supportive husband Bob
IR: To Max, Millie, Rob, Jack, and Jill

Contents

1	**Introduction**	1
	References	5
2	**Mental Health Online: Fact or Fiction?**	7
	Introduction	7
	Online Mental Health Resources	8
	Internet Use by Persons with Mental Health Diagnoses	9
	Types of Mental Health Resources	10
	Websites	10
	YouTube	13
	Podcasts	14
	Apps	16
	Social Media/Networks	18
	Summary	23
	References	23
3	**Mental Health Treatment Online**	27
	Tele-Mental Health: Pre- and Post-COVID	30
	Cognitive Behavioral Therapy (CBT)	33
	Tele-Mental Health with Children and Adolescents with Mental Health Conditions	34

vii

viii Contents

Self-Diagnosis Online	36
Internet Support Groups: Helpful or Toxic?	38
Toxic Groups	47
Therapeutic Relationships in the Digital Age	50
Summary	53
References	54

4 Social Media and Forms of Connectedness 59

Introduction	59
Being Connected	61
Fakers and Social Media	62
The Kindness of Strangers	66
Risky Behavior	69
Being Connected: Special Populations	71
Homeless Youth	73
Youth with Disabilities	74
Elderly Citizens	75
COVID-19	76
Summary	78
References	79

5 Digital Aggression, Cyberbullying, and the Impact of COVID-19 85

Introduction	85
The Evolution of Digital Aggression	87
Online Risks	90
Content-Related Risks	90
Contact-Related Risks	91
Conduct-Related Risks	91
Digital Aggression and Cyberbullying Before COVID-19	92
Cyberbullying and the COVID-19 Pandemic	94
Sexual Orientation (GLBTQ+)	95
Workplace	96
Building Resilience in Young People	98
Active Mediation	98
Co-viewing	99

	Restriction	99
	Responsibility for Resilience	100
	Workforce Resilience Post-COVID-19	102
	Summary	103
	References	104
6	**Information Overload and Zoom Fatigue**	109
	Introduction: Sheri's Morning Routine	109
	Sources of Online News and Information	112
	Mental Health Implications	115
	Children	116
	Adolescents	116
	Adults	117
	Fake News	119
	Summary	123
	References	123
7	**Artificial Intelligence, Virtual Reality, and Online Games**	127
	Introduction	127
	Artificial Intelligence	128
	AI for Suicide Prevention	133
	Virtual Reality	135
	Gaming	137
	Serious Games	139
	Commercial Games	140
	Summary	142
	References	142
8	**"The Self" Online**	147
	Introduction	147
	The Online Self and COVID-19	148
	The Distributed "Self"	149
	The Enmeshed "Self"	152
	The "Self" and Health	153
	Gender Games	157

x   Contents

What Am I Doing Now? Blogging, Social Media, and
Well-Being   160
Summary   161
References   162

9   **Conclusion**   167
Introduction   167
Digital Technologies Post-COVID-19: Are We Flourishing
or Languishing?   168
The "Enmeshed" Self   170
Reality or Not? How Enmeshed Are We?   171
    Setting the Scene   172
    The Dilemma   172
Where Do We Go from Here?   174
Conclusion   175
References   176

References   177

Index   203

About the Authors

Sheri Bauman is professor emerita in the College of Education at the University of Arizona. Prior to earning her doctorate in 1999, she worked in public schools for 30 years, 18 of those as a school counselor. She is a licensed psychologist (retired). Bauman conducts research on bullying, cyberbullying, and peer victimization, and also studies teacher responses to bullying. She is a frequent presenter on these topics at local, state, national, and international conferences. She is the author or co-author of nine books, over 75 publications in peer-reviewed journals, numerous book chapters, three training DVDs, and many publications in popular media. She is currently working on an international project that is investigating whether a teacher's willingness to intervene and their likely responses to a bias-based bullying situation vary across different types of identity-based peer exclusion and teacher characteristics. She is also engaged in a funded research project that seeks to increase our understanding of how teachers affect students' victimization and defending behaviors via the classroom ecology.

Ian Rivers is Associate Principal and Executive Dean of the Faculty of Humanities and Social Sciences at the University of Strathclyde, Glasgow. For 30 years he has been an active researcher in the field of developmental psychology, specializing in the study of bullying behavior. He is the author of *Homophobic Bullying: Research and Theoretical Perspectives*, and co-editor of *Young People Shaping Democratic Politics: Interrogating Inclusion, Mobilising Democracy* (Palgrave Macmillan). Ian is a fellow of the American Psychological Association, the Academy of Social Sciences, the British Psychological Society, and the Royal Society of Edinburgh.

List of Figures

Fig. 6.1	Proportion of US adults using various digital news sources	112
Fig. 6.2	Methods of news consumption by country	113
Fig. 6.3	Popular social networks accessed for news	113
Fig. 6.4	Zoom fatigue	120

1

Introduction

In this book, we define mental health as more than the absence of mental illness. There is a widespread focus on mental illness as a problem in individuals and society; this is a deficit perspective. Mental health is not merely the absence of mental illness but the presence of characteristics (symptoms) that reflect a positive state of being (the presence of life satisfaction, general well-being, resilience, positive relationships, and a sense of purpose). We argue that an equally, if not more, important goal of reducing mental illness is to enhance mental wellness in the population in the digital age.

Keyes (2007) argued that mental health is on a separate continuum from that of mental illness and called the two poles *languishing* and *flourishing*. That is, mental health is separate from, but correlated with, mental illness. Keyes provides definitions of mental health from the US Surgeon General: "A state of successful performance of mental function, resulting in productive activities, fulfilling relationships with people, and the ability to adapt to change and cope with adversity," and from the World Health Organization: "a state of well-being in which the individual realizes his or her own abilities, can cope with the normal stresses of life, can

© The Author(s), under exclusive license to Springer Nature Switzerland AG 2023
S. Bauman, I. Rivers, *Mental Health in the Digital Age*,
https://doi.org/10.1007/978-3-031-32122-1_1

work productively and fruitfully, and is able to make a contribution to his or her community" (Keyes, 2007, pp. 97–98). There are several models of the components (symptoms) of mental health: Keyes posits emotional well-being, psychological well-being, and social well-being, which together characterize mental health (Keyes, 2002). Just as there are measures of various mental illnesses, there is also a Mental Health Continuum Short Form (derived from the long form) that assesses the three domains of mental health and provides a guide to interpreting scores that indicate languishing, moderate, and flourishing mental health (Lamers, 2012). This scale was used in a study in Italy of health workers during the pandemic (Bassi et al., 2021). On the mental health measures, 33.4% were classified as flourishing, 57.7 % as moderate, and 8.9% as languishing. Flourishing participants were 3.85 times less likely to qualify for a provisional PTSD diagnosis while languishing participants were 3.0 more likely to qualify. That is, flourishing mental health was protective for PTSD while languishing mental health was a risk factor.

The COVID-19 pandemic, and the resulting restrictions and changes it made to our lives, have contributed to an increase in the need for mental health support around the globe. Some situations, such as working remotely, had positive psychological impacts on some but negative effects on others—especially those who lived alone.

In this new edition, we provide background information and research evidence from the literature on the impact of COVID-19 and post-pandemic issues that are related to the topic of the book. We review data on the availability of digital devices and access to cyberspace to illustrate the global reach of online communication. We describe the digital divide: inequitable access to both devices and connectivity and relate this to mental health. We introduce both benefits (e.g., access to information, support services, treatment options, etc.) and pitfalls (e.g., widespread misinformation, cyberbullying, pernicious environments, etc.) that will be explored more extensively in the following chapters. We will also consider the status of mental health issues around the globe, focusing on common conditions and available treatments as foundational concepts.

In Chap. 2, we discuss mental health on the internet. The vast amount of internet content related to mental health provides individuals with a plethora of information on mental health topics. While the internet is an easy, anonymous, and free portal to gain knowledge, there are inherent dangers as well as benefits in seeking out knowledge on the internet. With a significant portion of the world's population having internet access, and rates increasing rapidly in developing countries, the potential for information transference and the promotion of mental health and well-being has yet to be fully embraced and understood. Here, we focus on several major themes: the quality of online information, the concern about self-diagnosis, and the evidence for the effectiveness of online support mechanisms (vs. professional treatment). The impact of social media, specifically on mental health, will be covered in a subsequent chapter. The ethical issues related to mental health resources online are raised.

Chapter 3 focuses on digital treatment options for mental health disorders. Recently, and in part a response to the COVID-19 restrictions to in-person meetings, access to telehealth has added options for consumers that were not previously available. We describe some of those and their benefits and challenges and the variety of formats for digital mental health services, review research on the effectiveness of virtual treatments, and discuss guidelines for providing services in this context. The practice of therapists using the internet to gather personal information about clients without their knowledge and the parallel process of clients finding personal information about therapists is reviewed. Finally, we summarize the ways in which mental health professionals utilize digital media to reach the public (e.g., blogs, websites, YouTube channels) and suggest ethical issues that arise in this context.

There is no doubt that social media are an integral and influential aspect of the digital age. The number of social networks rapidly proliferates and changes in response to user practices and interests. In Chap. 4, we review the research on social media's impact on mental health. We then discuss several specific sites (e.g., Instagram, TikTok, Snapchat, Telegram, Twitter, Facebook, WhatsApp) that attract large audiences and identify the affordances (features) of these sites in an attempt to understand the nuances of attraction to various platforms and how users engage with them. We consider how "friendships" or, at the very least, online social interactions that have personal meaning, actually existed long before the emergence of the social networking and social media applications or "apps" we use today. We describe some sites that are specific to countries to understand whether they are related to mental health in ways like the more global networks. We also discuss the practical benefits of social media for mental health professionals and the ethical concerns with the professional use of internet and social media.

Digital aggression and cyberbullying are associated with mental health outcomes and we explore this in Chap. 5. Whether it is called cyberbullying or more general digital aggression, this is a problem that affects users of all ages. We explore the ways in which digital aggression is perpetrated, its taxonomy, and implications for well-being. Post-COVID, we explore how internet connectivity was used and abused, and consider how we can better support those who are targets of digital aggression and cyberbullying—intentional and unintentional. Finally, we explore current recommendations for harm reduction among particular groups.

The information available online is astonishing, and in Chap. 6 we look at both the advantages and problems associated with the wealth of ubiquitous digital information available. Given the almost universal availability and portability of digital connection, often via smartphone, it is nearly impossible to avoid being bombarded with difficult content. In this chapter, we talk about the mental health implications of distressing news (pandemic deaths, wars, humanitarian crises, local tragedies, etc.), hate speech, political vitriol, and the challenges of preventing this type of content from affecting one's mental health. We will include a section on virtual meetings (e.g., Zoom, Microsoft Teams, Google Meet, etc.) and the ways they affect mental health. We suggest guidelines for managing the challenges inherent in these circumstances.

Artificial intelligence (AI), virtual reality, and online gaming are increasingly being utilized for mental health. In Chap. 7, we address the issues related to AI, online gaming, and virtual reality that are often overlooked in discussions of mental health and the digital age. There are several issues regarding mental health that will be explored: the potential for addiction, internet addiction's status as a mental health disorder, and the creative aspects of gaming (including designing avatars). We will elaborate on games with large followings and how users may engage with them and introduce the growing practice of providing treatment in a virtual reality space.

Chapter 8 examines the development of online identities. For some users, the internet provides an opportunity to establish identities (via careful curating of posts) which may or may not resemble their offline selves. The online self is also devoid of some of the insecurities and self-perceived imperfections that free them from fears of judgment. The online self finds expression on dating sites as well as social media. We review what is known about the impact of online dating sites and their associations with mental health. In this chapter, we consider how online identities that are open and visible to the world have the potential to create a vulnerability that manifests itself offline. Following COVID-19, we reflect upon the fact that our physical world has changed, as have our professional and social lives. Being online is commonplace. We are already redefining and refining our lives following a period of enforced isolation. We ask the question, "Can we still assume that our offline selves have more salience than our online selves?"

In Chap. 9, we reflect upon our observations regarding mental health in the digital age. We reflect upon the benefits (e.g., access to information, support services, treatment options, etc.) and pitfalls (e.g., widespread misinformation, cyberbullying, pernicious environments, etc.) that exist online, and consider how much more our lives have become intertwined with technology—especially after COVID-19. While we recognize that COVID has not disappeared although rates of infection and hospitalizations are much diminished), we hope that we can apply what we have learned from this collective trauma to help address all our mental health needs in the future.

References

Bassi, M., Negri, L., Delle Fave, A., & Accardi, R. (2021). The relationship between post-traumatic stress and positive mental health symptoms among health workers during COVID-19 pandemic in Lombardy, Italy. *Journal of Affective Disorders, 280*, 1–6. https://doi.org/10.1016/j.jad.2020.11.065

Keyes, C. L. M. (2002). The mental health continuum: From languishing to flourishing in life. *Journal of Health and Social Behavior, 43*(2), 207–222.

Keyes, C. L. M. (2007). Promoting and protecting mental health as flourishing: A complementary strategy for improving national mental health. *American Psychologist, 62*(2), 95–108. https://doi.org/10.1037/0003-066X.62.2.95

Lamers, S. M. A. (2012). *Positive mental health: Measurement, relevance and implications*. PhD thesis, University of Twente. https://doi.org/10.3990/1.9789036533706

2

Mental Health Online: Fact or Fiction?

Introduction

The digital universe is home to a vast trove of content about mental health and mental illness. A Google search on "mental health" in March 2023 found 3,860,000,000 hits in less than one second. While online mental health information extends and augments other sources of information, for many people it has become the sole source of material. That is easy to understand: online information is always available and includes copious amounts of data, which can be located easily, anonymously, and generally without cost. Access to the digital world has increased to the extent that most people in developed countries (and many in developing countries too) have either a personal device with internet connectivity (92% in the US, 97% in the UK) or free access via computers in public spaces such as a local library (Petrosyan, 2022a, b, 2023). A small study of UK adults (Stawarz et al., 2019) found that 78% of participants used smartphone apps to support their mental health, either alone or along with other technologies. It is important to remember that digital platforms are not regulated, unlike books or manuscripts in scholarly journals, which go through a rigorous review process. Social media content

© The Author(s), under exclusive license to Springer Nature Switzerland AG 2023
S. Bauman, I. Rivers, *Mental Health in the Digital Age*,
https://doi.org/10.1007/978-3-031-32122-1_2

also includes *misinformation*, which Shu et al. (2020) define as unintentional inaccurate information (i.e., an error) that is not intended to mislead the user, and this is distinguished from *disinformation*, which is deliberately false or misleading information intended to deceive the user. Thus, it is necessary for both mental health professionals and the public to scrutinize these tools carefully.

Online Mental Health Resources

Since the onset of the COVID-19 pandemic in 2020 and the attendant restrictions and stressors—digital offerings for mental health have become even more important. Many of the digital expansions and innovations that support mental health in response to the pandemic are likely to become permanent. Although their development may have been prompted by the pandemic, their availability has contributed to changes in the "attitudes, behavior, and skills" (International Telecommunications Union, 2022) of the public. Digital sources of information can have both positive effects and negative consequences; an understanding of how to recognize potentially harmful sources is a basic skill for using the internet. We discuss this issue later in the chapter.

Consistent with our perspective that mental health is more than simply the absence of mental illness, we discuss how digital tools can support well-being and resilience. As helpful as these tools are, however, access to them is far from universal. For those who rely on one device per household, as often is the case for low-income families, it may be difficult for an individual to spend enough time exploring and using these tools. Not only is access to a device needed but also reliable connectivity to the internet. Again, low-income and marginalized groups are more likely to lack dependable access. In addition, is important to look closely at the content; it may be that it is relevant only to the dominant group in society, ignoring important cultural differences (Gamble, 2022). People with disabilities may also be at a disadvantage; closed-captioning or voice-to-text may not be offered on all sites. Despite these limitations, we believe that being aware of digital wellness tools offers opportunities for growth and enhanced well-being.

Internet Use by Persons with Mental Health Diagnoses

Gowen (2013) conducted three focus groups with 27 participants to better understand how young adults (ages 18–20) diagnosed with a mental health condition used the internet to learn about their own disorders. Among the participants, 89% had looked up mental health information online, with 15% reporting they did so daily. Five major topics were the object of their internet searches: medications, diagnoses, treatment options, access to health care, and support and resources. Regarding medications, the most frequent topic of discussion, participants checked on medications that had been prescribed for them and sought additional information about potential medications for their conditions. Self-diagnosing and looking up symptoms of disorders with which they had been diagnosed was another area of interest. Other members were searching for information about treatment options and the variety of treatment approaches, while some accessed information about specific treatment facilities, insurance coverage, fees for services, etc. Finally, participants used the internet to locate ancillary services such as food assistance and other sources of needed services.

Participants in Gowen's (2013) study were also queried about the reasons for using the internet related to their mental health condition. Five themes were described: additional information, community, nowhere else to turn, preparing for a health visit, and anonymity. As noted above, many sought more specific and detailed information regarding their diagnoses. Others sought to locate others with similar disorders with whom to communicate to reduce their sense of isolation. Because the internet is always available, some participants used it at times when other sources of assistance were not available (weekends, holidays, or the middle of the night). When an appointment with a mental health provider had been scheduled, some of the participants in these groups indicated they would seek information about the clinician prior to the meeting. Finally, participants felt safer getting information online because they could be anonymous while doing so. Although these activities may not be treatment, they can augment or encourage treatment through information and community. Concerns about using the internet for mental health purposes were also raised in these focus groups and relate to concerns that are not confined to those with mental health diagnoses. Others in the groups were concerned about their ability to trust information from online sources.

Types of Mental Health Resources

There are several types and formats for mental health content: websites, blogs, podcasts, apps, text messages, and webinars. Although many such tools existed prior to the pandemic, the isolation and stress of that experience seem to have both increased usage of existing tools and inspired the creation of new and innovative approaches to supporting mental wellness. We describe these digital resources in general terms, and then provide some examples of well-respected and useful tools. Mental health professionals can find resources designed for their own growth; some may decide to produce podcasts or create websites to increase awareness of mental health. They also might want to be familiar with useful resources that they can then recommend to clients and/or use themselves.

Websites

Websites are excellent sources of information on attaining and maintaining mental health. Many sites have links to other platforms (YouTube, TED talks, positive psychology sites) and websites for and by professionals. Note that some websites that claim to be about mental health actually focus on mental illness. However, searching for "happiness" brings up numerous websites to explore. Verywellmind.com (https://www.verywellmind.com/what-is-happiness-4869755) has a section on Happiness that is quite useful and provides links to other media. The Positive Psychology (https://ppc.sas.upenn.edu/) site has opportunities for professionals to be educated in that field in addition to material for the general public. There is an option to complete various questionnaires that are interesting to do and at the same time contribute to their research

2 Mental Health Online: Fact or Fiction?

database. PsychCentral (https://psychcentral.com/) is well-known and respected site; although it has much information about specific disorders, it also has information that supports maintaining mental health. Readers can find recommendations and descriptions of useful sites at websites such as MyStory (https://yourstory.com/mystory/top-ten-best-mental-health-websites-2020/amp), although it is important to check for more current additions.

Websites for government agencies offer suggestions for improving mental health (e.g., https://medlineplus.gov/howtoimprovemental-health.html) that include links to other sites, with some that are available in Spanish as well as English. In the US, a useful wellness checklist is available from the National Institute of Health (www.nih.gov/wellness-toolkits). Other lists can be found, and most such sites include short descriptions and reviews of the programs they recommend (see *Best Mental Health Podcasts* at https://www.verywellmind.com/best-mental-health-podcasts-5097922). Remember that most websites in mental health have no evidence of effectiveness, so the user has no guarantees if they decide to engage. A few studies of effectiveness have been published, but given the number of sites available and the exploratory nature of the research, it is impossible to present empirical evidence that using the site will result in positive outcomes. One Australian study (Manicavasagar et al., 2014) examined the *Bite Back* website, designed as a positive psychology program for youth in a sample of 154 adolescents (aged 12–18). Quantitative findings demonstrated that compared to subjects in the control condition (neutral entertainment website), Bite Back users who used the website for at least 30 minutes per week (over six weeks) had significant decreases in depression and stress and improvements in well-being. The qualitative data showed that 79% of the experimental group had positive experiences and 89% reported they would continue using the site after the study concluded. While this is encouraging, much more research with larger and more representative samples is needed on this and other similar websites.

Morahan-Martin and Anderson (2000) have suggested guidelines for evaluating websites. A key criterion is whether the site is sponsored (supported financially). Those sites that are supported by profit-making entities should be closely examined to be sure they are not including information (or excluding information) intended to boost their profits. One clue is whether there are advertisements on the site; the owners of the site may include only information that encourages the use of their product or paid services. Glowing testimonials are likely to have been selected (or created) to promote something for sale. Knowing who has written the information on the site allows you to check their credentials to ensure they are qualified. To determine whether a site is biased, the author's information is helpful for evaluating how the author's experiences or affiliations may result in material that is not completely objective. For example, when research on the efficacy of a new drug is conducted and sponsored by the drug company that manufactures the drug, we are likely to be cautious and skeptical. In contrast, when the research has been done by independent researchers and funded by a source that does not stand to profit from the findings, our confidence is justifiably higher. Other important considerations: How comprehensive is the material? Does the site cover your particular interests, or will you have to seek multiple sources?

Additionally, a framework is recommended by Chan et al. (2015) with several criteria that are not mentioned above. They suggest that the security of the site should be ensured, especially when the user provides personal information (e.g., to take an online survey). Privacy is also essential; Chan et al. suggest checking the site's privacy policy, and to be cautious if that is not available. In addition, the site should be easy to use without special skills. Does the site include features to sustain attention and interest?

Finally, some sites are not accessible to persons with disabilities and may also present biases towards marginalized groups. These are important features that should cause a user to consider whether these omissions and/or microaggressions should disqualify the site for their use.

In the resources described next, the phenomenon of *influencers* is especially pertinent when we reflect on the ways in which these online celebrities affect mental health. See a detailed discussion of this topic in Chap. 4.

YouTube

The number of videos on YouTube, founded in 2005 and the second most popular website (after Google), is overwhelming, with at least 800 million videos available and 150,000 new videos added per minute (https://www.wyzowl.com/youtube-stats/). YouTube includes approximately 38 million channels (home pages for personal accounts) and attracts 122 million active users per day, all over the world. The most popular purpose for watching YouTube is entertainment. In addition to viewing videos on the YouTube site, videos can be shared and often appear on other social media platforms. Viewers can make comments and show whether they dislike or like the video (Foster, 2013) Some creators of YouTube videos solicit subscribers (people who get notified of new material); there is a formula that provides monetary rewards for those who have a large group of subscribers.

Foster (2013) investigated aspects of YouTube among members of the National Alliance for the Mental Ill (NAMI) who were YouTube viewers. Members of that organization are often mental health treatment providers, persons with mental disorders, or family members of those with such disorders. Several interesting findings emerged: the majority of their sample (67%) sought videos that informed or educated viewers on mental health topics; 16% searched for YouTube groups where they could meet others with similar interests. However, most mental health videos were created by for-profit groups, while only 5% were from academic institutions. In terms of speakers in the videos, only 36% had professional knowledge, while 34% presented personal narratives.

Some of these videos support positive mental health, but given the vast number of possibilities, finding the best search terms and being patient are necessary. Searching for terms such as "mental wellness" or "positive mental health" brings up some videos worth examining more closely. Often an expert on mental wellness who is known for best-selling books or television appearances will post videos that expand or reiterate the themes. Admirers of these experts can view their videos multiple times to reinforce the messages.

Podcasts

Podcasts have become increasingly popular since the inaugural podcast in 2004. One recent study reported that among 12–34-year-olds, 29% listened to podcasts; for participants aged 35–54, 40% reported listening (Best & Clark, 2020). Surveys were conducted in January 2020 and May–June 2020 when UK schools were closed and lockdowns imposed. These researchers found that, in their large samples of young people (ages 8–18), the age group with the most reported engagement with podcasts was the 16–18 group. Boys listened more than girls, and White Travellers of Irish heritage listened more than any other ethnic group, although the difference was not statistically significant. Best and Clark observed that young people are potential audiences for podcasts that could tap into youth interest in hearing from others that are both similar and different from themselves. One of the quotes from an anonymous respondent illustrates the overlap in the different resources: "I didn't listen to podcasts before but I have discovered that my favorite YouTubers have a podcast so I listen to them now."

Podcasts, downloadable audio files, are convenient, as one can listen while doing other things (walking, jogging, doing chores, commuting etc.) and many are free, although the listener usually has to subscribe to a podcast to download it. Many also are serial programs with new episodes available at regular intervals; they also vary by length of episode. Some are linked to other publications (e.g., journals, magazines). Casares and Binkley (2021) propose that podcasts serve a similar function to that of bibliotherapy, a technique that uses books as an adjunct to counseling or psychotherapy. One might view the popularity of self-help books in a similar way. One of the advantages of podcasts is that the listener does not need to be literate—think dyslexia or little education—to benefit from a podcast. Podcasts are available many languages, with some descriptions even indicating the accent used. Podcasts are also reminiscent of *cuentos* (1986) therapy, which uses folktales from the Latinx or other traditions to convey ideas and values. These are culturally sensitive, so might resonate with native speakers of the language.

2 Mental Health Online: Fact or Fiction?   15

The process of finding a podcast can be simplified by using sites that review a selection of programs. For example, choosingtherapy.com has a list of the 21 best mental health podcasts for 2022, with descriptions of each. Recommendations from organizations, mental health professionals, trusted friends, and family may also lead to a suitable podcast. Austria (2007) developed criteria for evaluating podcasts. Although we are not suggesting that readers conduct a rigorous evaluation process with every podcast of interest, it is informative to consider these standards. There are many lists of recommended podcasts, including some that are specific to minority listeners. Those that appear high on many lists might be worth exploring. The following are points to think about (adapted from p. 183 in Austria, 2007):

* Author: Is the author qualified on this topic? What are the author's credentials? Do those credentials qualify the person to be offering information on the current topic? When the author is someone whose work has been subjected to critical review by peers (searching on Google Scholar can ascertain whether that is the case), there is evidence of expertise. How extensive is the expertise? A scan of the titles of publications can provide that information. Does this mean that practitioners' and/or individuals' sites should be considered invalid? Not at all. It means that the author of the material should be vetted for relevant experience and unbiased presentation.
* Accuracy: Can information in the podcast be verified in other sources? Does the author or producer provide contact information?
* Audience: To whom is this podcast directed? Professionals, general public, students, etc.? Is it suited to your needs?
* Bias: Is the podcast sponsored by a group or organization with a special interest in recruiting customers? Does the program reflect inclusiveness and diversity?
* Currency: How recently was the podcast made/released? The more recent releases may have information lacking in older programs.
* Listening: Do the speakers speak clearly? If in a language other than English, is the accent or dialect one that you understand?
* Introduction: Does the podcast offer sufficient information at the beginning and/or in advertisements for you to know what it is about?

- Technical: Is the audio quality good overall? Are there problems downloading the podcast?

We offer our own additional suggestions:

- First, seekers of information must use the correct search terms. If they have specific questions, it is usually more fruitful to include the entire question rather than just a word or short phrase.
- Second, the searcher should peruse the links beyond the first page of "hits" as some of the sites with high traffic (which will therefore appear on the first page of search results) may be commercial ones rather than the most accurate. Sometimes the sites that appear first on search results have paid to ensure that spot or used other maximization strategies to elevate their placement in search results. The best sites may be found on later pages.

Apps

Smartphone apps are programs designed for use on digital devices, typically smartphones or tablets (Strauss et al., 2022). They are obtained through app store on iPhone products and Google Play for Android users. Many of the apps are free, but some have a one-time fee, and others require a subscription. Among other advantages, these apps extend mental health resources to populations with limited resources. Although many apps focus on assisting those with mental health concerns, others offer convenient ways to monitor symptoms and offer guides to meditation, mindfulness exercises, and strategies to manage stress.

Smartphone apps are so popular that it is difficult to keep track of new additions to the collection. There are many apps that support mental health and well-being (including many for mindfulness and well-being, coping with stress, etc.). An excellent list of mental health apps can be found at https://www.verywellmind.com/best-mental-health-apps-4692902. We provide the list here, with the caveat that the site should be checked for updates:

10 Best Mental Health Apps of 2023:

- **Best for Talk Therapy:** BetterHelp
- **Best for Depression:** Talkspace
- **Best for Mindfulness:** Headspace
- **Best for Stress Relief:** Sanvello
- **Best for Kids:** Breathe, Think, Do with Sesame
- **Best for Addiction:** I Am Sober
- **Best for CBT:** MoodKit
- **Best for Better Sleep:** Calm
- **Best for Positive Thinking:** Happify
- **Best for Anxiety:** Worry Watch

It is important to remember that these apps are not regulated, nor are most apps evaluated by any outside agency. Despite the proliferation of apps, there are only a few studies that have investigated the efficacy of these apps using empirical data. One such study conducted by Bakker and colleagues (Bakker et al., 2018) examined three apps designed to enhance mental health. The community sample was randomly assigned to use one of the three apps. Data were collected at the start of the study and 30 days later. They found that all three groups had increased well-being at post-test compared to wait-list control group and concluded that increase in self-efficacy for coping was the underlying mechanism for the improvement. Happify.com is another good example of an app designed to enhance well-being. A study investigated 4485 new users (86% female, aged 19–24) of Happify who were randomly assigned to use Happify or a psychoeducational platform over an eight-week period (Parks et al., 2018). The researchers considered whether users of Happify engaged with the app at the recommended rate or a lower rate. Overall, they concluded that Happify users demonstrated improved well-being, with the best outcomes found in users who accessed the app at the recommended rate (2–3 times/week). The homepage of *MoodMission* exhibits several empirical studies with favorable outcomes. *MoodKit* targets depression based on CBT principles, but also includes a variety of activities designed to improve mood and acquire skills to enhance wellness. *MoodPrism* is similar to the other but includes regular check-ins to track mood, with immediate feedback and colorful visuals.

As with any other type of digital platform, using the guidelines described above for other platforms will help the user make an informed decision about the suitability and utility of a given app.

Social Media/Networks

The terms *social media* and *social networks* are frequently confused; they refer to different kinds of digital communication. Social media represent one-way channels that provide information, whereas social networks are interactive, designed for two-way communication. In this section, we refer primarily to social networks but retain the authors' terminology.

There is an ever-increasing array of social networks designed for users to create and share text or images, comment on or re-post others' posts, communicate with others, create and join online communities, maintain relationships and make new connections. As of July 2022, estimates indicate that 4.7 billion people around the globe use social media, and that number increases daily. Moreover, many people have accounts on an average of 7.4 social networks, possibly inflating those figures. On the other hand, figures from social media companies do not count users under age 13, perhaps leading to underestimation (*Global Social Media Statistics*, 2022). The same source reports that Facebook is still the most used platform worldwide, followed by YouTube, WhatsApp, Instagram, WeChat, and TikTok. Connecting with friends and family is the primary reason people give for using social networks (based on users ages 16–64) (*Global Social Media Statistics*, 2022), with variations by age and gender. Note that some of these platforms require permission before a new "friend" or viewer can obtain access to one's posts. However, many social media platforms (e.g., Twitter, Instagram) do not require permission to follow someone; professionals must keep that in mind when they post on their own sites. They cannot control who views their material.

As mental health professionals realize the potential impact of social media, some have taken to creating content, both text and videos, to share information (Phillips, 2022). A perhaps surprising source of useful

2 Mental Health Online: Fact or Fiction?

information about mental health is social media. For example, a licensed mental health counselor first made YouTube videos she hoped would educate viewers about mental health but soon switched to TikTok because of the popularity of the platform. As of March 2022, videos found with the hashtag #mentalhealth had 29 billion views (Phillips, 2022). The counselor's initial attempts were humorous and musical, but she gained a much larger following when she posted a video introducing herself and describing her practice. Other therapists have posted on TikTok to dispel myths and misunderstandings about mental health. Other mental health professionals attempt to use this medium to support self-healing and growth, and to point viewers to additional resources.

Scholars and the public tend to focus on the negative impact of social media use for mental health, with an emphasis on children and adolescents (e.g., O'Keefe & Clarke-Pearson, 2011), but there are also positive opportunities and resources that social networks provide to enhance mental well-being. It is impossible to conclude that social networks are either beneficial or harmful; like other digital tools, it depends on the platform, the user, and the context. Nevertheless, mental health professionals need to be familiar with social networks to understand their clients' world, including their digital world; the public needs to know when social media are legitimate platforms for mental health information. They also must be deliberate in deciding which social networks to use, and what kind of content to post. In this section, we point out commonly mentioned concerns about social media, and then discuss the positive opportunities they offer.

Uhls et al. (2017) pointed out several developmental mechanisms for adolescents who interact with social networks: social comparison, self-disclosure, and impression management. Peer relationships at this stage are of primary importance and these researchers suggest that social networks are a useful tool for these tasks. They cite research that has found associations with time on social media and increased self-esteem, and users of social networks report feeling closer to friends. Because of the interactive nature of social networks, peer approval is magnified, which may enhance self-esteem. Uhls and colleagues conclude that social media offers a venue for youth to pursue their identity search while practicing skills that are valuable for their development.

Multiple research studies have found associations between social media use and mental health concerns such as anxiety, depression, suicidal thoughts, and behaviors (e.g., Bauman et al., 2013), but others do not find such relationships (Royal Society for Public Health & Young Health Movement, 2017). The varied research methods, sampling strategies, analytic approaches, and other factors make it difficult to compare across studies. Some research includes dosage effects (time on social media per day), while others consider the emotional intensity of involvement on social media. An example is a study of 1027 American adults by Bekalu et al. (2019), who argue that routine use of social media is associated with beneficial mental health outcomes, while *emotional* connection (checking apps constantly, feeling isolated when not on social media, intense fear of missing out) is negatively related to social well-being, positive mental health, and self-rated health. Furthermore, many of these studies are cross-sectional, making it impossible to make causal conclusions.

Although the practice has a negative influence on mental health, many youths (and adults) keep their smartphones close by when sleeping, which can interfere with restful sleep. Sleep deficits can contribute to both physical and mental health disturbances. Another commonly noted problem associated with social networks is distress about body image, which may lead to low self-esteem and increased likelihood of eating disorders. Social comparison with photos that are often curated and/or altered to present what appears to be a perfect image lead some viewers to feel they inferior (Uhls et al., 2017). Interestingly, there are sources of recommendations for helpful Instagram sites (and other platforms) that professionals should be familiar with, even if you would primarily be suggesting these to others. The website https://bedthreads.com/blogs/journal/best-mental-health-instagram-accounts-to-follow describes 19 Instagram accounts that may be worthwhile to look at and perhaps follow. The info on the link has a brief illustrated description of each of those accounts that gives enough information to decide if it is of interest. A list of mental health *influencers* on TikTok, along with excellent tips for evaluating a site can be found here: https://www.everydayhealth.com/emotional-health/under-pressure/the-top-mental-health-tiktok-influencers-and-why-theyre-important/. Their top recommendation is TikToks posted by Dr. Julie Smith, an English psychologist whose videos

2 Mental Health Online: Fact or Fiction?

provide encouraging suggestions for mental well-being. Readers should note that new influencers appear and recommendations might change; checking for updates is advised.

Risks for young people who use social networks include cyberbullying, symptoms of anxiety and depression, and exposure to content that is inappropriate or harmful. Furthermore, those who engage with these sites may not be aware of the kind of data (metadata) collected by site owners and advertisers, who use the information to insert various commercial promotions which detract from the social purpose of the sites (Uhls et al., 2017). There are also legitimate concerns about internet addiction that may include obsessive checking of social media along with absorption by online gaming.

Books and numerous articles have been written about cyberbullying, and the media have publicized some instances that led to tragic consequences. See Chap. 5 for detailed discussion of misuse of digital tools. While it is unlikely that cyberbullying can be eradicated, arming social network users with strategies to respond (or not) when that occurs might minimize the negative impact. For example, the "fear of missing out" (FOMO) which refers to the belief that if one does not constantly check social media, they will miss an event or discussion that will negatively impact their social status and relationships. A variation of this danger is that viewing posts and images of vacations, accomplishments, etc. may cause some users to feel their life is dull and boring by comparison.

The International Telecommunications Union report (International Telecommunications Union, 2022) noted that one of the advantages of social media is that health and mental health information is easily accessible, often at no cost. At the same time, the possibility of finding inaccurate or misleading information means that caution is needed. This organization notes that youth (and adults) may be subjected to offensive content, which can have a negative impact on mental health.

While counselors and psychologists can use social media to increase understanding of mental health, they also need to be aware of the dangers inherent in such platforms. Comments from viewers are a feature of most sites, which means that someone may choose to post derogatory or hateful material, which can be disturbing to read. They should also know that with a following on social media, as with podcasts, compiling many followers brings an expectation of regular posts. This may prove to be burdensome for the mental health professional; they need to consider their reasons for using social media and how much time they can devote to maintain interest and update content.

A study of mental health content on TikTok (Miodus & Jimenez, 2021) found that TikToks with the #mentalheath hashtag generally provide accurate content. For example, 56% of content about ADHD was found to be accurate with 8% inaccuracy; the remainder were personal experiences. A similar pattern was found for other disorders. However, only 2.4% of content was contributed by mental health professionals. Mattoon (2021) describes a faculty member at Johns Hopkins University who uses TikTok to post creative but accurate bits of information; she quickly accrued over a million followers! Dr. Shepard strives to demystify mental health and encourage those in distress to seek counseling; she is emphatic that she is not providing direct mental health service via Tik Tok. Dr. Shepard, a psychiatrist, recognizes that there are going to be negative comments to her videos, but has compassion for the trolls, and is a member of a network of other medical professionals who use the site. The concern is that such content could appear to be a marketing tool; clinicians need to be very clear about the purpose of the content they post and the possibility of offensive comments.

TikTok recently announced new features that purport to protect the well-being of users. For example, the site has updated their mechanism for alerting the user that a video contains sensitive content. However, it does not restrict individuals with mental health challenges from posting about their own journey, arguing that personal stories inspire others. TikTok also has developed new guides to well-being, developed in concert with several well-respected organizations. In theory, a feature in the TikTok algorithm searches for terms related to eating disorders or suicide and automatically makes a referral to local resources and such services as Crisis Text line. In Europe, there are laws that prevent posts that present images of bodies that have been altered. Researchers analyzed 100 TikTok videos; on average each video was viewed 13,406,931 times and had similarly mindboggling numbers of likes and comments. More than half of the sample of videos contained "general mental health" material with the next largest category being personal experience; other videos had comments providing support, and 62% mentioned personal mental health issues. Many comments also suggested ways to cope and strategies to improve mental wellbeing (Basch et al., 2022).

Summary

In this chapter, we have provided an overview of the various digital sources of information about mental health or wellness. Although many resources existed prior to the COVID-19 pandemic, their use was greatly expanded in response to the changes and restrictions imposed to limit transmission. Ultimately, it is up to the user (general public or mental health professional) to heed the advice suggested above to ensure their digital mental health journey is a positive one. The perfect digital resource is the one that meets the individual's needs and is accurate and culturally sensitive. Providers need to recognize that most of their clients probably use the internet and have smartphones; it behooves them to be aware of how their use might support and sustain their mental health by familiarizing themselves with websites, apps, podcasts, etc. that they can suggest. In addition to the sources for mental health information and support, the internet provided options for mental health treatment when in-person treatment was curtailed. In the next chapter, we examine the ways in which treatment can be delivered in the digital age.

References

Austria, J. L. (2007). Developing evaluation criteria for podcasts. *Libri, 57*(4). https://doi.org/10.1515/LIBR.2007.179

Bakker, D., Kazantzis, N., Rickwood, D., & Rickard, N. (2018). A randomized controlled trial of three smartphone apps for enhancing public mental health. *Behaviour Research and Therapy, 109,* 75–83. https://doi.org/10.1016/j.brat.2018.08.003

Basch, C. H., Donelle, L., Fera, J., & Jaime, C. (2022). Deconstructing TikTok videos on mental health: Cross-sectional, descriptive content analysis. *JMIR Formative Research, 6*(5), e38340. https://doi.org/10.2196/38340

Bauman, S., Toomey, R., & Walker, J. (2013). Relations among bullying, cyberbullying and suicide in high school students. *Journal of Adolescence, 36*(2), 341–360. https://doi.org/10.1016/j.adolescence.2012.12.001

Bekalu, M. A., McCloud, R. F., & Viswanath, K. (2019). Association of social media use with social well-being, positive mental health, and self-rated health: disentangling routine use from emotional connection to use. *Health Education & Behavior, 46*(2_suppl), 69S–80S.

Best, E., & Clark, C. (2020). *Children and young people's engagement with podcasts before and during lockdown* (p. 13). National Literacy Trust.

Casares, D. R., & Binkley, E. E. (2021). Podcasts as an evolution of bibliotherapy. *Journal of Mental Health Counseling, 43*(1), 19–39. https://doi.org/10.17744/mehc.43.1.02

Chan, S., Torous, J., Hinton, L., & Yellowlees, P. (2015). Towards a framework for evaluating mobile mental health apps. *Telemedicine and E-Health, 21*(12), 1038–1041. https://doi.org/10.1089/tmj.2015.0002

Cosantino, G., Malgady, R. G., & Rogler, L. H. (1986). Cuento therapy: A culturally sensitive modality for Puerto Rican children. *Journal of Consulting and Clinical Psychology, 54*(5), 639–645.

Foster, C. B. (2013). *Mental health on YouTube: Exploring the potential of interactive media to change knowledge, attitudes and behaviors about mental health.* PhD diss., University of South Carolina. https://www.proquest.com/docview/1438102253/abstract/871EF7835D414FEFPQ/1

Gamble, C. (2022). Rethinking the accessibility of digital mental health. *Counseling Today, 65*(1), 48–51.

Global Social Media Statistics. (2022). DataReportal—Global Digital Insights. https://datareportal.com/social-media-users

Gowen, L. K. (2013). Online mental health information seeking in young adults with mental health challenges. *Journal of Technology in Human Services, 31*(2), 97–111. https://doi.org/10.1080/15228835.2013.765533

International Telecommunications Union. (2022). *Global connectivity report 2022* (p. 186). International Telecommunications union.

Manicavasagar, V., Horswood, D., Burckhardt, R., Lum, A., Hadzi-Pavlovic, D., & Parker, G. (2014). Feasibility and effectiveness of a web-based positive psychology program for youth mental health: Randomized controlled trial. *Journal of Medical Internet Research, 16*(6), e140. https://doi.org/10.2196/jmir.3176

Mattoon, E. R. (2021, April 10). TikTok therapy: Hopkins professor addresses mental health on social media. The Johns Hopkins News-Letter. https://

www.jhunewsletter.com/article/2021/04/tiktok-therapy-hopkinsprofessor addressesmental-health-on-social-media

Miodus and Jimenez. (2021). TikTok Therapy: An Exploratory Study on Popular TikTok Mental Health Content. TMS Proceedings 2021. https://doi.org/10.1037/tms0000137

Morahan-Martin, J., & Anderson, C. D. (2000). Information and misinformation online: Recommendations for facilitating accurate mental health information retrieval and evaluation. *CyberPsychology & Behavior, 3*(5), 731–746. https://doi.org/10.1089/10949310050191737

O'Keeffe and Clarke-Pearson. (2011). Clinical report. The impact of social media on children, adolescents end families. *American Academy of Pedriatics, 127*(4), 799–805.

Parks, A. C., Williams, A. L., Tugade, M. M., Hokes, K. E., Honomichl, R. D., & Zilca, R. D. (2018). Testing a scalable web and smartphone based intervention to improve depression, anxiety, and resilience: A randomized controlled trial. *International Journal of Wellbeing, 8*(2), 22–67. https://doi.org/10.5502/ijw.v8i2.745

Petrosyan, A. (2022a, October 18). Internet usage in the United Kingdom (UK) – Statistics & Facts. https://www.statista.com/topics/3246/internet-usage-in-the-uk/#dossierContents__outerWrapper.

Petrosyan, A. (2022b, July 7). Percentage of teenagers in the United States who have been cyber bullied as of April 2018, by age and frequency. https://www.statista.com/statistics/207508/teenagers-personal-experiences-of-bullying-on-social-media-websites/

Petrosyan, A. (2023, February 24). Number of internet and social media users worldwide as of January 2023. https://www.statista.com/statistics/617136/digital-population-worldwide/

Phillips, L. (2022, March 25). The rise of counselors on social media. *Counseling Today.* https://ct.counseling.org/2022/03/

Royal Society for Public Health & Young Health Movement. (2017). Status Of Mind social media and young people's mental health and wellbeing. Retrieved from https://www.rsph.org.uk/uploads/assets/uploaded/62be270a-a55f-4719-ad668c2ec7a74c2a.pdf

Shu, K., Bhattacharjee, A., Alatawi, F., Nazer, T. H., Ding, K., Karami, M., & Liu, H. (2020). Combating disinformation in a social media age. *WIREs Data Mining and Knowledge Discovery, 10*(6). https://doi.org/10.1002/widm.1385

Stawarz, K., Preist, C., & Coyle, D. (2019). Use of smartphone apps, social media, and web-based resources to support mental health and well-being: Online survey. *JMIR Mental Health, 6*(7), e12546. https://doi.org/10.2196/12546

Strauss, J., Zhang, J., Jarrett, M. L., Patterson, B., & Van Ameringen, M. (2022). 18—Apps for mental health. In D. J. Stein, N. A. Fineberg, & S. R. Chamberlain (Eds.), *Mental health in a digital world* (pp. 395–433). Academic Press. https://doi.org/10.1016/B978-0-12-822201-0.00006-X

Uhls, Y. T., Ellison, N. B., & Subrahmanyam, K. (2017). Benefits and costs of social media in Adolescence. *Pediatrics, 140*(Supplement_2), S67–S70. https://doi.org/10.1542/peds.2016-1758E

3

Mental Health Treatment Online

In the previous chapter, we examined the variety of ways mental health information and support can be accessed online. The increase in the prevalence of mental health disorders associated with the pandemic has been of widespread concern (e.g., Kessler et al., 2022; Pierce et al., 2020); anxiety, depression, substance abuse, suicidal behaviors, PTSD, and vicarious PTSD are some of the more frequently reported disorders. Overall, it appears that the increase in prevalence did not return to pre-pandemic rates by 2022 when the rates of infection and deaths had declined. Today, there are many more people who report subclinical levels of these disorders that impact their well-being and quality of life. The pandemic (and attendant isolation and uncertainty) has exacerbated existing mental health conditions for some, but many who did not have a disorder prior to the pandemic have developed one during this stressful period (Penninx et al., 2022). There is evidence that those who have recovered from COVID-19 report ongoing sleep disturbances, fatigue, and cognitive changes along with anxiety, depression, and PTSD. For example, although working in health care is a stressful occupation, the unprecedented pressures, extended work hours, exposure to COVID-19, and repeated encounters with death and trauma contributed to the high

© The Author(s), under exclusive license to Springer Nature Switzerland AG 2023
S. Bauman, I. Rivers, *Mental Health in the Digital Age*,
https://doi.org/10.1007/978-3-031-32122-1_3

levels of mental health disorders in healthcare workers (Greenberg, 2020; Walton et al., 2020).

The psychological impact of COVID-19 on the overall population is impossible to quantify. In addition to healthcare workers, workers whose jobs were considered essential experienced elevated levels of distress. These groups were exposed to the public and understandably often feared for their own health and that of their families should they transmit the virus to them. Indeed, COVID-19 patients report psychological effects associated with the contraction of the virus, especially those who were hospitalized for a period of time. Recall that most hospitals had strict quarantine and visitation protocols in place, so the comfort of having loved ones close by was not available.

Some people with pre-existing mental health disorders experienced increased severity of symptoms. Given the high death rate, many people experienced the loss of loved ones at a time when usual rituals and customs were prohibited. Some families lost more than one member; many children lost their parents. Economic stressors impacted many who struggled with job losses and inflation. Some people were faced with multiple stressors at the same time, easily becoming overwhelmed.

The ways in which these situations affected people varied with their unique circumstances. For example, the move to working remotely was a positive experience for some who reported enhanced autonomy and flexibility, the absence of a stressful and time-consuming commute, the ability to wear more casual attire, and increased job satisfaction and productivity (Shimura et al., 2021). Conversely, some found increased stress from lack of dedicated workspace at home, difficulties in maintaining separation of work versus family time, an increased distraction from others in the household, and increases in substance abuse and domestic violence, perhaps due to the constant contact and inability to engage in many previously helpful activities. Chirico et al. (2021) conducted a systematic review and concluded that a decline in worker efficiency and productivity was found, along with increases in burnout, violence, and aggression. The reader must keep in mind that the few studies available were conducted at different time points and in different countries, so it is not surprising that the results are inconclusive. However, we already see that as restrictions ease, many workers who worked remotely for the past

3 Mental Health Treatment Online   29

several years are resisting a return to previous schedules and workplaces (*Reworking Work*, n.d.)

Although virtual mental health treatments were available prior to the pandemic, the increased need inspired expansions and innovations in the digital age. The change from face-to-face to online services occurred abruptly, and many professionals (and clients) were unprepared for the need to quickly adapt to the virtual formats and strained to acquire the skillsets required (Feijt et al., 2020), including the development of a "website manner" (Moreno et al., 2020). In the US, prior to COVID-19, only 1% of outpatient treatment was provided via telehealth, whereas in March and April 2020, 40% of outpatient therapy (Lo et al., 2022) was delivered online. In 2021, more than 10,000 mental health apps were available (Naslund & Aschbrenner, 2021). In the UK, providers to the National Health Service (NHS) include *ieso* (www.iesohealth.com) (Hollis et al., 2015), an online treatment portal that offers text and video therapy for a variety of problems and is often free to NHS patients. Also available are websites that rate and describe online therapy services to assist in deciding which apps or services are best (e.g., https://www.very-wellmind.com/best-online-therapy-4691206). Other sites provide matching services (client and online counselor), but many of these have fees and/or recommendations that are restricted to counselors in their network. In this chapter, we explore mental illness and treatment online, noting both positive innovations that enhance treatment and potentially harmful influences.

Online treatment has been found to be as effective (Andersson, 2022) as traditional therapy. For some clients, the time and costs saved by not having to commute are important; even if a client relocates, the service is not interrupted. For others, the format allows for more flexible scheduling and reduced cost. For clients who live in rural areas where therapists are few, or who have a condition that requires specialized treatment that is not readily available, access to e-services is a welcome benefit. However, Moreno et al. (2020) observed that racial and ethnic disparities may be amplified in the context of COVID-19, as vulnerable populations may not have the access or skills to utilize tele-mental health options; these groups are most likely to suffer from the effects of the economic declines and other indirect effects of restrictions imposed to limit the spread of infection. The disruption of routines and reduced contact with support systems can exacerbate other stressors.

Practitioners report that for some clients, self-disclosure is sometimes easier in virtual sessions. Others are pleased with some of the affordances available to improve the options in virtual meetings (e.g., screen-sharing). Finally, clinicians gather additional perspectives when seeing the client in their usual (often home) environment. On the other hand, providers report that there is a lack of technical support and infrastructure and frequent connection problems that interfere with the flow of a session. They also note the loss of non-verbal communication as a problem with tele-mental health (Feijt et al., 2020).

In this section, we review the formats via which teletherapy is delivered, discuss the research on effectiveness, and describe the challenges clinicians face when using digital means for treatment. Finally, we comment on training for providers who use online methods in their clinical work. A caveat: although the data are primarily qualitative and anecdotal, online treatment is not suitable for every person or disorder. Feijt et al. (2020) note that online treatment has been found to be effective for depression, anxiety, and PTSD, but that is not the case for psychotic clients, labile clients prone to crises, those with comorbid disorders of more severe symptoms, and those needing family therapy.

The absence of specific training in tele-mental health for mental health professionals should be remedied, as it is quite likely that the end of the pandemic will not mean the end of online treatment (Poletti et al., 2021). Such training should also take into account the fact that during and after the pandemic, clinicians are also likely to experience increased stress, fears of infections, losses, etc., and strategies for managing those challenges are needed.

Tele-Mental Health: Pre- and Post-COVID

The most notable change in mental health treatment following COVID has been the increased use of various online communication strategies to replace face-to-face treatment. The safety restrictions imposed caused a pivot to online tools during the pandemic; the advantages of this format

3 Mental Health Treatment Online 31

are likely to encourage some clients and practitioners to continue to use distance services after the pandemic restrictions have been rescinded. Not only has COVID-19 prompted increased use of digital mental health, but it also addressed many existing challenges in delivering in-person therapy: time constraints, difficulty getting to in-person treatment locations, prohibitive costs, and fear of stigma (Hull & Mahan, 2017). For many new users of video-conferencing modalities (real-time interactive formats) for mental health treatment, however, there was a period of adjustment or learning curve involved in using the tools.

Prior to COVID-19, most practitioners had not received training in best practices for using the technology in this way, and not all entities that license practitioners require such training. Shore et al. (2018) identify various resources and training opportunities for clinicians to consider so that the online treatment they provide is as equivalent to an in-person treatment as possible. There is solid evidence that online treatment results are quite similar to those achieved in face-to-face treatment (Dueweke et al., 2020; Sweeney et al., 2019). A review and meta-analysis of smartphone interventions for anxiety concluded that the research included in their analysis demonstrated that greater improvement was reported in smartphone interventions than in control conditions (Firth et al., 2017).

Recommendations for practitioners using e-mental health are provided by Shore et al. (2018) and include the following:

* Verify the identity and physical location of the client and obtain verified contact information.
* Informed consent should include a policy for between-session contact.
* A protocol for managing emergencies must be in place prior to the start of treatment. Knowing the physical location of the client gives information needed to contact local responders, if necessary.
* Have a plan for digital interruptions (loss of internet connection, for example).
* Select a platform that ensures data privacy and security. In Europe, the General Data Protection Regulation provides guidelines.
* Carefully consider the location of the digital "office" so that it shows a pleasant, welcoming, and safe place.

- Discuss the importance of the client connecting from a private place. If the client is a minor, the caregiver should be informed of the need for privacy.
- Consider cultural differences online as is done in person.

Security of data and communication is of the utmost importance. Clinicians who conduct tele-mental health should investigate methods to protect all communication and data and use only the most secure platforms. Andersson (2022) advises providers to use only technologies that include encryption and/or require two-step authentication to access the platform.

In addition to synchronous virtual therapy sessions, asynchronous text therapy has also shown positive outcomes (Hull & Mahan, 2017). An advantage of this format is that the client and clinician can each participate at a time and place that is convenient for both. Hull and Mahan report successful outcomes with eating disorders, medication management for schizophrenic patients, and depression. Hull and Mahan conducted a small study of persons using the *talkspace.com* platform for 3–4 months. Most clinicians identified their theoretical orientation as cognitive behavioral therapy (CBT). Outcomes were assessed using the Working Alliance Inventory (WAI) and the General Health Questionnaire (GHQ-12). Study participants reported decreased life distress after an average of almost four months of text therapy. Compared to prior face-to-face therapy, 88.4% to 100% rated the online experience as cumulative (continued growth from a previous treatment), the same, or better. Convenience (86.5%) was the aspect selected by the largest percentage, who rated the experience "much better" while almost half rated the effectiveness of the treatment as somewhat or much better. Andersson (2022) summarizes quantitative and qualitative studies that found therapeutic alliance is as high in online formats as in face-to-face environments. This is important because overall, positive outcomes are associated with high therapeutic alliance.

Lest it seem that all online programs are effective, a study evaluating a self-help application for smartphones (DBT Self-Help; Washburn & Parrish, 2013) found that while many aspects of the app, designed to be used in conjunction with in-person treatment, were good to excellent, the ease of use of the program was problematic. Research on specific platforms and services available online is sparse, and given a large number of offerings, it is unlikely that sufficient empirical evidence to prove the effectiveness of any one platform or approach can be obtained. We hope that readers will utilize the information in this chapter to make informed choices about which treatment options best suit their needs and circumstances.

Cognitive Behavioral Therapy (CBT)

Cognitive Behavioral Therapy (CBT) is an evidence-based approach to treating a variety of mental health disorders (Fordham et al., 2021; Hayes & Hofmann, 2018). Although approaches to online therapy can be based on a variety of theoretical perspectives, CBT is particularly suited to the online context, and one of very few with empirical research to evaluate the approach (e.g., Mahoney et al., 2021; Rauschenberg et al., 2021). There are various ways in which CBT can be offered online. There are self-guided programs that do not involve a professional at all, and mixed-format approaches that have some face-to-face meetings interspersed with digital interactions with a clinician. Other programs use asynchronous communication between client and counselor, which gives both an opportunity to formulate their responses and the therapist time to review notes and earlier conversations. For example, a randomized controlled trial in Oman compared outcomes of six weekly sessions of online CBT therapy during COVID with a control group (self-help) who received a newsletter with similar content. The results demonstrated that the intervention group had greater symptom reduction than those in the control group (Al-Alawi et al., 2021).

CBT treatment components typically include psycho-education (reading assigned content), "awareness training though self-monitoring and writing exercises, relaxation training, positive self-verbalisation, social skills training through behavioural experiments, time management and relapse prevention" (Ruwaard, 2013, p. 142). In a series of randomized controlled studies by Ruwaard, CBT was found to be efficacious for work-related stress, depression, panic disorder, and bulimia. Since participants volunteered to be part of the research, he also used anonymized records from a mental health clinic to evaluate online CBT for a variety of disorders in a naturalistic context. Findings supported the positive outcomes for all disorders.

Tele-Mental Health with Children and Adolescents with Mental Health Conditions

Although adolescents and children are typically quite comfortable with technology, providing mental health services online presents some unique issues. The quality of the therapeutic alliance in online therapy is a concern. However, a small study in the UK concluded that more than half of participants who used a free online counseling service rated the therapeutic alliance as medium and 17.4% rated it as high (Hull & Mahan, 2017).

Cognitive Behavioral Therapy (CBT) is widely used with youth, and positive outcomes have been reported, although results are far from conclusive (Firth et al., 2017). Smart et al. (2021) considered the findings of a randomized controlled trial of the BRAVE for Teenagers-ONLINE, a therapist-supported online CBT program for Australian adolescents with anxiety. The program includes ten weekly sessions of about one-hour duration, and two follow-up sessions (at one month and three months post-treatment). The components of the program are similar to most CBT protocols. Then, Smart et al. (2021) conducted a qualitative study with users who had completed the program to gain information that would assist in program improvement. One of the concerns mentioned by interviewees was that technology or connectivity problems interfered with the process to varying degrees. Others commented that the number of reading assignments was burdensome. A difference between the younger and older adolescents emerged—some of the activities were engaging for the younger group but appeared somewhat juvenile to the older group. Email contact with the therapist was generally considered to be quite positive. Overall, the researchers concluded that although the program was effective for some teens, another format might be more appropriate for those with difficulties with concentration, reading, or motivation.

As with adults, a critical first step is to ensure the software used for online treatment complies with all laws regarding the privacy and security of the sessions. Clinicians treating children and adolescents would do well to heed the advice of Dueweke et al. (2020). We summarize those recommendations here:

- It is helpful to be more animated and expressive during sessions than in in-person meetings.
- If handouts are going to be used, it is helpful to provide them ahead of time to the client and their caregiver.
- Even though the client may be a digital native, take time to orient them to this format and obtain consent or assent as appropriate.
- Model how to use the technology effectively (e.g., showing full-face view, removing (or silencing) distractions).
- Work with the youth and caregiver to stress the importance of a private location for sessions.
- Headsets are helpful for privacy, as can be a signal or code to alert the clinician that someone has entered the space.
- It is essential to set up an emergency protocol with youth and their caregivers.
- Establish beginning and ending routines for sessions.
- Use as many interactive activities as possible. Dueweke et al. (2020) have a website that includes excellent free resources (games, quizzes, etc.) in both English and Spanish for practitioners (www.mental-healthfortrauma.com).
- Take breaks as needed, especially with younger children.
- Take advantage of objects in the child's vicinity (dolls or other toys) and incorporate them into the session.
- Adapt paper worksheets and activities for online use.
- Be observant about the child's environment. This provides important information that would not be available in face-to-face meetings in the clinician's office.
- Utilize features of the platform (e.g., chat or whiteboard) to enhance engagement.
- Be creative!

Self-Diagnosis Online

People with mental health problems (like those with physical health problems) may seek to diagnose their problem using online resources. This is appealing because one does not have to wait for an appointment, talk about embarrassing symptoms to a professional in the room, or pay a fee for service.

To determine the viability of online screening for depression, for example, researchers adapted a well-known depression screening measure (The Center for Epidemiological Studies-Depression, CES-D) to an online format (Houston et al., 2001) and made it available to visitors to a consumer health information site with a mental health section. Over the eight months of the test, 24,479 persons completed the measure, more than half of whom met the cut-off score for depression. Less than half of those who were positive for depression had received any treatment for the disorder prior to taking the measure; 58% indicated that they thought treatment would be helpful, and similar percentages expressed a preference for counseling and medication in the follow-up survey. Although representative of the US population demographic, there were more young persons and minorities completing the measure than in other public screening events. Since this study was completed, the digital divide has become smaller, and access to the internet has increased; it is possible that larger percentages of younger (< age 30) or minority persons would complete the measure if it were given now. The available data did not determine how many participants actually sought treatment following the feedback about their level of depression.

While the practice of self-diagnosis online could have a positive outcome, such as locating a therapist who specializes in the disorder, it may also encourage *Cyberchondria*, a term coined by White and Horvitz (2009). This condition occurs when symptoms are interpreted to be evidence of a disorder when in fact they are common symptoms that may not indicate a disorder at all. An analogy in physical medicine is the self-diagnosis of a brain tumor based on a headache. Although brain tumors are quite rare (approximately 0.2% in the population; Porter et al., 2010), 25% of sites that resulted from a search for "headache" gave brain tumor as a potential cause (Johnston, 2010). Such information is likely to provoke unnecessary alarm. In mental health, most people experience anxiety at times, but it is also a symptom of serious disorders. Without contextual information, and a complete history, it is unwise to form a diagnostic opinion based on limited information.

There is no shortage of online tests to diagnose a wide range of mental health problems, from mood disorders to personality disorders. Published tests used by trained mental health professionals are subjected to careful testing to determine reliability (consistency of scores) and validity (how accurately the test measures what it purports to measure), and most companies that sell these tests require evidence of the proper training of the clinician who intends to use them. On the other hand, self-tests might not be reliable or valid, but users may assume the results are accurate, and may become more concerned than the reality warrants. Many symptoms listed in the diagnostic criteria are matters of degree, which may elude the non-professional user of the information. The dangers of self-diagnosis are captured in this humorous blog post by Jolene Philio (2012), used with permission:

- The great pleasure I find in the order and symmetry of the picture above is a sure sign of obsessive-compulsive disorder.
- My penchant for list making could be another sign of obsessive-compulsive disorder, or it could be a coping mechanism I employ to hide early onset Alzheimer's.
- I probably have an eating disorder because one of the marks of an eating disorder is obsessively thinking about food. And I think of food at least three times a day, sometimes more.
- Kids can be traumatized in many ways, and one of them must have happened to me during childhood so I must have PTSD.
- Taking out all the garbage, cleaning the bathrooms, doing the laundry, and emptying the dishwasher before going on vacation points to a yet undiscovered, reverse housecleaning phobia which I hope they name "Philophobia" after me.
- The desire to name a mental illness after myself pretty much proves I have a narcissistic complex.
- All this worrying about having a mental illness points to an anxiety disorder, don't you think?

38 S. Bauman and I. Rivers

Some people will use information from websites and self-diagnose to seek help. That help may be from a professional mental health provider but also may be from online resources. In the next section, we describe one source of online help—online support groups.

Internet Support Groups: Helpful or Toxic?

Online support groups extend to cyberspace a format that has been effective in the face-to-face context—support groups. The therapeutic factors (Yalom & Leszcz, 2020) identified for therapy groups also apply to support groups (which may not have a professional leader), and studies have determined that these factors operate in online groups just as they do in traditional ones (Tate & Zabinski, 2004):

* The support group helps members see that they are not alone in their troubles, that others have similar problems and often experience similar feelings.
* Hearing from others who have made significant progress can instill hope in those just beginning to face a problem.
* The need to belong is a basic human drive, and support groups foster a sense of trust and belonging among members.
* In a support group, members may offer support or advice that is helpful and appreciated by others, which in turn boosts the self-esteem of that member (King & Moreggi, 1998).
* In many cases, the lack of effective communication skills contributes to or exacerbates the presenting problem; a group is a safe and supportive environment to learn and practice new skills.
* Within the group, there may be role models whose skills provide an example for others in the group to emulate.
* Members of support groups may also increase their self-understanding by exploring their motivations with encouragement and reactions from group participants.
* Emotions, even those long stifled, may find a safe place for expression in support groups, releasing the pressure and energy used to keep them under control.

3 Mental Health Treatment Online   39

- Finally, members receive information and education about the problem in the group and also have an opportunity to receive feedback from others in an honest manner.

In addition to having similar therapeutic factors, online groups appear to exhibit similar dynamics and processes as are found in face-to-face groups (Colón & Stern, 2011). The online environment in synchronous groups also demonstrates the unique effects of that platform, with earlier and greater self-disclosure, often leading to the more rapid development of cohesion among members. Relevant to this discussion is the influence of the online disinhibition effect (Suler, 2004) on online groups. Suler noticed that in an online environment, people often disregard societal norms about appropriate disclosure. In an online group, this can have mixed effects. A participant who finds the anonymity to be freeing may choose to disclose more personal information than would be the case in a face-to-face group (Bell, 2007). Sharing too much too soon in a group can generate feelings of vulnerability, which may then result in the person pulling back from group interactions. When a person reveals significant personal content, they may hope for something from the group that is not provided (e.g., sympathy, concern, empathy, etc.); the disappointment can discourage further participation. On the other hand, group members may be overly harsh or judgmental in their feedback to others as a result of the online disinhibition phenomenon. If the group is professionally led, these dynamics would be processed, and members would be helped to understand and learn from their own and others' behavior. In an online support group that is leaderless or peer-led, the skills to manage these situations may be absent, increasing the potential for significant psychological harm.

Online groups can be particularly valuable for those who have mobility problems or who reside in isolated areas, where attending a face-to-face meeting may require time and resources (such as transportation) that are absent. Others may have low-incidence mental disorders, so that finding a group of others with similar concerns in a local area is unlikely. In addition, some online groups are available 24/7 and include members from around the world, allowing members to find support in times of crisis. Online groups may also appeal to those who experience fear and anxiety about face-to-face groups, or who are extremely shy around others. The anonymity available in many online groups can reduce those worries. In addition, in online groups that do not incorporate video, one's gender, race, socioeconomic status, and disability are not apparent to other members, providing a broader sense of anonymity than occurs in face-to-face groups (Finfgeld, 2000). Furthermore, shy individuals can participate in the group as silent observers, giving them a chance to observe the dynamics of the group and the type of interactions that are normative without feeling pressure to become more active. Finally, some participants, particularly in asynchronous groups, may value the opportunity to compose, and reflect and edit, their contributions before posting them.

Online support groups are prone to the same miscommunication challenges as any communication that lacks non-verbal cues to the intent of the sender. Group facilitators are trained to manage and use conflict therapeutically, but the potential for conflict caused by miscommunication suggests that the facilitator needs to be particularly vigilant for these types of interactions. In leaderless or non-professionally led groups, this is a concern that consumers should be made aware of. There is some concern that for vulnerable individuals, the ready availability and easy access to the groups may promote or foster internet addiction problems (Finfgeld, 2000). The online environment may also reinforce social isolation in shy or withdrawn individuals rather than encouraging them to expand their horizons.

Perhaps more salient are the concerns that apply to support groups that are not led by mental health professionals. Aggressive attacks can occur, and inaccurate or false information can be presented as truth. However, these same dangers exist in in-person groups, and as in those groups, other group members can and do protect each other, rebuke members who make unhelpful attacks, and develop and communicate norms of acceptable behavior (King & Moreggi, 1998).

Online groups include a range of formats. For example, in the offline world, there are self-help groups that are organized and managed by members, with no mental health professional involved. There are also groups that are facilitated by professionals, which function very much as they do in face-to-face settings. Online groups may be synchronous

3 Mental Health Treatment Online   41

(members interact in real time, similar to conversations) or asynchronous (members post or read comments that are posted at various times). With asynchronous communication, members have a chance to compose and edit their messages before posting to ensure their communication is accurate. Asynchronous groups offer constant availability, including in the middle of the night, and those that use email or message boards offer the opportunity to save and review important posts for later reference or further reflection. This format also means that a member may post an important message, and then have to wait until someone responds. For some, the lag time may exacerbate any self-doubts (my post was misunderstood, no one in the group cares about me) the client may have. In synchronous groups, the interactions are immediate, providing timely feedback and support. This also allows members to practice skills using role plays (Tate & Zabinski, 2004).

Groups can be organized on a variety of platforms, such as email listservs, web forums, news groups, chat rooms, virtual communities, and using media that allow multiple participants to interact with voice and/or video (such as Zoom, Microsoft Teams, Skype, Google+ hangout, etc.). In addition, the way most platforms are constructed, there is likely to be a host of any group. If this group is asynchronous and interactions occur by text, the owner/host of the group (the clinician) should moderate posts frequently to prevent harmful interactions. If a user posts harmful content, there should be a mechanism to intervene, including direct contact with the person or removing them from the group.

An additional decision the group facilitator must make is how and whether to use the chat feature of many platforms. If the chat is available to all members and allows for posts to be visible to the whole group or to send private messages to another member, the practitioner must consider the potential challenges. If the chat is used exclusively to report technical issues, it can be a distraction from the group process if the leader is alert to those and responsible for troubleshooting. The alternative—having a non-member manage the technical issues, will require careful planning and preparation with technicians to ensure that person is unable to hear or see the group interactions and understands the importance of confidentiality. If members are able to send private chats to another member, two problems can arise: first, the members sending/receiving the messages are distracted and can appear to be attempting to form sub-groups. Second, a member may attack or make inappropriate comments to another member without the group knowing. One of the authors participated in an online group using Zoom, with audio and video features. In the third session, the atmosphere in the group changed noticeably. A very vocal member suddenly became silent and unresponsive. When this was noticed and commented upon, the member declined to explain the change. After the session ended, the facilitator spoke to the quiet member and discovered that another member was using the private chat to make extremely vicious and nasty remarks to the other. The situation was difficult to resolve with the group.

Actions can be taken to protect the privacy of group interactions. First, entry into the group can require a password, and encryption can be used to increase security. Second, well-designed and clear information to members about their roles and responsibilities should be distributed to all potential members. One of the guidelines that should be imposed and discussed is the importance of keeping cameras on in synchronous groups. There are good reasons some members do not want to do so—including embarrassment about their surroundings, self-consciousness about their appearance, and so on. Note that on Zoom, one can choose to blur the background so only the participant can be seen. When one person does not enable video, the other members often wonder whether they are actually there, whether they are paying attention, and whether they are invested in the group. Even in the limited view of the face and upper torso, much non-verbal information is conveyed by posture, facial expression, or gestures, and the group may be uncomfortable when those cues are missing. Finally, trust and risk-taking are important to the development of a working group; it may be more difficult to establish those without all members being visible.

There is surprisingly little in the way of empirical research on online groups in the mental health field. One study examined the impact of internet-based peer support groups for depression (Houston et al., 2002). One hundred three volunteers from the US, Canada, Australia, and Europe were recruited from five support groups via the list owners. Due to logistical needs, the participants had been involved in the groups for a minimum of one month prior to completing baseline data collection.

3 Mental Health Treatment Online   43

Follow-up data were collected six and twelve months later; in addition to demographic information, measures of depression, and social support, participants were asked how many hours they spent with the group in the previous two weeks. The results indicated that slightly more than half of the sample spent at least five hours over two weeks involved with the group. The participants cited social support as the most important reason to participate and reported their symptoms were reduced because of the help received. A preference for the support group was indicated by 38% of participants, while 50% preferred face-to-face counseling and 12% had no preference. Most users continued to receive professional treatment for depression (76% at six months and 79% of respondents at 12 months). The vast majority told their therapists about the group, and 63% of those said the group had influenced them to ask a question of their provider. The researchers were interested in whether members of the groups would withdraw from other forms of social support over time while participating in the group. A comparison of frequent and infrequent users of the group on the social support survey found no difference on the amount of social support they obtained outside the group. In general, at the one-year follow-up, between 26% and 50% of social support of members came from their participation in these groups. Finally, more frequent users of the group had a significantly greater number of cases of "resolved" depression in one year.

A team from the Veteran's Affairs offices in the US studied both processes and outcomes in group therapy when delivered via video teleconferencing to rural combat veterans with PTSD. Participants were randomly assigned to conditions (Greene et al., 2010). In the process part of the study, the researchers compared the strength of the relations of the therapeutic alliance and attrition in anger management groups delivered via conventional and tele-modes. They found that there was a weaker alliance between members and therapists in the distance condition, but on a 1–5 scale, with higher numbers meaning a stronger alliance, the mean for the tele-condition was 4.2 with the mean for the in-person participants at 4.5. No differences were detected in attrition, treatment adherence, or treatment satisfaction. The researchers concluded that teleconferencing delivery was not inferior to in-person delivery.

44   S. Bauman and I. Rivers

Much of the information available on support groups is anecdotal. However, there is some useful information to be gleaned from the scholarly literature. For example, Hsiung (2000) outlines the roles and functions of facilitators of online groups, from the more technical tasks related to maximizing the potential of the platform hosting the group to facilitation skills similar to those used in any counseling or therapy group.

The most common self-help groups, online or offline, are 12-step groups, which originated with Alcoholics Anonymous and expanded to include other substances, other addictions, and family and friends of persons with those disorders (whether or not the addict is involved). A website (www.intherooms.com) is a hub of information about groups and information with portals for those seeking help (active users), those who are recovering from an alcohol or other drug addiction, and family and friends. It bills itself as "the worlds [sic] largest recovery social network."

Online 12-step meetings are particularly helpful for geographically isolated persons or others who are homebound for a variety of reasons. Members can continue to attend meetings even if they relocate (King & Moreggi, 1998). They suggest that visiting the Rooms website and watching video testimonials have prompted some visitors to acknowledge their own problems and begin to engage in the recovery process. The anonymity on 12-step sites that is augmented by the digital format may free some members to disclose shameful experiences that would be difficult to do in a face-to-face meeting. There is some criticism of the site because the owners do sell products (e.g., T-shirts), which the site owners purport to use to support the site. AA.org, the official site of Alcoholics Anonymous, offers a link to a directory of online meetings (http://aa-intergroup.org/directory.php) that allows the visitor to search by format (e.g., email, chat, audio/video) and special interest groups (Deaf/Hard of Hearing, GLBT, military). AA also has products for sale.

There are some issues that must be addressed in professionally led support groups online. One of those is anonymity. If members are permitted to participate without any verification of their offline identity, the facilitator has no way to intervene in an emergency (e.g., threat of suicide). In this environment, it is possible persons can pretend to have the disorder or issue that brings the group together. They could garner attention and concern that should go to honest members. Furthermore, trolls (persons

3 Mental Health Treatment Online 45

whose purpose is to cause havoc and distress using the internet) could infect the group and cause serious damage to the group process and/or individuals in the group, with no accountability. For this reason, we recommend that a screening process be conducted in the same manner as for a face-to-face group, with personal identifying information collected and verified before a person enters the group. Furthermore, the facilitator should provide group guidelines to all members that include information about the role of the facilitator and the expectations of members.

Some online groups have an unlimited membership, so the groups can become quite large and postings difficult to follow. Those groups also have difficulty maintaining a core of stable members who model the norms of the group for new members. The size also seems to inhibit commitment on the part of the members, as their individual contribution may seem trivial or unimportant. Professionally let groups might want to limit the size and duration of the group, and define beginning and ending dates. Such groups are more likely to provide the therapeutic factors and conditions described above.

With the increasing availability of free or inexpensive live chat options with video (Zoom, Teams Skype, Google Meet), a facilitator may choose to utilize this format to more closely simulate the face-to-face environment. For those who choose online formats because they do not want their appearance to influence others' perceptions of them, this presents an obstacle. However, for others, it may ease concerns about fellow members being "real people." If the facilitator decides to use such media, all members should have individual training meetings (which could double as screening interviews) to ensure they are able to manage the technology and have sufficient internet connection speed to participate. If the facilitator chooses not to use video but rather leads either a voice-based or text-based interaction (or synchronous chat), the establishment of some norms will increase the sense of safety of members. For example, when members enter or leave the meeting, they should announce this to the group. If the group is open and accepts new members, entries are a time for introductions, and as members leave, that decision should be known to all members so that all have an opportunity for closure.

Important decisions for online groups relate to use of chat and video features. If the chat is available during the meeting, members can have side conversations that distract those members from the group interactions. A member might attack another while the rest of the group is unaware, creating strange dynamics. To avoid such disruptions, we recommend that the chat feature be set so that only the facilitator can send and receive chat messages, and those should be restricted to such things as difficulties with technology.

The ability to turn off one's video can become contentious. Members may argue that they are unhappy with their appearance, which inhibits their participation. Although this makes sense, when some members do not have a camera on, the others may feel exposed, or may believe that the invisible members are not engaged with the group but rather can pretend to be present while actually doing something else (e.g., playing video games). The inconsistency (camera on, camera off) makes it difficult to establish a climate of trust, and creates an imbalance among members. Others may be uncomfortable with their surroundings being visible, particularly if their environment signals their socio-economic status (i.e., poverty). In Zoom, it is easy to blur the background to show only the face of the speaker, or to select from choices of background images.

An avenue of interest for future research is the effect of member-created mental images of other group members and leaders in groups without video access. Colón and Stern (2011) see this process as one likely to increase the presence of *projection* in the group, in which members project their unconscious needs onto others in the group. This process can be used therapeutically in psychodynamically oriented groups but requires a skilled leader to recognize and utilize this process to the benefit of members.

Mental health providers need to be aware of the popularity of self-help groups online and should inquire whether clients are using such sites. For clients who find 12-step meetings helpful (AA, NA, etc.), the difficulty of finding a group at a convenient time and location is greatly reduced, since the geographical setting is not relevant. It would be prudent for clinicians to be familiar with other high-quality sites to be able to recommend suitable resources to interested clients. Rather than dissuading clients from pursuing online support, these experiences can be helpful adjuncts to treatment. It is now easier and more convenient for newly sober members to attend "90 meetings in 90 days."

Toxic Groups

The intention of online groups described above is to provide a safe and supportive environment in which members can obtain information, feedback, and emotional support for mental health issues. There are, however, people who perceive some psychological disorders as "lifestyle choices" that do not require treatment, and which should be encouraged. We discuss below groups that actively promote what most consider to be disordered behavior (or "extreme communities," Bell, 2007), but it is essential that readers be aware that individuals with these views might choose to join more traditional groups to "recruit" members for their own agendas. Leaderless groups could be more vulnerable to such strategies; we hope that professional leaders would be alert to this possibility and quickly intervene if such behavior emerges.

Most western countries place a high value on freedom of speech. This freedom means that individuals have the right to express themselves even if doing so is considered offensive by others. This basic value, coupled with the essentially unrestricted nature of cyberspace, means that groups to "support" behaviors that others find unacceptable are generally within the bounds of legal activity. No laws have outlawed sites that promote eating disorders, but promoting suicide online or describing techniques for suicide are against the law in Denmark, Australia, Turkey, and South Korea (Boyd et al., 2011)

Although any group has the potential to be damaging to individuals, this section focuses on groups that are considered problematic by most "reasonable person" standards. We refer here primarily to groups that promote self-harm (including deliberate self-injury, eating-disorder behaviors, and suicide). Boyd et al. (2011) stress that the motives fueling self-harming behaviors are not uniform across behaviors or individuals, but often are predicated on a belief that one deserves punishment (which can be self-inflicted), difficulties expressing psychological pain, and a desire to alter one's present (unpleasant) psychological state. Many persons who engage in these behaviors report a sense of release of tension and anxiety following a self-injurious behavior (or an episode of purging or making a serious suicidal gesture).

48   S. Bauman and I. Rivers

Some self-help groups that concern these topics do advocate and support efforts to discontinue the self-harming behaviors. These groups typically include much self-disclosure by members who have struggled and are now recovering from these behaviors. On the other hand, there are groups that advocate and encourage (sometimes via graphic examples) self-harming behaviors.

Most participants in these pro-self-harm groups are teens (Boyd et al., 2011); these groups are attracting a vulnerable population. Because fulfilling the need to belong is generally an underlying motive for joining any group, members may find they engage in these behaviors as a way to feel closer to other members. These groups often explain how to conceal the behaviors from others and offer "instruction" in various techniques. Sites known as "pro-ana" (pro-anorexia) and "pro-mia" (pro-bulimia) are numerous and often include photos that present the "ideal" state of thinness.

Most approaches to understanding eating disorders espouse a biomedical (or biopsychosocial) model of the disorder. From that perspective, these disorders must be treated and ultimately resolved, because they are disorders, diseases, and mental health problems. Although anorexia in particular is very difficult to treat and has a high mortality rate, most treatment approaches have goals of restoring normal body weight and eating habits. Secondary goals include changing cognitive errors about food and thinness. Some approaches incorporate ideas regarding the social and cultural aspects of food and thinness, and others extend that issue to include the role and image of women in society. However, all approaches consider eating disorders as pathological to some degree and develop treatments designed to curtail the problem. Fox et al. (2005) engaged in an ethnographic study of pro-ana sites using participant observation and conducting interviews with some members of online pro-ana groups. They also engaged in text analysis of site content.

Like similar sites, the pro-ana sites include a warning on the home page informing the visitor that the site espouses the pro-ana view. The particular site used for Fox et al.'s (2005) analysis attracted predominantly females aged 17–20. The site makes it clear that the goal is not to cure the behavior. The site used a message forum with asynchronous communication among members. The researchers observed that the site

3 Mental Health Treatment Online 49

included recipes to use for what the site referred to as a "healthy" anorectic diet and advice about the use of weight-loss supplements to reach the desired state of thinness. There were also photos called "thinspiration," which were images of thin celebrities considered inspirations to maintaining the anorectic lifestyle. The theme of postings was that anorexia could be engaged in safely. Many postings were chronicles of members' journey to anorexia, and their need for understanding and support of their chosen path. Members appeared to see anorexia as a way to manage their lives and problems, that is, a coping mechanism. Their position is that, without this "effective" way to cope, they would be unable to function. The site does not judge them for their disorder, and in fact, provides validation and approval from others who share their worldview.

Similar approaches and philosophical arguments can be found on pro-self-mutilation and pro-suicide sites. Bell (2007) pointed out that the information about methods of self-harm or suicide may encourage some individuals to act upon ideation. Given their beliefs, it is unlikely that members of these sites would be good candidates for traditional mental health treatment, as participants in the sites reject the foundational assumptions to which mental health clinicians ascribe. It is also unlikely, given the high value of free speech, that legislation will be an effective response. However, studies such as that of Fox et al. (2005) do provide insight into the barriers that keep these people from treatment. For example, if people with anorexia believe their eating behavior is a way to cope with their pain, perhaps focusing on the pain and identifying other methods to alleviate the suffering will be more successful than demanding a return to more normal eating. That said, it is sometimes medically necessary to take measures to restore normal body weight in order to save the person's life. Bell (2007) cautioned that some sites borrow the therapeutic technique of personifying and externalizing the negative behavior (e.g., naming the problem and referring to it as outside the person). However, rather than considering the named entity as a problem, these sites may encourage considering the entity as a "companion" or "ideal" to strive for. This is alarming.

Bell (2007) also discovered online groups whose members were likely to be psychotic, and who support each other's pathology. They may agree that they are being controlled by external agents who use advanced mind control technology. Other delusional beliefs can also be validated in such groups. The enormous size of the internet means that a determined individual is able to find a community to support almost any behavior, regardless of how deviant or destructive the behaviors or ideas. The experience of social support in such groups may serve to reinforce these behaviors. Members of such sites may find that their unmet needs for understanding and social support can be fulfilled on such sites. In any case, it behooves mental health providers to be aware that such sites exist and proliferate, providing a sense of safety and community that the members are very reluctant to give up. Active involvement in such groups may make other types of intervention much more difficult to implement.

Therapeutic Relationships in the Digital Age

So far in this chapter, we have discussed the various formats for therapy that is delivered online and have outlined the advantages and disadvantages of each. One topic that has not yet been explored but one that has a practical and ethical impact is the ability of clients to gather information about their therapists, and vice versa. The internet provides access to abundant information, while also providing an outlet to express personal information visible to others (Kaluzeviciute, 2020; Sfoggia et al., 2014). The sparse literature on the topic has mainly come from the psychoanalytic perspective whose traditional approach relies on therapist anonymity and neutrality in order to elicit transference, an essential focus of analysis. In addition, the fast pace of life on the internet may lead to expectations of rapid results of therapy, which is contrary to the process of psychoanalysis.

The psychoanalytic authors acknowledge that their concerns are generally the same as those of practitioners who use different approaches. The therapeutic relationship may be altered by the ability of clients to discover details of the therapist's private life using online search engines, making anonymity impossible. This possibility changes the traditional elements of privacy, anonymity, and self-disclosure in treatment. The clinical interactions may be affected by information discovered online without the therapist's awareness, a process called *virtual impingement* by

Balick (as cited by Kaluzeviciute, 2020). On the other hand, therapists may use the same strategies to gather information about clients without their knowledge or consent. de Araujo Reinert and Kowacs (2019) refer to this as *patient-targeting googling* (PTG). These authors note a variety of reasons for PTG: curiosity, concern about a client missing appointments, following up post-treatment, and checking for possible suicidal ideation.

Sfoggia et al. (2014) provide six vignettes similar to those experienced by the authors in their clinical practices. These vignettes are very useful for discussions in either training or supervision of practitioners, especially because they reveal how complex these situations are. Based on guidelines from the American Medical Association about maintaining professional standards in the digital world, Sfoggia et al. (p. 8) suggest a set of guidelines for mental health professionals that are an excellent starting point. We summarize those recommendations here:

* Make sure to enable all privacy settings on all social networking platforms.
* Google yourself periodically to check for false information or photos and act immediately to have them removed.
* Be careful of content you include on websites or blogs, avoiding an information about clients, comments about other professionals, or pending administrative or legal cases.
* Do not post any unprofessional images.
* Although information you find about clients online is public, clients may experience your search as intrusive and disrespectful of boundaries. Thoughtful reflection about the value of and motives for gathering information should be carefully considered.
* Do not create relationships with clients on social media. Many clinicians create separate accounts for personal and professional contact.
* Recognize that the determined and tech-savvy searcher can likely find the source of apparently anonymous content; the clinician who uses dating sites must be prepared for a client discovering and reacting to that information.
* Training programs should include these topics and ethical implications in their materials, including ethical decision-making in this digital climate (de Araujo Reinert & Kowacs, 2019).

52 S. Bauman and I. Rivers

Additional suggestions are proffered by Holmes and Taube (2016):

* Include the use of social media in the informed consent document provided to clients at the initial meeting, inviting clients who do gather information about therapists to discuss that in sessions.
* Ask clients about their use of social media to indicate this is an acceptable topic of discussion.
* Attend ongoing training to ensure current knowledge of technological skills to protect privacy.
* Do not accept friend requests from anyone unknown to you.
* Be aware that your family members (e.g., teenage children) may be the source of information about you, and urge them to be particularly cautious about what they share on social media.
* Be conscious of what activities you engage in online that might indirectly reveal more than you intend about your personal life. Therapists who are active in groups or discussion about political topics need to be aware that some clients might discontinue treatment if they have opposing views (Kaluzeviciute, 2020).

The only attempt at an empirical examination of the question of clients using the internet to locate personal information about the therapist was conducted by Holmes and Taube (2016). A survey was completed by 332 participants who acknowledged having searched for personal information online about a mental health provider at some time. Information about the family was accessed most frequently; sizeable numbers also looked for the therapist's age, education, and of particular concern, home address and photos. Eighty-one percent indicated that they were motivated by curiosity. Most respondents sought out the information, although a small proportion came upon the information accidentally. Although a number of participant characteristics were tested, only those who had participated in group therapy were more likely to search. Some participants did their searches prior to making an appointment; the information they acquired helped them decide whether the therapist was a good fit. Finally, participants indicated whether the information they located had a positive, neutral, or negative impact on their therapeutic experience. The positive effects most often reported were skills and training and overall feelings about the clinician, whereas the most negative was availability to the client. Overall, most dimensions were rated as neutral.

The internet provides access to a great deal of information about both therapists and clients. It is probably safe to assume that many, if not most, clients have gathered personal information about their therapists. Therapists need to process that experience so that it does not impede treatment. They also must reflect on their motives for searching for information about clients before doing so. There is a dearth of research on how this process affects the clinician, the client, and the therapeutic relationship. Given that it is unknown, the suggestions provided above are important steps for clinicians to take to minimize the potential for a negative effect on the treatment process.

Summary

The answer to the question, "Is the internet a danger or an opportunity for improving mental health?" is, it depends. In this chapter, we examined the many variations of digital mental health treatment and reviewed evidence of effectiveness. We explored CBT in particular, as it has both empirical support and an approach that is amenable to online delivery. We agree with Rauschenberg et al. (2021) that an approach that utilizes both online material and contact with a mental health professional is optimal. In addition to positive outcomes, this blended strategy allows clinicians to serve more clients at a time when there is a shortage of professionals and an increase in need for treatment.

However, there are also sites that can lead one astray, and it is essential that the consumers use best strategies for locating reliable and valid current information. Clinicians need to be familiar with harmful sites as well as helpful sites so they can recommend appropriate online resources when they are indicated.

The availability of support groups in a variety of digital formats greatly increases the accessibility of such services. There are many advantages to online formats, including the elimination of problems with transportation, scheduling, and other barriers to participation. However, those groups that are not read or monitored by a mental health professional increase risk for harm in such groups, and we recommend that mental health professionals discuss any involvement with their clients. At the same time, we hope group members will encourage each other to add professional treatment to their group involvement to improve the prognosis of participation.

The internet is both a danger and an opportunity to improving mental health. There are numerous options for obtaining treatment online; it is important to be very particular about which of those options is best for which individuals.

References

Al-Alawi, M., McCall, R. K., Sultan, A., Balushi, N. A., Al-Mahrouqi, T., Ghailani, A. A., Sabti, H. A., Al-Maniri, A., Panchatcharam, S. M., & Sinawi, H. A. (2021). Efficacy of a six-week-long therapist-guided online therapy versus self-help internet-based therapy for COVID-19–induced anxiety and depression: Open-label, pragmatic, randomized controlled trial. *JMIR Mental Health, 8*(2), e26683. https://doi.org/10.2196/26683

Andersson, G. (2022). 17—Internet-based psychotherapies. In D. J. Stein, N. A. Fineberg, & S. R. Chamberlain (Eds.), *Mental health in a digital world* (pp. 377–394). Academic Press. https://doi.org/10.1016/B978-0-12-822201-0.00008-3

de Araujo Reinert, C., & Kowacs, C. (2019). Patient-targeted "googling:" When therapists search for information about their patients online. *Psychodynamic Psychiatry, 47*(1), 27–38. https://doi.org/10.1521/pdps.2019.47.1.27

Bell, V. (2007). Online information, extreme communities, and internet therapy: Is the internet good for our mental health? *Journal of Mental Health, 16*, 445–457.

Boyd, D., Ryan, J., & Leavitt, A. (2011). Pro-harm and the visibility of youth-generated problematic content. I/S: *A Journal of Law and Policy for the Information Society, 7*, 1–32.

Chirico, F., Ferrari, G., Nucera, G., Szarpak, L., Crescenzo, P., & Ilesanmi, O. (2021). Prevalence of anxiety, depression, burnout syndrome, and mental health disorders among healthcare workers during the COVID-19 pandemic: a rapid umbrella review of systematic reviews. *J Health Soc Sci, 6*(2), 209–220.

Colón, Y., & Stern, S. (2011). Online counseling groups. In Kraus, Stricker & Speyer (Eds.), Online Counseling: A Handbook for Mental Health Professionals. San Diego, CA: Academic Press/Elsevier.

Dueweke, A. R., Wallace, M. M., Nicasio, A. V., Villalobos, B. T., & Rodriguez, J. H. (2020). Resources and recommendations for engaging children and adolescents in telemental health interventions during COVID-19 and beyond. *The Behavior Therapist, 43*(5), 171–176.

Feijt, M., de Kort, Y., Bongers, I., Bierbooms, J., Westerink, J., & IJsselsteijn, W. (2020). Mental health care goes online: Practitioners' experiences of providing mental health care during the COVID-19 pandemic. *Cyberpsychology, Behavior, and Social Networking, 23*(12), 860–864. https://doi.org/10.1089/cyber.2020.0370

Finfgeld, D. L. (2000). Therapeutic groups online: The good, the bad, and the unknown. *Issues in Mental Health Nursing, 21*(3), 241–255. https://doi.org/10.1080/016128400248068

Firth, J., Torous, J., Nichols, J., Carney, R., Rosenbaum, S., & Sarris, J. (2017). Can smartphone mental health interventions reduce symptoms of anxiety? A meta-analysis of randomized controlled trials | Elsevier Enhanced Reader. *Journal of Affective Disorders, 218*, 15–22. https://doi.org/10.1016/j.jad.2017.04.046

Fordham, B., Sugavanam, T., Edwards, K., Stallard, P., Howard, R., Nair, R. D., Copsey, B., Lee, H., Howick, J., Hemming, K., & Lamb, S. E. (2021). The evidence for cognitive behavioural therapy in any condition, population or context: A meta-review of systematic reviews and panoramic meta-analysis. *Psychological Medicine, 51*(1), 21–29. https://doi.org/10.1017/S0033291720005292

Fox, N., Ward, K., & O'Rourke, A. (2005). Pro-anorexia, weight-loss drugs and the internet: An 'anti-recovery' explanatory model of anorexia. *Sociology of Health & Illness, 27*, 944–971.

Greene, C. J., Morland, L. A., Macdonald, A., Frueh, B. C., Grubbs, K. M., & Rosen, C. S. (2010). How does tele-mental health affect group therapy process? Secondary analysis of a noninferiority trial. *Journal of Consulting and Clinical Psychology, 78*, 746–750. https://doi.org/10.1037/a0020158

Greenberg, N. (2020). Mental health of health-care workers in the COVID-19 era. *Nature Reviews Nephrology, 16*(8), 425–426. https://doi.org/10.1038/s41581-020-0314-5

Hayes, S. C., & Hofmann, S. G. (2018). *Process-based CBT: The science and core clinical competencies of cognitive behavioral therapy*. New Harbinger Publications.

Hollis, C., Morriss, R., Martin, J., Amani, S., Cotton, R., Denis, M., & Lewis, S. (2015). Technological innovations in mental healthcare: Harnessing the digital revolution. *British Journal of Psychiatry, 206*(4), 263–265. https://doi.org/10.1192/bjp.bp.113.142612

Holmes, K., & Taube, D. O. (2016). Client discovery of psychotherapist personal information online. *Professional Psychology: Research and Practice, 47*(2), 147–154. http://dx.doi.org/10.1037/pro0000065

Houston, T. K., Cooper, L. A., Vu, H. T., Kahn, J., Toser, J., & Ford, D. E. (2001). Screening the public for depression through the Internet. *Psychiatric Services, 52*(3), 362–367.

Houston, T. K., Cooper, L. A., & Ford, D. E. (2002). Internet support groups for depression: a 1-year prospective cohort study. *American Journal of Psychiatry, 159*(12), 2062–2068.

Hsiung, R. C. (2000). The best of both worlds: An online self-help group hosted by a mental health professional. *CyberPsychology & Behavior, 3*, 935–950.

Hull, T. D., & Mahan, K. (2017). A study of asynchronous mobile-enabled SMS text psychotherapy. *Telemedicine and E-Health, 23*(3), 240–247. https://doi.org/10.1089/tmj.2016.0114

Johnston, J. (2010, January 6). Don't be a cyberchondriac: Use the internet to self-screen. Not self-diagnose. https://www.psychologytoday.com/us/blog/the-human-equation/201001/dont-be-cyberchondriac-use-the-internetself-screen-not-self-diagnose

Kaluzeviciute, G. (2020). Social media and its impact on therapeutic relationships. *British Journal of Psychotherapy, 36*(2), 303–320. https://doi.org/10.1111/bjp.12545

Kessler, R. C., Chiu, W. T., Hwang, I. H., Puac-Polanco, V., Sampson, N. A., Ziobrowski, H. N., & Zaslavsky, A. M. (2022). Changes in prevalence of mental illness among US adults during compared with before the COVID-19 pandemic. *Psychiatric Clinics, 45*(1), 1–28.

King, S. A., & Moreggi, D., (1998). Internet therapy and self-help groups – the pros and the cons. In J. Gackenbach, J. (Ed.), Psychology and the internet: Intrapersonal, interpersonal, and transpersonal implications (pp. 77–109). San Diego, CA: Academic Press.

Lo, J., Panchal, N., & Miller, B. P. (2022, March 15). Telehealth has played an outsized role meeting mental health needs during the COVID-19 pandemic. *KFF.* https://www.kff.org/coronavirus-covid-19/issue-brief/telehealth-has-played-an-outsized-role-meeting-mental-health-needs-during-the-covid-19-pandemic/

Mahoney, A., Li, I., Haskelberg, H., Millard, M., & Newby, J. M. (2021). The uptake and effectiveness of online cognitive behaviour therapy for symptoms of anxiety and depression during COVID-19. *Journal of Affective Disorders, 292*, 197–203. https://doi.org/10.1016/j.jad.2021.05.116

Moreno, C., Wykes, T., Galderisi, S., Nordentoft, M., Crossley, N., Jones, N., Cannon, M., Correll, C. U., Byrne, L., Carr, S., Chen, E. Y. H., Gorwood, P., Johnson, S., Kärkkäinen, H., Krystal, J. H., Lee, J., Lieberman, J., López-Jaramillo, C., Männikkö, M., et al. (2020). How mental health care should change as a consequence of the COVID-19 pandemic. *The Lancet Psychiatry, 7*(9), 813–824. https://doi.org/10.1016/S2215-0366(20)30307-2

Naslund, J. A., & Aschbrenner, K. A. (2021). Technology use and interest in digital apps for mental health promotion and lifestyle intervention among young adults with serious mental illness | Elsevier Enhanced Reader. *Journal of Affective Disorders Reports, 6,* 100227. https://doi.org/10.1016/j.jadr.2021.100227

Penninx, B. W. J. H., Benros, M. E., Klein, R. S., & Vinkers, C. H. (2022). How COVID-19 shaped mental health: From infection to pandemic effects. *Nature Medicine, 28*(10), 10. https://doi.org/10.1038/s41591-022-02028-2

Philio, J. (2012, February 27). The danger of self-diagnosis. https://jolenephilo.com/a-self-diagnosis-crisis/

Pierce, M., Hope, H., Ford, T., Hatch, S., Hotopf, M., John, A., Kontopantelis, E., Webb, R., Wessely, S., McManus, S., & Abel, K. M. (2020). *Mental health before and during the COVID-19 pandemic: A longitudinal probability sample survey of the UK population. 7*, 11.

Poletti, B., Tagini, S., Brugnera, A., Parolin, L., Pievani, L., Ferrucci, R., Compare, A., & Silani, V. (2021). Telepsychotherapy: A leaflet for psychotherapists in the age of COVID-19. A review of the evidence. *Counselling Psychology Quarterly, 34*(3–4), 352–367. https://doi.org/10.1080/09515070.2020.1769557

Porter, K. R., McCarthy, B. J., Freels, S., Kim, Y., & Davis, F. G. (2010). Prevalence estimates for primary brain tumors in the United States by age, gender, behavior, and histology. *Neuro-oncology, 12*(6), 520–527.

Rauschenberg, C., Schick, A., Hirjak, D., Seidler, A., Paetzold, I., Apfelbacher, C., ... & Reininghaus, U. (2021). Evidence synthesis of digital interventions to mitigate the negative impact of the COVID-19 pandemic on public mental health: rapid meta-review. *Journal of medical Internet research, 23*(3), e23365.

Reworking work. (n.d.). https://www.Apa.Org. Retrieved March 17, 2023, from https://www.apa.org/monitor/2022/01/special-reworking-work

Ruwaard, J. J. (2013). The efficacy and effectiveness of online CBT. Universiteit van Amsterdam [Host].

Sfoggia, A., Kowacs, C., Gastaud, M. B., Laskoski, P. B., Bassols, A. M., Severo, C. T., Machado, D., Krieger, D. V., Torres, M. B., & Teche, S. P. (2014). Therapeutic relationship on the web: To face or not to face? *Trends in Psychiatry and Psychotherapy, 36*, 3–10.

Shimura, A., Yokoi, K., Ishibashi, Y., Akatsuka, Y., & Inoue, T. (2021). Remote work decreases psychological and physical stress responses, but full-remote work increases presenteeism. *Frontiers in Psychology, 12.* https://www.frontiersin.org/articles/10.3389/fpsyg.2021.730969

Shore, J. H., Yellowlees, P., Caudill, R., Johnston, B., Turvey, C., Mishkind, M., Krupinski, E., Myers, K., Shore, P., Kaftarian, E., & Hilty, D. (2018). Best practices in videoconferencing-based telemental health April 2018. *Telemedicine and E-Health, 24*(11), 827–832. https://doi.org/10.1089/tmj.2018.0237

Smart, K., Smith, L., Harvey, K., & Waite, P. (2021). The acceptability of a therapist-assisted internet-delivered cognitive behaviour therapy program for the treatment of anxiety disorders in adolescents: A qualitative study. *European Child & Adolescent Psychiatry.* https://doi.org/10.1007/s00787-021-01903-6

Suler, J. (2004). The online disinhibition effect. *Cyberpsychology & Behavior, 7*(3), 321–326. https://doi.org/10.1089/1094931041291295

Sweeney, G. M., Donovan, C. L., March, S., & Forbes, Y. (2019). Logging into therapy: Adolescent perceptions of online therapies for mental health problems. *Internet Interventions, 15*, 93–99. https://doi.org/10.1016/j.invent.2016.12.001

Tate, D. F., & Zabinski, M. F. (2004). Computer and Internet applications for psychological treatment: Update for clinicians. *Journal of Clinical Psychology, 60*, 209–220.

Walton, M., Murray, E., & Christian, M. D. (2020). Mental health care for medical staff and affiliated healthcare workers during the COVID-19 pandemic. *European Heart Journal. Acute Cardiovascular Care, 9*(3), 241–247. https://doi.org/10.1177/2048872620922795

Washburn, M., & Parrish, D. E. (2013). DBT self-help application for mobile devices. *Journal of Technology in Human Services, 31*(2), 175–183. https://doi.org/10.1080/15228835.2013.775904

White, R. W., & Horvitz, E. (2009). Cyberchondria: studies of the escalation of medical concerns in web search. *ACM Transactions on Information Systems (TOIS), 27*(4), 1–37.

Yalom, I. D., & Leszcz, M. (2020). *Theory and practice of group psychotherapy* (5th ed). New York: Basic Books.

4

Social Media and Forms of Connectedness

Introduction

There is no doubt that social media platforms are an integral and influential aspect of the digital age. The number of platforms available to users has rapidly proliferated and changed in response to user practices and interests. In this chapter, we review research relating to social media's impact on mental health. We discuss many of the applications and platforms that attract large audiences and identify those features that attract users and how they engage with them. We then consider how online social interactions that have personal meaning are established and how such relationships relate to mental health. Finally, we discuss some of the learning that has taken place following the COVID-19 pandemic.

Social media includes an array of applications and platforms where users create personal profiles (often including photos), with additional, often personal information (like/dislikes, occupation, location) that is visible to followers. Some applications require confirmation that a prospective follower is a friend or contact (e.g., Facebook) while others have

© The Author(s), under exclusive license to Springer Nature Switzerland AG 2023
S. Bauman, I. Rivers, *Mental Health in the Digital Age*,
https://doi.org/10.1007/978-3-031-32122-1_4

the capability to access contacts lists and integrate them—confirming whether contacts also have profiles on particular platforms (e.g., WhatsApp, Snapchat, Instagram). Some platforms allow users to see or follow someone without consent (e.g., Twitter, Instagram, TikTok); however, this is dependent upon security settings. Typically, users are able to post public comments that can be seen by anyone using the applications, and some allow users to send private or direct messages (DMs) that can only be viewed by the recipient. Some users prefer to remain anonymous or create profiles that may not correspond to their offline names or their identities on other social media. Today, most applications and platforms can be accessed on smartphones and this degree of accessibility and portability enhances their appeal.

Once a profile has been created, users are then able to upload text, images, recordings, and live streams that reflect their interests (everything from politics to cookery to travel), likes and dislikes, opinions, or their daily lives. Some users use social media as a means of diarizing their everyday experiences or those experiences/journeys of discovery that they believe others will find interesting/entertaining. Along the way, we also encounter a group of users who are known as influencers, who post content regularly and have built up a following (often many hundreds of thousands or millions of users) as a result of their expertise, knowledge, or commentary on specific subjects. The power of influencers is such that the role has become monetarized with sponsorship from brand names or partnerships with companies wishing to attract audiences. In an article published in the *Harvard Business Review*, the influencer industry in 2022 was estimated to be $16.4 billion (Leung et al., 2022). Many companies now set budgets aside to engage with influencers, and as Leung and colleagues demonstrated using the platform Weibo, for the Chinese market returns of investment are positively related to those influencers who have large followings, are original, post frequently, post endorsements (with links) that fit the influencer brand, and seek to extend the market attraction of an existing product.

Being Connected

Through the evolution of the World Wide Web and the creation of accessible social media platforms, several authors have argued that our understanding of what constitutes friendship and who we class as "friends" has changed. This transformation has, to a certain degree, emerged as a result of the notion that following another person on social media or connecting with them via social networking sites results in an online social interaction that has personal meaning and a degree of investment that results in a range of emotional reactions from physical attraction (Fox & Anderegg, 2014) to depression and anxiety (Alsunni & Latif, 2021).

While there is a long history of research focusing on the formation of friendships online (see Parks & Floyd, 1996 as an early example), studies have continued to question whether there exist differences in the quality of friendships formed online as opposed to those formed offline (Amichai-Hamburger et al., 2013; Anthenunis et al., 2012; Yau & Reich, 2018). Amichai-Hamburger et al. (2013) recognized that while friendship is essential to well-being, the digital age has redefined the way in which we look at friendship so that issues such as intimacy and closeness, companionship, the nature of social support (its tangibility and ability to offer protection), exclusivity, and conflict resolution have had to be recast in non-corporeal ways.

The ability of an online friendship to be intimate and offer closeness and support in times of need has been questioned in ways that, historically, letters and relationships through correspondence have never really been explored. Does the presence of a piece of paper, a thoughtful note, or a secret bundle of intimate letters change the meaning of a relationship between two people who, for whatever reason, cannot meet? Chan and Cheng (2004) studied 162 internet users in Hong Kong. They asked participants to think about two friends, one they knew face-to-face and the other they knew via the internet, and describe the qualities of those friendships. Initially, results suggested that offline friendships were more interdependent, and were greater in terms of breadth, depth, understanding, and commitment. However, they also found that not only did the quality of relationships improve with duration (offline and online) but the qualitative differences between the two types of friendship also diminished. They also noted that, as online friendships did not have to conform to the social and cultural expectations or limitations that might exist offline, those friendships between people of the opposite sex were qualitatively richer than those of members of the same sex.

The emotional support that online friendships bring should however not be underestimated. Sherman and Greenfield (2013) found that teen mothers and pregnant teens went online to find emotional support from similar others through message boards when perhaps those around them were less than supportive. Together with emotional support and compassion, the researchers also found that message boards provided a medium where instrumental support (direct one-to-one communication), as well as advice and guidance on the early stages of pregnancy or what to do if a user has concerns about being pregnant, was offered. Sherman and Greenfield also reported that the young women who posted to message boards about teen pregnancy also had to deal with animosity, negative content, and so-called *fakers*.

Fakers and Social Media

The challenge we all face on social media is to determine whether or not the profile with which we interact is reflective of the person who created that profile. However, over the past few years, we have come to understand the phenomenon of "fake news"—a means of spreading disinformation without supporting evidence with the aim of causing harm to an individual's reputation (see Chap. 6 for a detailed discussion of fake news). Social media has been then the major conduit for the spreading of fake news, to such an extent that fake news accounts outperform real news accounts in terms of readership and circulation (Meel & Vishwakarma, 2020). However, there are other forms of fakers who also appear on social media and these fakers include both members of the general public and influencers. Saura and Punzo (2020) provide a taxonomy of six types of fakers that can be found currently on social media. Each type of faker has one goal, to increase influence through the number of followers they collect and provide platforms that promote:

4 Social Media and Forms of Connectedness 63

1. conspiracy theories;
2. personal beliefs and attitudes;
3. self-promotion;
4. chaos through dissension;
5. character defamation;
6. alternative "facts" (often invented).

Machine learning algorithms are being increasingly used to detect fake accounts when they are created and close them down. Fake accounts are set up for many different reasons. They can be set up to stalk an individual, collect embarrassing information about them, shame them through online ridicule, as well as hide the true identity of the profile owner. One of the most significant examples associated with the creation of a fake identity to harass and ultimately cause the death of another is recounted by Rivers and Noret (2010) in their article on text and email bullying.

> Megan Meier was a 13-year-old young woman with a history of clinical depression, who began an online relationship with a 16-year-old boy 'Josh Evans' on Myspace. 'Josh Evans' was the pseudonym for the mother of one of Megan's former friends. The intention of creating this false account was, it has been argued, to lull Megan into a false sense of security, to obtain private information from her, and then use it to humiliate her. The final message Megan received from 'Josh Evans' included the statement, 'the world would be a better place without you'. Megan took her own life on 17 October 2006. Lori Drew, the mother who posed as 'Josh Evans' was prosecuted and found guilty of accessing a computer without authorisation on three occasions in 2009. (pp. 668–669)

It should be noted that, after the trial, Lori Drew's conviction was vacated on the basis that the Computer Fraud and Abuse Act used to secure a conviction was never intended for the purpose of criminalizing the behavior of Drew. However, the story of Megan Meier illustrates the power users of social media and social networking platforms can have over one another.

Generally, research shows that there is value in online friendship, both for those who are confident in their relationships offline and for those who show more anxiety. Additionally, other forms of networking through message boards provide a support mechanism where there may not be one in physical space (this is discussed further below). However, the question remains, what exactly is friendship in online environments? Are there different forms of friendship online, and how do these compare with the different forms of friendships that exist offline?

In their study of friendships on social networking sites, Zhang et al. (2013) explored whether or not there were qualitative differences in online friendships that could be categorized or classified. Building upon Spencer and Pahl's (2006) work, which identified eight different forms of friendship, Zhang and colleagues explored whether similar variants of friendship could be found online. In Spencer and Pahl's work, friends were classified as follows:

1. *Associates*—people who are not well known to each other but share a common interest.
2. *Useful contacts*—people who share information or advice, usually work related.
3. *Fun friends*—people who socialize for fun, but the nature of the relationships may not be deep.
4. *Favor friends*—people who offer practical help but not emotional support.
5. *Helpmates*—people who both socialize together and offer practical help.
6. *Comforters*—helpmates who also provide a level of emotional support.
7. *Confidants*—people who enjoy each other's company, share personal information, and offer emotional support.
8. *Soulmates*—people who embody all of the above characteristics.

Zhang et al. (2013) also considered whether friendship types developed through social networking sites bore any similarities to those found by Kelley et al. (2011) in their study of Facebook friends. According to Kelley et al., Facebook friendships fall into six categories: *general friends* (location-based, generic, and friends of friends), *college friends* (general and club/group), *other education friends* (high school or grade school), *family*, *church*, and a *don't know* category of friend. Based upon data

4 Social Media and Forms of Connectedness   65

gathered from 104 students undertaking an MSc program in either Information Studies or Information Systems (96% of whom has more than one social networking site account), they found 17 different types of online friends similar to those found by Kelley et al. (2011). These included school friends, work-related friends, friends with similar interests, family members, close friends, unneighborly friends, roommates, boy/girlfriends (relationships), useful contacts, competitors, and virtual friends.

Zhang et al. (2013) also provided a description of the different forms that friendship took online using 11 categories:

1. *School friends*—people who went to the same school or were in the same class.
2. *Hang-out friends*—people who socialize or have fun together, have dinner and drinks.
3. *Work-related friends*—people met through work.
4. *Same organization friends*—members of the same club, church, or group.
5. *Mutual friends*—people known through a common friend.
6. *Confidants*—people with whom a person can confide or offer emotional support.
7. *Common interest friends*—people who share a common interest or pastime (e.g., football).
8. *Online friends who have never met offline*—people known only through a social network site.
9. *Information-sharing friends*—people who offer advice or information on practical issues (where to dine or where to buy an item cheaper).
10. *Online friends who have met offline*—people who have subsequently met offline (e.g., *tweet-ups*).
11. *Neighborly friends*—people who will look after pets or water plants.

Both studies conducted by Zhang et al. (2013) and Kelley et al. (2011) demonstrate that, for most participants, online friendships were reinforced by offline interactions. Whereas this research suggests that very few participants had friends that were exclusively online and that the

66   S. Bauman and I. Rivers

nature of our existence is or was "enmeshed" (Jurgenson, 2011), however with the advent of COVID-19 things changed.

The Kindness of Strangers

It is very easy to demonize social media by drawing attention to those instances where it is used to belittle, oppress, or, indeed, abuse others (see the following chapter); however, there are also examples where online communities have come together to support a member in distress, either through providing emotional support or by seeking financial support through the circulation of crowdfunding pages.

Crowdfunding is a way in which it is possible to fund a project or endeavor by asking many individuals to make a small monetary contribution. Twitter has been extremely successful in crowdfunding projects, particularly ones resulting from injustice or where deliberate harm has been done. For example, call for funds have 'gone viral' on Twitter where animal shelters have been burnt down or where a person has been burgled, assaulted, or where a family has lost everything through no fault of their own. One example of such an outpouring followed a fire at a dog shelter in the North-West of England in 2014. Within hours of the fire being discovered, social media (including Twitter) sprang into action and from a modest request for funds to support the work of the shelter in caring for the dogs in their care (£5000), over £1.5million was raised from well-wishers in over 40 countries.

The power social networking sites have in bringing together like-minded individuals is tremendous. For example, Hughes and Palen (2009) studied the influence Twitter has in an emergency. In such events as in others, we see an outpouring of concern and support for those who are distressed. Additionally, we see offers of financial or other material support (e.g., shelter) where once perhaps all expectations rested on the emergency services providing food, warmth, and accommodation. Twitter has also shown itself to be a means of distributing important information quickly and effectively, so much so that the uptake of Twitter increases after such events.

4 Social Media and Forms of Connectedness 67

In terms of personal well-being, while there remains very little research on the support mechanism offered by Twitter, anecdotally we see that it does provide a necessary support in times of difficulty. For example, one Twitter user wrote:

A woman in recovery from chemo[therapy] once told me she was never alone. Late nights, unable to sleep, she made a ton of new friends.

Another wrote:

It's far easier to find like-minded groups & people than other platforms.

Examples of how Twitter has been effective in saving lives are often usually anecdotal, but a few have shown that posting information can attract the attention of healthcare professionals in times of extreme need. For example, Griffith (2011) recounted how one evening the following tweet was received:

NEED HELP NOW!! Grandma w/ RUPTURED AORTA needs Card Surgeon/ OR ASAP, STAT can you accept LifeFlight NOW!!?

Griffith responded:

please either call 911 or have your grandma's doctor call our transfer service to get immediate help: 404-686-8334.

This very basic information allowed the user, Matthew, to get emergency help when it was needed and a link to specialist care. As Griffith stated:

What was most important here was giving Matthew information he could act on. When using Twitter, messages can only be 140 characters, so it was critical to include the most necessary information for him to get immediate assistance.

For healthcare providers, Griffith (2011) provided a series of recommendations if a service is going to be used via social media, and especially Twitter:

* Are you listening constantly and able to act immediately?
* Do you have contacts for every standard issue? That is, is there a person you can reach immediately in every department that may be required to assist you with resolution?
* Do you keep key contact information in your line of vision and reach?
* Have you considered every possible one-off emergency that could come your way?
* If every necessary contact in your process disappeared, do you have a back-up plan?
* Do you have a way to communicate to teams in your healthcare facilities (if decentralized) to keep them in the loop?
* Do you have a method to reach other healthcare facilities in the region if you are unable to help?
* Could you remove spatial barriers to appropriate teams? Are your teams strategically located to aid in social media efficiency?
* Is there a feedback loop in place to allow you to proactively stay informed once a hand-off has been made?

Griffith (2011) went on to argue that healthcare providers need to feel that they can respond immediately, show empathy and authenticity, and be empowered to act. However, we have yet to capitalize on the reach of platforms such as Twitter or TikTok for effective frontline health care.

Platforms such as Twitter are undoubtedly powerful in connecting people across the globe. Unlike Facebook, it connects us to events in the world that are not mediated by offline friendships, or by corporates (e.g., news agencies), and offers us an opportunity to see the lived experience of those who face oppression or hardship in whatever form it takes. Twitter provides a platform for us to reach out and help others immediately, and it is important that we harness the opportunities brought about by social networking sites such as Twitter and explore how they can be used to effectively help those in need. However, Twitter, like so many social networking platforms, has its drawbacks too. It too is owned by a corporate and has something of a checkered history when it comes to challenging false news distributed by individuals (Vosoughi et al., 2018).

Other platforms such as Facebook have been positively associated with a variety of measures of well-being and appear to provide positive social and psychological outcomes for most users (Fox & Moreland, 2015). For example, college students in one study completed online surveys, and researchers found that the intensity of Facebook use was associated with *bonding* (close ties that can provide emotional support), *bridging* (weak ties that provide information and ideas but not emotional support), and *maintained* social capital (the ability to continue existing weak relationships despite geographical distance), which was then correlated with satisfaction with their campus life (Ellison et al., 2007). These researchers also found that those with lower school satisfaction and self-esteem had lower bridging social capital and less intense Facebook use.

Risky Behavior

When the use of computers for interpersonal communication became widespread, there were concerns that it would lead to many superficial relationships at the expense of close personal contact in the offline world, and in fact this was confirmed by early research (Valkenburg & Peter, 2009). These researchers note, however, that in the 1990s, only a proportion of the population was online, limiting those with whom one might exchange online communications, and at that time, a good deal of online communication occurred in impersonal settings such as public chat rooms and multi-user games. With the advent and popularity of social networking came the realization that the offline and online worlds often merge and that most communication occurs with online friends who are also known offline. Once that shift was understood, studies found positive relationships between adolescents' use of social networking and their well-being (Clark et al., 2018).

Valkenburg and Peter (2009) suggested that the positive effects are due to the enhanced social disclosure that occur on these platforms. They theorize that the absence of visual, auditory, and social status information allows users to overcome inhibitions to disclosure because they are less concerned about how they are perceived. The opportunity to self-disclose intimate concerns is akin to catharsis in therapy, whereby expressing intimate thoughts and associated emotions releases energy to free the person for growth. These digitally supported disclosures support offline friendship quality, which in turn increases well-being.

One concern related to mental health of Facebook and, more recently, TikTok users is that risky offline behaviors (sexual acting out, substance use, violence, etc.) may be promoted among vulnerable users (Ahlse et al., 2020; Bonifazi et al., 2022). While posting about those behaviors is not inherently harmful, it can be that responses to those posting lead to negative consequences with mental health implications. For example, an online survey of Dutch adolescents aged 10–19, who had profiles on a popular friend networking site, found that when users had positive feedback on their profiles, their social self-esteem was enhanced (Valkenburg et al., 2006). A large number (78%) of respondents reported that they always or mostly received such positive feedback. The 7% who received negative feedback, however, had a negative effect on self-esteem. Interestingly, the number or types of friendship formed on the site were not related to social self-esteem, but rather the valence of the feedback was the influential factor.

A study of college students at one college institution addressed the concerns about Facebook and risky behavior by extracting a random sample of 161 student profiles (using a feature available on Facebook in 2006), and coding the content contained in profiles, wall content, and photos (Shelton, & Skalski, 2014). The researchers also extracted demographic and personal information included on the site. Their results were startling: 11% of the profiles listed "drinking" as an interest, plus almost 7% identified "partying" as an interest. Drug use references were found in 1.9% of sites and 2.4% included profanity in describing their interests. More than half the profiles in the study (53%) had photos with alcohol, and of those, 14% showed alcohol being consumed by either the profile person or others. A quarter of the sites included sexually suggestive contact. In terms of providing personal information, 15% gave their address and 14% included their mobile phone numbers. Although this study was published in 2014, the data were collected several years earlier. We wonder whether the strong message about the dangers of posting compromising information would yield different findings today. However, the next study we describe suggests that these behaviors persist despite the warnings of adverse consequences.

A National Survey in the US found that teens that spend time on social networking platforms are five times as likely to use tobacco, three times more likely to use alcohol, and twice as likely to use marijuana (CASAColumbia, 2011). They also found that 40% of teens in their survey had seen photos of other teens using drugs, drinking, or passed out; many first saw these people when they were younger than 13. More recently, Cookingham and Ryan (2015) found that 54% of the social media profiles posted by adolescents (13–19 years of age) referred to highly risky behaviors, including the posting of sexually explicit self-images as well as references to alcohol, drug, or tobacco use. Subsequent studies have found that social media has also had a negative impact on adolescent girls' body image (Papageorgiou et al., 2022).

Being Connected: Special Populations

For some groups within society, being connected to others online can mean the difference between life and death. The ability to find like-minded or sympathetic others in a virtual space when a physical space may be toxic is important, not only in terms of one's own sense of self-worth but also in terms of one's own mental health. Historically, people with concealed stigmas (e.g., being gay, lesbian, bisexual, trans, queer/questioning plus) could only find others who were like them through word-of-mouth or unofficial networks that were generally hidden from the general population. Additionally, when out among their local communities, those who belonged to stigmatized groups could recognize allies by attending certain venues on certain dates at certain times, or by wearing clothing or insignia that was meaningful only to like-minded others. For many marginalized groups, the evolution of the internet changed this. Where once there had been no means of contacting a support group without exposing oneself to the risk of being discovered, email and message boards provided those who felt isolated with an opportunity to chat with people who understood their experiences and could offer support both in terms of advice and guidance, but also in terms of providing them with information about safe venues in which to meet. Thomas (2002), in his qualitative study of internet chat room participation and coming-out among gay men, showed how early social networking through IRC, AOL chat rooms, and gay dating sites such as Gay.com provided opportunities for men who had not "come out" to ask questions, share experiences, and ultimately feel good about themselves:

> [The chat room was] a crutch to get [me] into the gay society. I used that crutch, I walked with it for a few days, and it was gone. Look at me now. I don't care what you think of me. I will go out in public how I want to go out. I will act the way I want to act and if you don't like it tough shit. Before I even started on AOL I would have never thought that. I would have thought I was a piece of shit. Everybody would walk on me and spit on me. And I was afraid. I was very self-conscious, very insecure about everything about me. And now I don't care. (pp. 89–90)

Perhaps the most important result to emerge from Thomas' work is the understanding that being able to chat online had a significant effect upon the well-being of this marginalized group and resulted in the invisible becoming visible: at first online and then offline. For marginalized groups, visibility is an important issue, as with visibility comes resource and the World Wide Web was and is the starting point for many marginalized groups coming together to lobby for recognition and resource.

Today there remain populations that are isolated from others; this can be because they no longer have the social capital they once had, or because they are disabled, or simply because society has forgotten about them. In the next sections of this chapter, the role of social media in supporting three groups is explored. These three groups are: homeless youth, disabled youth, and elderly citizens. For each of these groups, the internet not only has an important role to play in keeping them connected with the world, but it also has a value in providing them with information and support when it is needed.

Homeless Youth

We often think of the homeless as being isolated physically from society, perhaps, because of the link with extreme poverty with little or no access to technology. However, it may come as a surprise to find that homeless youth do use social media as means of keeping in touch with family members, friends, case workers, and even potential employers. Of course, the definition of homelessness includes those who, while not having a permanent residence, can also move around the homes of friends and extended family members, or "sofa surfing." While this increases their likelihood of encountering and using technology such as PCs and laptops, one study found that nearly 50% of homeless youth survey used public library to get online, or through an agency service. In fact, only 11% accessed the internet from the place they were staying that night (Rice & Barman-Adhikari, 2014). In one study, Von Holtz et al. (2018) looked at internet and social media access by 87 homeless youth. Overall, 56% reported that they were able to access the internet at least once a day, with 86% reporting accessing it at least once a week. Those young people with access to a smartphone were three times more likely to access the internet. Among those surveyed, while experiencing homelessness, participants also reported decreased internet access and social media use. Ten youth completed the semi-structured interviews, and various themes were identified that were linked to internet usage, including personal concerns about health and interest in resources for young people experiencing homelessness.

The unregulated nature of the World Wide Web also means that some homeless youth (particularly those without any form of shelter) may use social media as a means of selling their bodies for sex. There is a wealth of research on homelessness and prostitution, but less so on the utilization of websites and platforms by homeless youth to sell sex. For example, Barman-Adhikari and Rice (2011) noted that 27% of the homeless youth they surveyed reported talking about sex online, though 40% had sought out HIV-STI testing services, suggesting that these youth were not only sexually active (approximately 81% said they were sexually active) but also engaging in risky sexual behavior. Baird and Connolly (2023) in

74   S. Bauman and I. Rivers

their review of studies addressing the sex trafficking of minors in the United States and Canada noted that homeless youth are particularly vulnerable, and the most commonly cited recruitment location was online. Consequently, while there is clear need for and value in providing online resources for these young people in terms of assisting them to find accommodation, employment, and access to health care, it is also important that we do not ignore the potential for the sexual exploitation of homeless youth via the internet.

Youth with Disabilities

Young people with disabilities often find themselves isolated from their non-disabled peers because of the limitations they face in terms of communication, mobility, or simply because of stigma. Various studies have reported that there is some value in online communication and social networking for young people with disabilities and particularly those who have difficulties interacting with others socially or find it difficult to communicate (see Grace et al., 2014. Raghavendra et al., 2013). However, the degree to which online communication has been found to be beneficial is equivocal for those young people with complex communication needs. Grace et al. noted in their study of five young people between the ages of 11 and 18 years that while a tailored intervention with assistive technology had increased those young people's engagement with others online, feelings of loneliness and poor self-concept remained. Thus, for these youth, there remains a need to interact physically with others, a fact that has been noted on many message boards by parents of children who have autism.

In her study of 23 disabled young people living in Norway, Söderström (2009) noted that young people are expected to be connected digitally continuously and that the social ties that young disable people forge online and offline are reinforced by being able to access information and communication technologies (ICT) and social media platforms, resulting in them feeling more connected to a world that still struggles to integrate them physically. Being connected online reduces feelings of loneliness and offers an opportunity to escape the offline identity of being disabled.

4 Social Media and Forms of Connectedness 75

We should also acknowledge that there are now social influencers who are disabled themselves and attract a significant following. According to Bonilla del Río et al. (2022), social networks allow disabled influencers to not only become part of the digital world but also make their interests visible, interact with followers and, importantly, be a positive role model celebrating diversity and inclusion. In this context, social media platforms become tools to empower people with disabilities and break down those barriers that have existed in the physical world.

Elderly Citizens

Elderly citizens often face isolation as a result of retirement, the passing of loved ones, or increasingly frailty. However, both researchers and commercial organizations have turned their attention to the elderly and the role of technology in promoting inclusion. As a result, several initiatives have been introduced to ensure that not only are the elderly connected to the internet but that they too can develop or maintain social support networks through technology.

In one cross-national study conducted in Italy and the UK by Morton et al. (2015), the researchers provided vulnerable older adults the opportunity to learn to use a modified computer package developed specifically for them called *The Easy PC*. The research teams in both countries believed that the ability to engage socially with others using the internet would offer significant benefits for cognitive and mental health and well-being. The results from this study were very positive. Using data collected from participants themselves, as well as notes from trainers and reports from carers and care homes, the picture that emerged was a very positive one, and one that showed that not only could elderly citizens engage with technology but also use it effectively to keep in touch with others. For example, one carer noted of one elderly man:

> He became passionate about using PCs and through the computer he was able to meet satisfy many of his interests and curiosities. This has significantly improved his self-esteem. (p. 51)

A trainer described how one elderly woman began to use Facebook as a result of the friendship she had developed with another participant in the project:

> At the beginning of the training, she initially showed much reluctance to use social media. Then, thanks to her friendship with another participant in the project, she began using Facebook and e-mails. (p. 51)

Even for those elderly participants resident in care homes and facilities, the opportunities brought about by the project were significant, not only in terms of keeping connected with family members but also in terms of cognitive skill.

> Facebook is used constantly to keep in touch especially with the family members the lady kept in contact with very often using Skype as well. Both the lady and some of her family members noticed an improvement in her memory and ability to concentrate. (p. 53)

Morton et al. also noted that once these tools were mastered, some participants used them to learn new skills:

> A lady, for instance, has used the Internet to find tutorials to learn how to sew, something that interested her. (p. 53)

Additionally, various studies have reported that internet use had a significant impact on well-being (Yang et al., 2022) and its benefits were also found to improve quality of life (Benvenuti et al., 2020).

COVID-19

In the spring of 2020, fears that a pandemic was spreading across the globe were realized and everyday life as we knew it ended. Over the course of the next two years, education, employment, and social interaction moved online. Very quickly we became proficient in using technologies that we had never encountered before (e.g., Zoom and Microsoft Teams),

4 Social Media and Forms of Connectedness   77

and we became adept at ensuring that social distance was maintained from loved ones, friends, and colleagues. Across the two years that followed, we learned much more about that value of the internet and the value of social media (Jones et al., 2021). We also learned a great deal about social isolation, its impact upon those who lived alone and those who had lost the practical support (day care centers, respite care) that had sustained them. Some countries fared better than others. In particular, Estonia, that had for years built an online infrastructure—*e-estonia*—was able to transition from face-to-face to online readily when COVID-19 forced the shutdown of daily life (https://e-estonia.com; see Chap. 9). Other countries "pivoted" swiftly from in-person meetings, crowded offices, factories and shops with appropriate distancing protocols put in place, with face masks and hand sanitization becoming commonplace. In the midst of this, we began to re-evaluate our relationship with the online world. For two years it became our reality. Early in the pandemic, Döring (2020) considered how COVID-19 would impact sexualities, relationship quality and, ultimately, sex itself. She looked at the way media narrative romanticized lockdown with stories of quarantine honeymoons, the so-called Coronavirus Baby Boom and, of necessity, the reduction in casual sex. Behind these narratives, another narrative also emerged—that of sex online with the development of a number of online platforms that provided free or, more likely pay to view, sexual imagery, videos—often bespoke—where models interacted in real time with those who signed up to the pages or paid for personal content. To a degree, the reduction in physical casual sex and the uptake of online platforms for sexual experiences was to be welcomed (though many might disagree), as it significantly reduced that chances of being infected with COVID-19 or sexually transmitted diseases. Indeed, elsewhere online, health professionals actively engaged with social media platforms and advertising companies to ensure that important public health messages were heeded. Governments too worked with social media companies such as Facebook, Twitter, and Instagram to ensure that false information was kept to a minimum (Limaye et al., 2020).

As a result of the physical restrictions that were put in place, we also saw a rise in the need for online communities to support those with ongoing and/or chronic conditions. For example, Nutley et al. (2020)

reported that the changes in daily routines, exercise routines, and help-seeking opportunities resulted in increased anxiety and frustration among individuals with a lifetime history of eating disorders. However, Reddit forums provided a means of sharing personal experiences, advice, and peer support during this pandemic. For others with pre-existing mental health conditions (such as depression, anxiety, and obsessive-compulsive disorder), issues such as a fear of returning to normality, isolation, and a lack of social support were commonly posted on open forums (Brewer et al., 2022). The importance of forums and other communication platforms is summarized aptly by Cheded and Skandalis (2020) who said, "digital spaces provided us with a much-needed sense of connection with other people." However, they also noted that these spaces "also contributed to a sense of frustration at the end of online social interactions. when closing the laptop, this meant a return to a space that felt terribly empty" (p. 345).

Summary

COVID-19 taught us that being connected to the world around us is increasingly important. Increasingly, our online and offline lives are enmeshed and not easily separated. While evidence suggests that online friendships cannot entirely compensate for the lack of offline friendships, personal well-being and feeling of social connectedness derive from successful online *and* offline relationships. Initiatives that promote digital inclusion have been shown to have benefits, not only in maintaining and developing social networks, but also in sustaining or improving quality of life. For those with disabilities, while loneliness may still be a feature of daily life offline, the ability to go online and talk to others is a great course of support, building confidence, and the social skills necessary to form offline friendships too. For homeless youth, the ability to stay connected offers a way out of poverty but comes with its own significant risks. The provision of computers in public libraries and youth agencies must remain a priority if we are to assist them in finding shelter and employment. While there are dangers in online communication (and these are discussed in greater detail in Chap. 5), this chapter has shown that social media has a significant role to play in maintaining and developing lines of communication and support for all those facing life's challenges—and no more so than when we faced, as a global community, the threat of COVID-19.

References

Ahlse, J., Nilsson, F., & Sandström, N. (2020). *It's time to TikTok*. https://www.diva-portal.org/smash/get/diva2:1434091/FULLTEXT01.pdf

Alsunni, A. A., & Latif, R. (2021). Higher emotional investment in social media is related to anxiety and depression in university students. *Journal of Taibah University Medical Sciences, 16*(2), 247–252. https://doi.org/10.1016/j.jtumed.2020.11.004

Amichai-Hamburger, Y., Kingsbury, M., & Schneider, B. H. (2013). Friendship: An old concept with a new meaning? *Computers in Human Behavior, 29*(1–2), 33–39. https://doi.org/10.1016/j.chb.2012.05.025

Anthenunis, M. L., Valkenburg, P. M., & Peter, J. (2012). The quality of online, offline, and mixed-mode friendships among users of a social networking site. *Cyberpsychology: Journal of Psychosocial Research on Cyberspace, 6*(3), 6. https://doi.org/10.5817/CP2012-3-6

Baird, K., & Connolly, J. (2023). Recruitment and entrapment pathways of minors into sex trafficking in Canada and the United States: A systematic review. *Trauma, Violence, & Abuse, 24*(1), 189–202. https://doi.org/10.1177/15248380211025241

Barman-Adhikari, A., & Rice, E. (2011). Sexual health information seeking online among runaway and homeless youth. *Journal of the Society for Socail Work Research, 2*(2), 88–103. https://doi.org/10.5243/jsswr.2011.5

Benvenuti, M., Giovagnoli, S., Mazzoni, E., Cipressoo, P., Pedroni, E., & Riva, G. (2020). The relevance of online social relationships among the elderly: How using the web could enhance quality of life. *Frontiers in Psychology, 11*, 551862. https://doi.org/10.3389/fpsyg.2020.551862

Bonifazi, G., Cecchini, S., Corradini, E., Giuliani, L., Ursino, D., & Virgili, L. (2022). Investigating community evolutions in TikTok dangerous and non-dangerous challenges. *Journal of Information Science*. https://doi.org/10.1177/01655515221116519

Bonilla del Río, M., Castillo Abdul, B., García Ruiz, R., & Rodríguez Martín, A. (2022). Influencers with intellectual disability in digital society: An opportunity to advance social inclusion. *Media and Communication, 10*(1), 222–234. https://doi.org/10.17645/mac.v10i1.4763

Brewer, G., Centifanti, L., Castro Caicedo, J., Huxley, G., Peddie, C., Stratton, K., & Lyons, M. (2022). Experiences of mental distress during COVID-19: Thematic analysis of discussion forum posts for anxiety, depression and obsessive-compulsive disorder. *Illness, Crisis & Loss, 30*(4), 795–811. https://doi.org/10.1177/10541373211023951

CASAColumbia. (2011, August 24). *2011 National teen survey finds teens regularly using social networking likelier to smoke, drink, use drugs.* http://www.casacolumbia.org/newsroom/press-releases/2011-national-teen-survey-finds

Chan, D. K.-S., & Cheng, G. H.-L. (2004). A comparison of offline and online friendship qualities at different stages of relationship development. *Journal of Social and Personal Relationships, 21*(3), 305–320. https://doi.org/10.1177/0265407504042834

Cheded, M., & Skandalis, A. (2020). Touch and contact during COVID-19: Insights form queer digital spaces. *Feminist Frontiers, 28*(S2), 340–347. https://doi.org/10.1111/gwao.12697

Clark, J. L., Algoe, S. B., & Green, M. C. (2018). Social networking sites and well-being: The role of social connectedness. *Current Directions in Psychological Science, 27*(1), 32–37. https://doi.org/10.1177/0963721417730833

Cookingham, L. M., & Ryan, G. L. (2015). The Impact of social media on the sexual and social wellness of adolescents. *Journal of Pediatric and Adolescent Gynecology, 28*(1), 2–5. https://doi.org/10.1016/j.jpag.2014.03.001

Döring, N. (2020). How is the COVID-19 pandemic affecting our sexualities? An overview of the current media narratives and research hypotheses. *Archives of Sexual Behavior, 49*, 2765–2778. https://doi.org/10.1007/s10508-020-01790-z

Ellison, N., Steinfield, C., & Lampe, C. (2007). The benefits of Facebook "friends:" Social capital and college students' use of online social network sites. *Journal of Computer-Mediated Communication, 12*, 1143–1168. https://doi.org/10.1111/j.1083-6101.2007.00367.x

Fox, J., & Anderegg, C. (2014). Romantic relationship stages and social networking sites: Uncertainty reduction strategies and perceived relational norms on Facebook. *Cyberpsychology, Behavior, and Social Networking, 17*(11), 685–691. https://doi.org/10.1089/cyber.2014.0232

Fox, J., & Moreland, J. J. (2015). The dark side of social networking sites: An exploration of the relational and psychological stressors associated with Facebook use and affordances. *Computers in Human Behavior, 45*, 168–176. https://doi.org/10.1016/j.chb.2014.11.083

Grace, E., Raghavendra, P., Newman, L., Wood, D., & Connell, T. (2014). Learning to use the Internet and online social media: What is the effectiveness of home-based intervention for youth with complex communication needs? *Child Language, Teaching & Therapy, 30*(2), 141–157. https://doi.org/10.1177/0265659013518565

Griffith, M. (2011, April 27). *Can Twitter help save lives? A health care social media case study.* http://advancingyourhealth.org/highlights/2011/04/27/can-twitter-help-save-lives-a-health-care-social-media-case-study-part-i/

Hughes, A. L., & Palen, L. (2009). Twitter adoption and use in mass convergence and emergency events. *International Journal of Emergency Management, 6*(3–4), 248–260. https://doi.org/10.1504/IJEM.2009.031564

Jones, R., Mougouei, D., & Evans, S. L. (2021). Understanding the emotional response to COVID-19 information in news and social media: A mental health perspective. *Human Behaviour and Emerging Technologies, 3*(5), 831–842. https://doi.org/10.1002/hbe2.304

Jurgenson, N. (2011). *Amber case: Cyborg anthropologist (a critique).* http://thesocietypages.org/cyborgology/2011/02/10/amber-case-cyborg-anthropologist-a-critique/.

Kelley, P. G., Brewer, R., Mayer, Y., Cranor, L. F., & Sadeh, N. (2011). An investigation into Facebook friend grouping. In *Human-computer interaction – INTERACT 2011: 13th IFIP TC 13 international conference, Lisbon, Portugal: Proceedings, Part III* (pp. 216–233). Springer.

Leung, F. F., Zhang, J. Z., Gu, F. F., & Palmatier, R. W. (2022). Does influence marketing really pay off? *Harvard Business Review.* https://hbr.org/2022/11/does-influencer-marketing-really-pay-off

Limaye, R. J., Sauer, M., Ali, J., Bernstein, J., Walh, B., Barnhill, A., & Labrique, A. (2020). Building trust while influencing online COVID-19 content in the social media world. *The Lancet, 2*(6), E277–E278. https://doi.org/10.1016/S2589-7500(20)30084-4

Meel, P., & Vishwakarma, D. K. (2020). Fake news, rumor, information pollution in social media and web: A contemporary survey of state-of-the-arts, challenges and opportunities. *Expert Systems with Applications, 153*, 112986. https://doi.org/10.1016/j.eswa.2019.112986

Morton, T., Genova, A., Neild, B., Wilson, N., Haslam, C., Dell'Atti, A., Sansonetti, S., & Di Furia, L. (2015). *AGES 2.0: Activating and guiding the engagement of seniors through social media: Final report.* http://www.ages2.eu/sites/default/files/page/Ages-final-report-EN.pdf

Nutley, S. K., Falise, A. M., Hendeson, R., Apostolou, V., Mathews, C. A., & Striley, C. W. (2020). The impact of COVID-19 on disordered eating behavior: A qualitative analysis of social media users' response to the global pandemic. *JMIR Mental Health*. https://preprints.jmir.org/preprint/26011

Papageorgiou, A., Fisher, C., & Cross, D. (2022). "Why don't I look like her?" How adolescent girls view social media and its connection to body image. *BMC Womens Health, 22*(1), 261. https://doi.org/10.1186/s12905-022-01845-4

Parks, M. R., & Floyd, K. (1996). Making friends in cyberspace. *Journal of Communication, 46*(1), 80–97. https://doi.org/10.1111/j.1460-2466.1996.tb01462.x

Raghavendra, P., Grace, E., Newman, L., & Wood, D. (2013). 'They think I'm really cool and nice' the impact of Internet support on the social networks and loneliness of young people with disabilities. *Telecommunications Journal of Australia, 63*(2), 2. http://www.swinburne.edu.au/lib/ir/onlinejournals/tja/

Rice, E., & Barman-Adhikari, A. (2014). Internet and social media use as a resource among homeless youth. *Journal of Computer Mediated Communication, 19*(1), 232–247. https://doi.org/10.1111/jcc4.12038

Rivers, I., & Noret, N. (2010). 'I h8 u': Findings from a five-year study of text and email bullying. *British Educational Research Journal, 36*(4), 643–671. https://doi.org/10.1080/01411920903071918

Saura, J. R., & Punzo, J. G. (2020). Defining types of "fakers" in social media. *Marketing and Management of. Innovations, 11*(4), 231–236. https://doi.org/10.21272/mmi.2020.4-18

Shelton, A. K., & Skalski, P. (2014). Blinded by the light: Illuminating the dark side of social network use through content analysis. *Computers in Human Behavior, 33*, 339–348. https://doi.org/10.1016/j.chb.2013.08.017

Sherman, L. E., & Greenfield, P. M. (2013). Forging friendship, soliciting support. A mixed-method examination of message boards for pregnant teens and teen mothers. *Computers in Human Behavior, 29*(1), 75–85. https://doi.org/10.1016/j.chb.2012.07.018

Söderström, S. (2009). Offline social ties and online use of computers: A study of disabled youth and their use of ICT advances. *New Media & Society, 11*(5), 709–727. https://doi.org/10.1177/1461444809105347

Spencer, L., & Pahl, R. E. (2006). *Rethinking friendship: Hidden solidarities today*. Princeton University Press.

Thomas, A. B. (2002). *Internet chat room participation and the coming out experiences of young gay men: A qualitative study*. Unpublished PhD thesis. The University of Texas at Austin.

Valkenburg, P. M., & Peter, J. (2009). Social consequences of the Internet for adolescents. *Current Directions in Psychological Science, 18*(1), 1–5. https://doi.org/10.1111/j.1467-8721.2009.01595.x

Valkenburg, P. M., Peter, J., & Schouten, A. P. (2006). Friend networking sites and their relationship to adolescents' well-being and social self-esteem. *CyberPsychology & Behavior, 9*, 584–590. https://doi.org/10.1089/cpb.2006.9.584

Von Holtz, L. A. H., Frasso, R., Golinkoff, J. M., Lozano, A. J., Hanlon, A., & Dowshen, N. (2018). Internet and social media access among youth experiencing homelessness: Mixed methods study. *Journal of Medical Internet Research, 20*(5), e184. https://doi.org/10.2196/jmir.9306

Vosoughi, S., Roy, D., & Aral, S. (2018). The spread of true and false news online. *Science, 359*(6380), 1146–1151. https://doi.org/10.1126/science.aap9559

Yang, Y., Zeng, D., & Yang, F. (2022). Internet use and subjective well-being of the elderly: An analysis of the mediating effect based on social capital. *International Journal of Environmental Research and Public Health, 19*, 12087. https://doi.org/10.3390/ijerph191912087

Yau, J. C., & Reich, S. M. (2018). Are the qualities of adolescents offline friendships present in digital interactions? *Adolescent Research Review, 3*(3), 339–355. https://doi.org/10.1007/s40894-017-0059-y

Zhang, X., Gao, Q., Khoo, C. S. G., & Wu, A. (2013). Categories of friends on social networking sites: An exploratory study. In *Proceedings of the 5th international conference on Asia-Pacific library and information education and practice* (pp. 244–259). University of Khon Kaen.

5

Digital Aggression, Cyberbullying, and the Impact of COVID-19

Introduction

Digital technology has brought numerous benefits to society, but as with any innovation, it brings both opportunity and risks. We define risk as the possibility of exposure to danger, harm, hazards, or peril. Note that harm does not automatically occur, but risk brings with it the potential for negative outcomes.

Since the internet and mobile/cell phones have become commonplace features of modern life, there have been worries about the potential for harm, particularly for children and adolescents. This has led to an explosion of coverage of negative consequences, in the nature of "I told you so," proffered as exemplars of the dangers that await naïve users of technology. Many appeals to protect children from these ubiquitous dangers continue to be featured in the media. There are two fallacies in this focus: today's children and adolescents are not naïve about the dangers. In fact, they are quite technologically sophisticated, and many are able to teach adults about technological strategies for protection from harm. It is true that young people lack experience in making difficult decisions and may also lack the mature brain structures required to generate careful plans

© The Author(s), under exclusive license to Springer Nature Switzerland AG 2023
S. Bauman, I. Rivers, *Mental Health in the Digital Age*,
https://doi.org/10.1007/978-3-031-32122-1_5

and consider options. But this is balanced by their technological skill and knowledge, bolstered by the many media messages and educational programs designed to ensure the safe use of technology.

The second fallacy is that attention should be focused solely on young people. The fact is that many adults and older adults are also at risk. Older adults are latecomers to technology and often lack knowledge of measures they can employ to protect themselves and of technological remedies to difficult situations they encounter; their ignorance renders them vulnerable.

We wish to stress that we in no way intend to suggest that the risks present in modern technology should overshadow the many benefits and positive enhancements that technology brings. Young people engage in physical activities and sports which are important to their development, but such activities have inherent risks. Typically, adults provide protective equipment and ensure that the children in their charge are trained in requisite skills. We agree with the Telnor Group (2013):

> In general, the increase in children's access to online services is overwhelmingly positive, bringing with it educational and developmental benefits as well as security, giving parents the ability to keep track of their children wherever they are and to communicate easily with them when plans change or they are running late. Expansion of internet access to this cohort also generates long-term socio-economic benefits, increasing digital literacy and building skills they will need to succeed in the 21st century. (p. 3)

Adults drive cars, an activity that carries the risk of injury or death from collision or mechanical malfunction of the vehicle, but the advantages of independence and mobility attendant to driving do not prevent most adults from acquiring and using the skill to drive. They use seat belts, ensure that vehicles are serviced regularly, and drive carefully. But they drive. We wish to emphasize that we view the risks of technology from a similar perspective—acknowledging that there are risks in using digital technology, but that there are advantages too, and we would not discourage people from enjoying the many ways in which one's life can be enriched by the digital world.

The Evolution of Digital Aggression

In her pioneering book, *Life on the Screen*, MIT professor Sherry Turkle (1995) was perhaps one of the first to understand the challenges we face engaging with online environments. In one chapter, she tackled the issue of online violence and critiqued the discussions she saw taking place about engagement with others in multi-user domains (MUDs). She explored whether online sexual interactions between users that were, at the time, textual, could be described as abusive or even rape. In the offline world, the act of forcing someone to engage in sexual acts against his or her will would clearly constitute an act of rape. It is less clear about sexual aggression in an online environment. Turkle recounts how the "behavior" of one user—*Mr Bungle*—not only reduced one of his victims to tears as she recounted her experiences to a journalist, but the narration of her story brought together a mix of emotions that were described as, "murderous rage with eye-rolling annoyance" (p. 252). Julian Dibbell—the journalist—was perplexed by this, as his interviewee's emotional response did not entirely make sense in terms of what he might have expected in "real life" or in terms of what he understood virtual reality to be (p. 252). While the incident was clearly upsetting in its retelling, it also evoked calls for *Mr Bungle's* castration together with an acceptance that people can be annoying online. Ultimately the question of whether *Mr Bungle* had "raped" another person online was raised. There also seemed to be confusion as to whether there was a tangible cause for *Mr Bungle's* victim to be upset. As one defender of *Mr Bungle* wrote:

> MUDs are Fantasy. MUDs are somewhere you can have fun and let your hidden self out. (p. 252)

In those early days of internet use when online interactions were devoid of images and videos, our first attempts to understand how people engaged with others online included an assumption that some form of distinction existed between the material or offline world and the virtual or online world. For example, Robert Young (1996a, b) argued that while the material world limited the ways in which we express ourselves, no such limits exist online:

> One of the most striking features of email forums and letters is that people can experience almost no impediment to expressing themselves – for good or ill – because it all feels as if it's happening in the head. (Young, 1996b)

These early suggestions that online interactions with others were no more than a form of fantasy ultimately meant that we gave license to those who questioned or even dismissed the potential harm caused by a confrontational or abusive exchange or downplayed another's hostile intentions because it was, to all intents and purposes, without physical form.

However, advances in technology, the ability to post and send images and share videos and movies, and the emergence of social networking sites and applications have all brought the offline and online worlds closer together or, more likely, torn down boundaries that we once believed existed. For example, over the last few years, we have become familiar with *revenge porn*, where images and clips that are sexual in nature and once shared between partners, are posted openly by one partner to humiliate another. In one study conducted in the UK in 2022, 27% of those who were targeted with, what is described as *image-based sexual abuse*, were women aged between 30 and 39 years (it was only 7% for men in the same age bracket). For women between the ages of 21–29 years, the reported rate of victimization was 15% (2% for similarly aged men). For 40–49 years old, the number of women who were targeted was 10% (3% for men), among 50–59 years olds reported rates were 12% and 2%, respectively. Among older women and men aged 60 years plus, rates were 7% and 2%. Notably among under 16s, where there is the potential for the person posting images or clips to be prosecuted under laws relating to the distribution of child pornography, the rates were 10% for girls and 0 for boys (Statista, 2023). The long-term implications for the mental health of revenge porn have only recently come to light through a handful of studies. Using in-depth qualitative interviews conducted with 18 female targets of revenge porn, Bates (2017) found that the women she interviewed experienced ongoing issues with trust (especially trust of a

5 Digital Aggression, Cyberbullying, and the Impact of COVID-19

partner), anxiety, depression, suicidal thoughts, and symptoms of post-traumatic stress disorder.

Through our engagement with social media platforms, we ideally wish to present ourselves to the outside world in a way in which we feel comfortable. As we have seen, this can be derailed where relationships with intimate others go sour. Sometimes our online personas are, at times, idealized versions of ourselves without the imperfections and confusions that arise in daily life; however, because they are personas in which we have invested and in which we hope others will invest by linking, following, or befriending us, we need to be able to monitor what is shared with others online. Those personas are us.

The same can be said of avatars in the multiplayer gaming world. Crowe (2012) has shown us that, even within fantasy environments with dragons, huntsmen, and sorcerers, there are elements of engagement that are not disembodied or "in the head"; they are real and result in physical reactions and emotional responses. As one gamer said:

It's like my life but more, and better. (p. 221)

The confused emotions expressed by *Mr Bungle's* victim demonstrate that in the 1990s we had some understanding (albeit rudimentary) of the potential for virtual space to invade our offline world in ways that made us feel violated; however, we were ill-prepared to deal with the ways in which social media has become part of our everyday existence and now impacts upon our own sense of self. This is most keenly illustrated by the tragic suicide, in 2006, of Megan Meier, a 13-year-old girl with a history of clinical depression (part of this story is recounted in Chap. 4). She began an online relationship with a 16-year-old boy called Josh Evans whom she met on *MySpace*—a social networking site. Although Megan was always supervised by a parent when she was online, no one could foresee the impact Josh would have on her. Alas Josh turned out to be the creation of the mother of one of Megan's former friends—a woman called Lori Drew who was aided in her online hoax by an employee. In court, it was argued that Drew's intention in creating Josh Evans was to establish a friendship with Megan and obtain private information which could then be used to humiliate her as punishment for gossiping about her daughter. Up until 16 October, all evidence suggests that the online relationship had been a positive one for Megan, but then the messages changed and became hostile. One of the last messages Megan received from Josh said, "the world would be a better place without you." Megan took her own life on 17 October.

While there is a myriad of issues to consider in this case, including Drew's extreme behavior towards a girl with whom her daughter had once been friends, the fact that Josh Evans could elicit feelings that led to Megan's death indicates that the online world has just as much salience as that we inhabit offline.

Online Risks

One useful way to examine digital risk is to use the schema proposed by Livingstone et al. (2013). They identify four types of risk:

* content-related risks,
* contact-related risks,
* conduct-related risks, and
* other risks (e.g., security, commerce).

Content-Related Risks

In their study of what bothers children online, Livingstone et al. (2013) found that 12% of the 9–16-year-olds in their sample from 25 European countries had been distressed by something they encountered online. The most frequently mentioned types of content were pornographic or violent content, with 14% of the sample indicating they had viewed sexually explicit content online. Pornography was upsetting because it was not being sought but was encountered accidentally (or appeared on the screen unbidden) and thus was unexpected and shocking, particularly to younger children. The next most frequent concern is the violent and aggressive, or gory material they saw. Some young people noted they were particularly upset by the cruelty, killings, and mistreatment of animals. Some of this material was found on sites such as YouTube, which is a user-generated platform for videos. Others mentioned finding upsetting content on websites and on social networking sites. Games were mentioned too. Young people who reported being upset by pornography indicated they were disgusted and fearful. When the content was violent, the most often mentioned emotional reaction was fear, followed by disgust. One concern is that unintentionally viewing pornographic or violent material can be so frightening to young people that anxiety disorders might develop. The experience might cause a young person to abandon their optimistic view of humanity, resulting in depression. On the other hand, the availability of these types of material for young people who seek them out because of curiosity makes it possible that they would find validation or normalization in the volume of content of this nature.

Contact-Related Risks

Contact-related risks include people online assuming fictitious personas, attempts at inappropriate offline contact, particularly sexual contact, face-to-face meetings following online contact, unwanted messages and other communication, and other people accessing personal data or being tracked by "cookies." A very small number of children mentioned that they feared being targeted by religious or ideological zealots who might seek to persuade them to do unacceptable things.

Conduct-Related Risks

Conduct-related risks include a number of aggressive behaviors that include unwelcome intrusion or interference, hacking or the misuse of personal data, people saying bad things or attempting to cause damage to reputation, sharing images of photos of a user, sharing another's personal information deliberately and unwelcome sexting. However, the most commonly cited form of conduct-related risk cited by children and young people is cyberbullying. In the following section, we focus on this issue in

Digital Aggression and Cyberbullying Before COVID-19

Cyberbullying refers to the use of digital technology to inflict harm. The definition is not universally accepted but will suffice for our purpose. There are features of cyberbullying that suggest it can be more harmful than other forms of (offline) bullying: there is the perception of anonymity, which means perpetrators are unlikely to be held accountable for their actions. Cyberbullying is not limited by time or geography but can be perpetrated at any time from wherever the aggressor is located. Two features are particularly associated with psychological harm: the enormous size of the audience and the permanence of content posted online, which can resurface years later to embarrass or torment the target.

It has been difficult to determine a realistic prevalence rate for this behavior because of the variety of measures that have been used. The *EUKids Online* study of youth in 25 countries reported that 6% of 9–16-year-olds have been bullied online, with 3% admitting having bullied others (Lobe et al., 2011). In most of the countries in which the survey was administered, a high proportion (70–90%) of children reported they were at least a little upset by it. However, the survey was administered in 2009, and the question did not take into account bullying via mobile phones. Using nationally representative data from the United States, Wang et al. (2009) indicated that approximately 14% of children in grades 6–10 were involved in cyberbullying either as perpetrator, target, or both. Statistica.com reports that in a 2023 survey of US youth, 87% of respondents indicated they had witnessed cyberbullying. The focus of the cyberbullying was physical appearance in 61% of cases, race (17%), or religion in 11%, and sexuality in 15% (Broadband Search, 2023). It is clear that while there is variation in prevalence rates across studies, cyberbullying is a significant problem.

5 Digital Aggression, Cyberbullying, and the Impact of COVID-19

Cyberbullying has the potential to be much more damaging than any other form of bullying because it is relentless. It stretches beyond the perimeters of the school or workplace and invades our homes, as the case of Megan Meier illustrates. Cyberbullying is also personal—much more so than schoolyard bullying. Messages are targeted and sent for maximum effect, often when the perpetrator knows the recipient will be alone, and they convey a meaning that is usually personal. As noted earlier, these messages can be sent at any time and are usually anonymous. Finally, these messages lack any form of social filter, thus resulting in more extreme threats to personal safety. Any rules relating to the offline world do not apply and, as a result, perpetrators' implicit attitudes and beliefs are aired (Hinduja & Patchin, 2020).

Cyberbullying has been linked to several negative mental health consequences, such as depression, sadness, social anxiety, and poor self-concept, in addition to increased school absences and decreased academic performance (Gradinger et al., 2012; Sourander et al., 2010). Before the advent of COVID-19 and the lockdown, researchers also found that targets of cyberbullying reported higher rates of depression than those who experience more traditional forms of offline bullying. Concerns about the well-being of targets of cyberbullying have intensified over the years, with data showing that young people are more likely to consider taking their own lives—especially if they believe they have no other option to relive the relentless torment that (Bauman et al., 2013; Bonanno & Hymel, 2013; Cénat et al., 2015; Litwiller & Brausch, 2013; Patchin & Hinduja, 2010; Sinclair et al., 2012).

Most studies of cyberbullying focused on youth or college students, but workplace cyberbullying is also a serious problem. One study of university employees conducted in the UK found that 80% had experienced cyberbullying in the previous six months, with 14–20% experiencing such mistreatment weekly or more often (Economic and Social Research Council, 2012). Workplace cyberbullying can involve demeaning or threatening emails, forwarding emails to others, using social media to spread rumors or embarrass the target. Sometimes the aggressor is a superior, but it often comes from colleagues who may be jealous of the target, or from business competitors. For example, one professional writer described negative reviews of her book posted on Amazon.com (Kay,

2013) by someone who had a personal agenda. Such reviews can be very damaging to the sales of a book.

Data from Statistica.com showed among US, UK, and German adult workers, US workers reported the highest frequency of four cyberbullying behaviors (Petrosyan, 2022). Those included being insulted by a colleague, discovering secret online discussions about the worker; rumors circulated using office digital communication and receiving unwanted romantic solicitation using digital devices.

Workplace cyberbullying can cause high levels of stress and strain that lead to both physical and psychological illness and can also result in reduced productivity on the job, reduced job satisfaction, anxiety, and increased absenteeism (Anonymous, 2013). Experts on workplace cyberbullying often advise reporting to supervisors or managers (unless, of course, the supervisor or manager is the aggressor) and working with Human Resources. This may be helpful, but many workers have left their jobs to escape cyberbullying. Workplace cyberbullying can lead to anxiety and depression, particularly when one's income and livelihood are threatened. It is essential that mental health workers do not diminish the power of cyberbullying among adults and offer support and empathy in addition to strategies to recover from the experiences.

Cyberbullying and the COVID-19 Pandemic

Internationally, lockdown saw a shift in the usage of online platforms for communication in order to support education and industry. For many people, the move online resulted in increased feelings of isolation and, concomitantly, the erosion of those social filters that had kept implicit attitudes and beliefs under wraps. With the closure of schools, we saw, as we might expect, reductions in offline bullying as there were few opportunities for social interactions outside the family circle. Some researchers also reported reductions in cyberbullying (Bacher-Hicks et al., 2021).

In one study conducted in Canada, a sample of 6578 students in grades 4 (9–10 years of age) to 12 (17–18 years of age) were recruited to explore the impact of COVID-19 on bullying behaviors (Vaillancourt et al., 2021). While higher rates of physical, verbal, and social bullying

5 Digital Aggression, Cyberbullying, and the Impact of COVID-19

were reported before the pandemic, Vaillancourt et al. found that there was little change in reports of cyberbullying. By way of contrast, Jain et al. (2020) explored the experiences of bullying (offline and online) among 256 Indian students before the pandemic (October 2019) with a follow-up of 118 students at the height of lockdown (June 2020). Their data showed that before the pandemic, those students who were more likely to interact with strangers online spent longer time on social media and began a relationship online were likely to be targets of online aggression. In June 2020, some additional factors came to the fore: these included a willingness to share opinions online; posting social media content via Instagram; and regular use of gaming platforms. Jain et al. also found that two other factors explained susceptibility to cyberbullying: age (i.e., youth) and sexual orientation.

Sexual Orientation (GLBTQ+)

Prior to the pandemic, in 2019, Hinduja and Patchin (2020) surveyed 4500 youth from across the United States and found that 87% of sexual minority youth (gay, lesbian, bisexual, trans, queer/questioning plus) reported having been bullied at school with 52% reporting that they had been bullied online. For heterosexual and cisgender youth, the rates were 72% and 35%, respectively. "Non-heterosexual" males were most likely to say they had been bullied at school (73.9%) with 30% reporting having been bullied online. Among trans youth, 33.3% reported being bullied online.

Following the lockdown (between April and June 2020), TIE (Time for Inclusive Education) initiated a national survey to assess the toll lockdown had on the well-being and mental health of Scotland's young people between the ages of 12 and 24 years. In total, 47% of young people said that they had been bullied online during lockdown. While 59% said they had witnessed an increase in prejudice-based posts, comments, and/or attitudes online, 45% had seen racism and 36% had seen homophobia. Additionally, 39% said that the closure of schools, colleges, and universities had negatively affected their mental health (Rivers et al., 2023).

Comparing the experiences of heterosexual and sexual minority young people (N = 352) during lockdown, it was found that 60% of sexual minority youth reported having experienced and/or seen online bullying (30% had "seen" it, 19% had "seen and experienced" it, and 11% "experienced" it). Among heterosexual youth, 38% reported that they had seen and/or experienced online bullying, with 27% having "seen" it, and 7% having "seen and experienced" it. Overall, 76% of sexual minority youth believed that more online bullying has taken place during lockdown; only 49% of heterosexual youth reported similarly (Rivers et al., 2023).

In terms of emotional well-being, before lockdown, 52% of sexual minority youth suggested that their emotional well-being was positive and 22% reported that it had been "Ok." Following lockdown, only 13% said their emotional well-being was positive and 18% believed that it was "Ok." Among heterosexual youth, before lockdown, 72% suggested that their emotional well-being had been positive, with 14% saying it had been "Ok." Once lockdown began, only 36% said their emotional well-being was positive, with 24% suggesting that it was "Ok" (Rivers et al., 2023).

Workplace

Within the workplace, we saw bullying and harassment of healthcare professionals who faced inordinate stresses during the pandemic (see, for example, Somani et al., 2022). Within the general workforce, one study by Sigursteinsdottir and Karlsdottir (2022) explored the importance of social support at work among Icelandic workers during the pandemic. Overall, 4, 973 people were surveyed (82% were women). The data showed that whilst 87% said they were "often" or "always" satisfied with their job, a small number (8%) had been bullied at work, 2% reported having been sexually harassed, and 3% had been subject to gender-based harassment. Social support was found to be a significant protective factor against bullying and sexual harassment at work, and of course, for many workers, the degree of social support they were used to was lost during the pandemic. The authors argued that worker well-being was of paramount importance and, as the world moved to new ways of working,

5 Digital Aggression, Cyberbullying, and the Impact of COVID-19

new ways of offering social support to workers needed to be found. In another study by Tsuno and Tabuchi (2022), 16,384 workers in Japan were surveyed from August to September 2020 to identify the risk factors for workplace bullying during the pandemic. A key finding from the study was that those employees who worked remotely from home during lockdown, who experienced pressure brought about by increased physical or psychological demands of their job, and who had a current or prior diagnosis of depression were more likely to report severe psychological distress, suicidal ideation, and work-related bullying. Indeed, Mehta and Maniar (2023) caution us to consider the impact COVID-19 has had upon the workforce in a stark warning:

> In spite of having pronounced benefits, the use of ICT produces unintended and unwelcome consequences including IT-based cultural domination, new colonization, technological slavery, attacks on privacy, hindrance to personal safety, insecurity, family conflict, mental pressure, health hazards, and hindrance to creative thinking. Long working hours that began with Covid-19 has led to high blood pressure, insomnia, mental disorders, fatigue and boredom. (p. 40)

COVID-19 highlighted the significant digital divide that exists within our countries and across countries. It highlighted the fact that few countries had the infrastructure ready to deal with an issue such as a pandemic, and that the well-being of the workforce was not paramount during a time when businesses struggled to keep going with significant numbers of the workforce working from home. As a consequence of the fact that there were fewer of us in the workplace, vulnerabilities emerged, and as a consequence of many of us working online and from home, new forms of cyber-mediated bullying emerged with people working unsustainable hours, with few breaks and little in the way of mechanisms to facilitate workforce well-being. Indeed, it is now, as we return to our workspaces, that we realize the toll of the pandemic not only in terms of lives lost but the emotional impact it has upon each and every one of us.

Building Resilience in Young People

Prior to the pandemic, one study of British 14–17-year-olds considered how we build resilience in young people who are exposed to online aggression (Przybylski et al., 2014). First, not only are youth who self-regulate their use of digital technology more resilient than those who rely on external regulation, they are more likely to take advantage of the opportunities available in cyberspace. For example, they learn technological and other skills, expand their social networks, gather useful information, and become aware of current events. Second, parents who restrict access to technology in order to protect their children or who employ various monitoring tools to oversee their child's digital activities are not as effective in building resilience as those who provide support and show interest in the child's activities. Finally, young people who perceive the digital world as positive and contributing to society are more likely to be resilient. This reinforces our position that engagement in cyberspace is overall a positive and necessary activity in the digital world.

Przybylski et al. (2014) point out that new technologies (telephone, radio, television) have historically prompted discussions of parental strategies to protect children from perceived dangers associated with new media. Thus, we can draw from wisdom acquired about those innovations to suggest parental strategies for digital media. Three overall strategies are useful:

* active mediation,
* co-viewing, and
* restriction.

Active Mediation

Active mediation refers to discussions between parents and children about what is available online, what children are doing, what harmful behaviors they have observed, and so on. Creating an open channel for communication about online activities, including risks and harmful material, is a way to support resilience by showing interest and concern.

A derivative of this strategy is seeking assistance from the child when the adult attempts new behaviors. For example, perhaps the adult is posting a photo online for the first time. Seeking a youth's advice, perhaps about which photo-sharing site is safest and most easily accessed by grandparents, or how to transfer photos from phone to computer, gives the youth the message that their knowledge is respected and that parents are concerned about safety in cyberspace as well.

Co-viewing

Co-viewing or using the technology together is the next strategy. The parent and child might both play the same online game, might be friends on social media, or might seek information online together about a shared activity (e.g., vacation activities or movie schedules at local theatres). While these can be very useful strategies, they are most effective when coupled with active mediation, which encourages the youth's self-efficacy and self-regulation while demonstrating that parents are interested in and care about the youth's digital world.

Restriction

Restrictive strategies include overall restrictions (such as not allowing broad categories of technology, such as cell phones, online games, social media), or content restriction (prohibiting specific activities such as Facebook, or particular websites), or time restrictions (no use of technology after 8 pm), or place restriction (computers or phones not allowed in the child's room). Przybylski et al. (2014) found that children were least resilient online when parents used general restrictive strategies. They pointed out that their findings do not tell us whether the restriction interferes with the development of resilience, or whether parents of resilient children are less likely to employ restrictive strategies.

Responsibility for Resilience

The Telnor report (2013) stresses that protection from risk is not solely the responsibility of users and parents, but schools can assist by teaching internet safety at school. Instruction should include protecting one's privacy in cyberspace, reporting offenses, being aware of possible actions to take when targeted, knowing what actions are illegal, how to preserve evidence, netiquette, and how to be a good digital citizen (Bauman, 2015). Content providers can clearly label adult content so children can easily recognize inappropriate material and can also assist by developing content that is enriching and engaging for the younger audience. They can also make reporting tools easy to locate and use so that users can take positive action when needed. They can provide moderation of chat rooms and discussion forums to ensure interactions in those spaces are not disrupted by trolls or others whose intent is malicious. Society in general can assist by providing help lines or other digital resources (text-based help services) to assist anyone challenged by harmful digital experiences. Finally, governments can create legislation banning online harassment and other behaviors without interfering with freedom of speech. Recent evidence suggests that parents are in fact doing many of these positive things to foster resilience in their children. For example, more youth report that parents discuss online dangers, and youth who have discussions of risks with parents are less likely to share personal information online (Williams, 2015).

One of the concerns expressed by young people in the *EUKids Online* study was that they could not learn how to navigate the internet safely if they were constantly shielded from less savory content by parents and teachers. As one 12-year-old girl sagely said:

> I think the fewer things a kid knows about the internet the greater the risks. Nevertheless, I may accidentally come across violent or inappropriate scenes while doing coursework online. Also, a stranger might bother me. (Livingstone et al., 2013, p. 14)

Recognizing the dangers and feeling able to talk about inappropriate content when it is encountered is as much a lifesaver as any net-nanny

5 Digital Aggression, Cyberbullying, and the Impact of COVID-19 101

application or blocking software. We need to be able to discuss these issues in meaningful ways at home and at work. Much more research is needed in exploring how and where we encounter danger online—it is not just in chatrooms and message boards, but in gaming environments too. Resilience arises from awareness not from ignorance. As we demonstrate in Chap. 9, even when a parent supervises a child's online activity, one can never be too sure who is truly sitting at the other computer or on another smartphone. It is not just children and young people who can be exploited online. As increasingly our banking and utility payments have moved online, there has been a concomitant increase in online scams. Adults need to be aware of the sophisticated ways in which such scams are run and be much more discerning in how we use and divulge personal information. The UK Council for Child Internet Safety has produced a very simple guide for our online lives that can be used by us all (see Rivers, 2013, p. 28):

Zip It – Keep your personal stuff private and think about what you say online.
Block It – Block people who send nasty messages and don't open unknown links and attachments.
Flag It – Flag up with someone you trust if anything upsets you or if someone asks to meet you offline.

Post-COVID-19, we also have to recognize the impact the pandemic had on the physical and mental health of our young people. In Scotland, for example, the Scottish Government has introduced a program to support young people, their families, and their teachers titled the *Mental Health Transition and Recovery Plan* (Scottish Government, 2020). This program includes counseling for young people through schools and dedicated support for those young people who were deemed vulnerable or who have complex support needs. The program also includes art-based therapies and targeted youth work as well as referrals to child and adolescent mental health services. A resource for all school staff was also produced and addresses issues such as understanding trauma and adversity, the importance of sleep, the impact of digital technologies and social media, and body image (https://www.cypmh.co.uk). The resource also addresses issues of diversity and discrimination and how to build stigma-free schools.

Workforce Resilience Post-COVID-19

As Mehta and Maniar (2023) have suggested, the pandemic has resulted in a workforce that, at times, has felt exploited and ill-used. While some may not agree with terms such as technological slavery, it is clear that working remotely or from home during national lockdowns took its toll both on the well-being of workers and our understandings of acceptable behavior. So how do we rebuild the workplace post-COVID? According to Parry et al. (2022), it is important to understand that the workforce might be differentially affected. For example, in their study, young workers were more likely to report physical health complaints when their absence from work was related to a mental health issue. Being older was found to be a protective factor when it came to mental health and well-being. Older workers were more likely to cope with changes to the work experience and have more coping strategies than younger workers. Thus, adaptability became a key feature of well-being. In terms of building a resilient workforce for the future, social and professional learning was core along with validation and reassurance for young workers (many of whom had heard stories of redundancy among peers as a result of long-term mental ill-health). Communication is also key, and that communication needs to be positive and supportive. Thus, a culture that allows bullying or any form of discrimination will impact workforce well-being and productivity. Much of this is obvious, but as we learn to work in new ways, learning new languages such as hybrid, flexible, and remote working, expectations of the workforce have to change. Indeed, there is a need for management to become fluent in how different forms of work pattern impact productivity and a sense of belonging (a notable factor in reducing bullying behavior).

5 Digital Aggression, Cyberbullying, and the Impact of COVID-19

Finally, mentoring and reverse mentoring seem to have relevance to promoting a resilient workforce post-COVID. As we have seen in Parry et al.'s (2022) study, older workers were able to adapt more readily to change than young workers, and this had a protective influence on well-being. Thus, formal or indeed informal mentoring schemes where not only technical but also soft and adaptive skills are taught would seem too crucial in supporting a thriving workforce post-COVID. Additionally, a study by Oksanen et al. (2021) has also shown that issues such as technostress (stress resulting from the use of or demands of technology) are greatest in those who are unfamiliar with social media applications. Furthermore, older people are less likely to use social media or know how to respond to incidents of digital aggression and cyberbullying. In this situation, young workers have a role in reverse mentoring their older colleagues, teaching them how to use technologies such as social media applications thus reducing stress levels and supporting older workers in tackling issues such as digital aggression and cyberbullying.

Summary

This chapter identifies the different ways in which digital aggression and cyberbullying has evolved and the ways in which we have used and abused the pivot to online and remote working following COVID-19. We have illustrated ways in which we can build resilience in both young people and the older workforce through guidance and mentoring, and it is important to acknowledge that as we become more reliant upon technology to support education, health care, and the economy, the opportunities for exploitation and harm increase. Notwithstanding data collected by Broadband Search (2023) does suggest that even considering COVID-19 and our move online, there has been a reduction in cyberbullying in the student population compared to the 2014 data presented in the first edition of our book. We must make sure that this trend continues.

References

Anonymous. (2013, May 5). Cyberbullying in the workplace. *Secure NU*. http://www.northeastern.edu/securenu/?p=1995

Bacher-Hicks, A., Goodman, J., Green, J. G., & Holt, M. (2021). *The COVID-19 pandemic disrupted both school bullying and cyberbullying*. National Bureau of Economic Research (Working Paper 29590). https://www.nber.org/papers/w29590

Bates, S. (2017). Revenge porn and mental health: A qualitative analysis of the mental health effects of revenge porn on female survivors. *Feminist Criminology, 12*(1), 22–42. https://doi.org/10.1177/1557085116654565

Bauman, S. (2015). Cyberbullying and sexting: School mental health concerns. In R. Witte & S. Mosley-Howard (Eds.), *Mental health practice in today's schools: Current issues and interventions* (pp. 241–264). Springer.

Bauman, S., Toomey, R., & Walker, J. (2013). Relations among bullying, cyberbullying and suicide in high school students. *Journal of Adolescence, 36*(2), 341–360. https://doi.org/10.1016/j.adolescence.2012.12.001

Bonanno, R. A., & Hymel, S. (2013). Cyber bullying and internalizing difficulties: Above and beyond the impact of traditional forms of bullying. *Journal of Youth and Adolescence, 42*, 685–697. https://doi.org/10.1007/s10964-013-9937-1

Broadband Search (2023). Key Internet usage statistics in 2023 (including mobile). https://www.broadbandsearch.net/blog/internet-statistics

Cénat, J. M., Blais, M., Hébert, M., Lavoie, F., & Guerrier, M. (2015). Correlates of bullying in Quebec high school students: The vulnerability of sexual-minority youth. *Journal of Affective Disorders, 183*(September), 315–321. https://doi.org/10.1016/j.jad.2015.05.011

Crowe, N. (2012). "It's like my life but more, and better!"—Playing with the Cathaby Shark Girls: MMORPGs, young people and fantasy-based social play. *International Journal of Adolescence and Youth, 16*(2), 201–223. https://doi.org/10.1080/02673843.2011.9748055

Economic and Social Research Council. (2012, November 2). *Cyberbullying in the workplace 'worse than conventional bullying.* http://www.esrc.ac.uk/news-and-events/press-releases/23829/cyberbullying-in-the-workplace-worse-than-conventional-bullying.aspx

Gradinger, P., Strohmeier, D., Schiller, E. M., Stefanek, E., & Spiel, C. (2012). Cyber-victimization and popularity in early adolescence: Stability and predictive associations. *European Journal of Developmental Psychology, 9*(2), 228–243. https://doi.org/10.1080/17405629.2011.643171

Hinduja, S., & Patchin, J. W. (2020). Bullying, cyberbullying, and sexual orientation/gender identity. *Cyberbullying Research Center (cyberbullying.org)*. https://cyberbullying.org/bullying-cyberbullying-lgbtq.

Jain, O., Gupta, M., Satam, S., & Panda, S. (2020). Has the COVID-19 pandemic affected the susceptibility to cyberbullying in India? *Computers in Human Behavior Reports, 2*(August–December), 100029. https://doi.org/10.1016/j.chbr.2020.100029

Kay, A. (2013, June 8). At work: Cyberbullies graduate to workplace. *USA Today.* http://www.usatoday.com/story/money/columnist/kay/2013/06/08/at-work-office-cyberbullies/2398671/

Litwiller, B. J., & Brausch, A. M. (2013). Cyber bullying and physical bullying in adolescent suicide: The role of violent behavior and substance use. *Journal of Youth and Adolescence, 42*(5), 675–684. https://doi.org/10.1007/s10964-013-9925-5

Livingstone, S., Kirwil, L., Ponte, C., & Statksrud, E. (2013). *In their own words: What bothers children online.* http://www.lse.ac.uk/media@lse/research/EUKidsOnline/EU%20Kids%20III/Reports/Intheirownwords020213.pdf

Lobe, B., Livingstone, S., Ölafsson, K., & Voleb, H. (2011). *Cross-national comparisons of risks and safety on the internet: Initial analysis from the EU Kids online survey of European children.* London School of Economics & Political Science.

Mehta, S., & Maniar, A. (2023). Technology during COVID-19: Boon or a curse. *International Journal of Management, Public Policy, and Research, 2*(Special Issue), 40–44. https://doi.org/10.55829/ijmpr.v2iSpecialIssue.135

Oksanen, A., Oksa, R., Savela, N., Mantere, E., Savolainen, L., & Kaakinen, M. (2021). COVID-19 crisis and digital stressors at work: A longitudinal study on the Finnish working population. *Computers in Human Behavior, 122*, 106853. https://doi.org/10.1016/j.chb.2021.106853

Parry, S. L., Carr, N. A., Staniford, L. J., & Walker, L. (2022). Rebuilding the workplace to promote young workers' mental health. *International Journal of Workplace Health Management, 15*(3), 307–319. https://doi.org/10.1108/IJWHM-10-2021-0188

Patchin, J., & Hinduja, S. (2010). Bullying, cyberbullying, and suicide. *Archives of Suicide Research, 14*(3), 206–211. https://doi.org/10.1080/1381111 8.2010.494133

Petrosyan, A. (2022, July 7). Percentage of teenagers in the United States who have been cyber bullied as of April 2018, by age and frequency. https://

www.statista.com/statistics/207508/teenagers-personal-experiences-of-bullying-on-social-media-websites/

Przybylski, A. K., Mishkin, A., Shotbolt, V., & Linington, S. (2014). *A shared responsibility: Building children's online resilience.* Oxford Internet Institute. https://parentzone.org.uk/sites/default/files/2021-12/PZ_Building_Online_Resilience_2014.pdf

Rivers, I. (2013). Cyberbullying and cyberaggression: Sexualised and gendered experiences explored. In I. Rivers & N. Duncan (Eds.), *Bullying: Experiences and discourses of sexuality and gender* (pp. 19–30). Routledge.

Rivers, I., Daly, J., & Stevenson, L. (2023). Homophobic and transphobic online harassment: Young people in Scotland during the COVID-19 pandemic. In H. A. Cowie & C.-A. Myers (Eds.), *Cyberbullying and online harms: Preventions and interventions form community to campus.* Routledge.

Scottish Government. (2020). Coronavirus (COVID-19): Mental health—transition and recovery plan. *Scottish Government.* https://www.gov.scot/publications/mental-health-scotlands-transition-recovery/

Sigursteinsdottir, H., & Karlsdottir, F. B. (2022). Does social support matter in the workplace? Social support, job satisfaction, bullying and harassment in the workplace during COVID-19. *International Journal of Environmental Research and Public Health, 19*(8), 4724. https://doi.org/10.3390/ijerph19084724

Sinclair, K. O., Bauman, S., Poteat, V. P., Koenig, B., & Russell, S. T. (2012). The association between cyber and bias-based harassment and academic, substance use and mental health problems. *Journal of Adolescent Health, 50*(5), 521–523. https://doi.org/10.1016/j.jadohealth.2011.09.009

Somani, R., Muntaner, C., Smith, P., Hillan, E. M., & Velonis, A. J. (2022). Increased workplace bullying against nurses during COVID-19: A health and safety issue. *Journal of Nursing Education and Practice, 12*(9), 47–53. https://doi.org/10.5430/jnep.v12n9p47

Sourander, A., Klomek, A. B., Ikonen, M., Lindroos, J., Luntamo, T., Koskelainen, M., et al. (2010). Psychosocial risk factors associated with cyberbullying among adolescents. *Archives of General Psychiatry, 67*(7), 720–728. https://doi.org/10.1001/archgenpsychiatry.2010.79

Statista (2023). Cyber bulling – Statistics & Facts. https://www.statista.com/topics/1809/cyber-bullying/

Telnor Group. (2013). Building digital resilience. http://www.telenor.com/wp-content/uploads/2013/04/Telenor-report-Building-Digital-Resilience.pdf

5 Digital Aggression, Cyberbullying, and the Impact of COVID-19 107

Tsuno, K., & Tabuchi, T. (2022). Risk factors for workplace bullying, severe psychological distress and suicidal ideation during the COVID-19 pandemic among the general working population in Japan: A large-scale cross-sectional study. *BMJOpen, 12*, e059860. https://doi.org/10.1136/bmjopen-2021-059860

Turkle, S. (1995). *Life on the screen: Identity in the age of the internet.* Simon & Schuster.

Vaillancourt, T., Brittain, H., Krygsman, A., Farrell, A. H., Landon, S., & Pepler, D. (2021). School bullying before and during COVID-19: Results from a population-based randomized design. *Aggressive Behavior, 47*(5), 557–569. https://doi.org/10.1002/ab.21986

Wang, J., Iannotti, R. J., & Nansel, T. R. (2009). School bullying among U.S. adolescents: Physical, verbal, relational, and cyber. *Journal of Adolescent Health, 45*(4), 368–375. https://doi.org/10.1016/j.jadohealth.2009.03.021

Williams, A. (2015, January 22). *How to protect your teen's online privacy.* Family Online Safety Institute. https://www.fosi.org/good-digital-parenting/helping-parents-protect-teen-privacy-online-/

Young, R. M. (1996a). *NETDYNAM: Some parameters of virtual reality.* http://human-nature.com/rmyoung/papers/paper17h.html

Young, R. M. (1996b). *Psychoanalysis and/of the internet.* http://human-nature.com/free-associations/psaint.html

6

Information Overload and Zoom Fatigue

Introduction: Sheri's Morning Routine

My morning routine begins with reading several newspapers online (while enjoying a cup of coffee). I then read the local print newspaper (with another cup). It is important to me that I stay abreast of important events in my country and the world. However, I often feel overwhelmed by the number of important happenings and issues that are in the headlines on the front pages alone. There is always a crisis or political issue or catastrophe that commands my attention. I am particularly vigilant about news about COVID-19 because I want to be sure I am doing the right things to avoid infection. Many of the articles on the topic, while including updates on positive progress (e.g., development of vaccines, development of drugs to reduce chances of hospitalization and death), also include grim statistics that are disturbing to see repeatedly. Then I move on to check Facebook and other social media to connect with friends and colleagues; more sensational news is on display. Today, there are several high-interest stories unfolding, and I find I am distracted and feel the need to keep checking for updates, which elevates my anxiety because I

© The Author(s), under exclusive license to Springer Nature Switzerland AG 2023
S. Bauman, I. Rivers, *Mental Health in the Digital Age*,
https://doi.org/10.1007/978-3-031-32122-1_6

am not getting my work done. I hope the reader gets the picture: this chapter describes me very well.

As I prepared to write this chapter, I began by doing a search on Google Scholar, which showed 20,000 results for "information overload" published from 2019 to the present. A regular Google search yielded 426,000,000 hits when I used "news fatigue" as my search term. I had similar results using other search terms. At that point, I experienced information overload and became quite anxious. Clearly, I could not check each possible source. What if I overlooked an important one? How do I decide which sources are absolutely necessary to read? I am experiencing serious information overload.

The Merriam-Webster dictionary defines *news* as "a report of recent events" or "previously unknown information." The Oxford Dictionary defines news as "newly received or noteworthy information, especially about recent or important events." Streckfuss (1998) contends that craving for news is a universal human characteristic, given its prevalence among isolated primitive villages as well as modern cities. Stephens (1988) explains that the desire for news is not just for knowledge but it satisfies a need for entertainment by the "bizarre and sensational."

Even after written language was invented about 5500 years ago, literacy was a privilege of the elite few, while most people still relied on oral accounts. News was carried by town criers, who traveled to villages and shouted such news as births, deaths, marriages, and so on that were important to the populace. During wars, messengers ran from combat zones to towns and settlements to inform the public of battlefield events. News was shared in gathering places such as markets and taverns and passed on by word-of-mouth. The invention of the printing press by Gutenberg in the 1450s made it possible for multiple copies of books to be produced, but even so, most people were illiterate until the nineteenth century when literacy became more common in industrialized countries.

Town criers and messengers are relics from an earlier period in human history. Newspapers were widespread by the nineteenth century. In the twentieth century, news could be heard on the radio, and then television became a popular source of news. The reporters of news on radio, television, and newspapers submitted their articles to editors who ensured sources were reliable and facts were accurate. Now news can be presented

6 Information Overload and Zoom Fatigue 111

in a variety of media, information can be posted and spread with no fact-checking. In addition, some internet sites use bots and other tools to spread unverified information. The arrival of the internet greatly expanded the breadth of news available online, especially as the variety and prices of devices made them accessible to much of the population. The resources now available digitally often replace more traditional sources but may also augment online material.

Abundant websites and social media posts can be updated or watched in real time (via live stream), and thus give the public instantaneous information. Although there are many newsworthy events in our history that attracted wide news coverage, the COVID-19 pandemic emerged at a time when internet use was commonplace, and when being well-informed was a matter of avoiding infection by a deadly virus. In addition, COVID-19 represents a long-term global event, affecting an enormous number of people. To date, we estimate that there have been nearly 7 million deaths related to COVID-19 (World Health Organization, 2023). Other collective trauma may be covered more extensively for a shorter time period of time, and in media of more local interest.

In this chapter, many of our sources are recent and focused on COVID-19, but the concepts would apply to any major catastrophe. Furthermore, the reader is urged to keep in mind that during the pandemic, there were other tragic events that were in the news. In addition to the mental health impact of the incessant COVID-19 coverage, some people were also being inundated by additional stressful news. It is logical to assume that the psychosocial effects would be amplified in those cases.

However, in addition to fear and uncertainty about the disease itself, the measures taken to reduce the spread, including isolation, restricted movement, changes in education and employment also contributed to the mental health issues experienced by many people around the world. As (Park, 2019) observed, a growing percentage of the population now gets news from social media instead of other sources. A study of 1000 adults in the UK found that 65% of respondents indicated that keeping track of so much information is a major concern, and 35% felt that keeping up with the vast amounts of news causes stress. Numerous research studies have investigated the mental health sequelae of the constant bombardment of news during this time. We next examine digital sources of news and information.

Sources of Online News and Information

News consumption online has increased, as have other options for retrieving news. Figure 6.1 shows the proportion of US adults who used various digital sources of news, and Fig. 6.2 visualizes which methods of news consumption are most often used in several countries. Figure 6.3 presents popular social networks that are accessed for news in various parts of the world. Note that Facebook is a primary source in all regions.

A recent report compiled by the Pew Research Center (www.pewresearch.org), indicated that 60% of American adults often use digital devices as a source of news, compared to 40% who use television often, 16% use radio, and only 10% use print publications often. Among the digital options, 34% use news websites or apps frequently, compared to

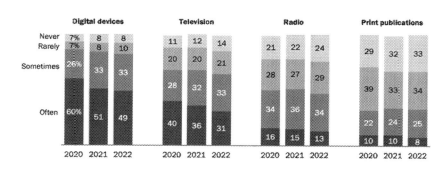

Fig. 6.1 Proportion of US adults using various digital news sources

6 Information Overload and Zoom Fatigue 113

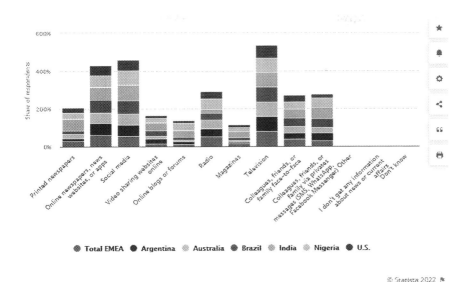

Fig. 6.2 Methods of news consumption by country

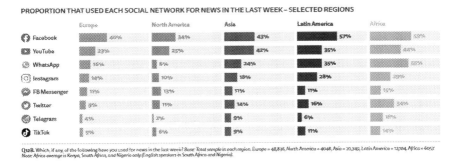

Fig. 6.3 Popular social networks accessed for news

23% that use search terms, 23% who access news on social media, and 6% for whom podcasts are a source of news.

These US figures are for the total sample; data were also calculated by demographic groups. The highest rate at which a group used social media for news was for users ages 18–29, while only 27% of participants age 65+ did so. News websites or apps were used most often by those aged 30–40 (68%), and by those with some college education (52%). Among racial groups, Blacks were most likely to rely on search engines (69%) at least sometimes, while only 26% of that group listened to podcasts for news. Among those who get news from social media, rates vary widely. In other parts of the world, the patterns are similar. In the EU, 72% of internet users use online sources of news Ellerbeck (2022) with social media most often used.

A striking recent development is the rapid increase in the use of TikTok for news. In 2020, 3% of respondents indicated they regularly get news from that platform; the rate was 6% in 2021 and 10% in 2022. The rates increased in all age groups (other than 65+ who use it at a very low rate). Respondents under 30 showed a notable increase from 9% in 2020 to 26% in 2022. This increase is in contrast with all other social media sites, which either decreased or stayed the same during that time period (Matsa, 2022).

It is important to keep in mind that these sources of online news are not independent of one another. Social media sites provide links to news websites, and news organizations scour social media for breaking news in order to be timely. Hermida (2016) noted that social media can provide immediate, often live, and emotionally layered accounts of a crisis incident; traditional news often relies on social media for information until they can get their journalists to the site of the event. Podcasts similarly often reflect current topics in the news, and television continues to serve its usual role, although they typically rely on fixed broadcast times (with rare interruptions for breaking news).

Keeping up with the news is a hallmark of democracy that requires a well-informed citizenry (Boukes & Vliegenthart, 2017; Park, 2019). During COVID-19, interest in news increased on all media, including websites and social media (Kellerman et al., 2022). The uncertainty and fear of the pandemic prompted increased use of media for gathering information. Sixty-three percent of Americans report that they find their news via Facebook (Keib et al., 2018). Kellerman et al. suggest that in addition to seeking information that might diminish distress, some people used media to escape from the news and reduce anxiety. It remains to be seen whether these patterns will persist over time.

Mental Health Implications

The information presented above provides a picture of how widely digital sources are available and utilized around the world. We are interested here in the impact of these circumstances on mental health. There is a body of literature that identifies *information overload* as "when informational input exceeds the human information processing capacity" (Schmitt et al., 2018, p. 3); it is an important contributor to the increase in mental health symptoms. Schitt et al. identify factors that influence an individual's vulnerability to information overload. Intrinsic factors include information processing ability and self-efficacy, time pressure, personal characteristics (e.g., gender, age, time spent looking at news online), and extrinsic factors (the characteristics and quality of the information, sources of information, etc.) that interact to create information overload. Research results have been mixed regarding age, with some studies finding older people to be more susceptible to information overload, and others reporting that younger adults experienced more information overload. Females have been consistently found to be more likely to have symptoms of information overload.

The pandemic, the torrent of news, much of it including negative headlines and dire statistics, updated around the clock, led to *news fatigue* (Fitzpatrick, 2022), with studies revealing that users felt emotional fatigue and distress from reading the news. A conundrum is that participants in the survey also believed the news coverage mitigated the spread of COVID-19. During COVID-19, many people were subjected to upsetting material even if they were not actively seeking it (de Hoog & Verboon, 2020). While social media might be used primarily to communicate with friends and family, as we saw information about COVID-19 crises and tragedies tended to be interspersed in feeds. According to Kellerman et al. (2022), in one study, the more news a sample of college students consumed, the more worry they reported, and that worry contributed to feelings of hopelessness. In addition, the increase in misinformation and disinformation on this (and other) topics may prompt users to seek even more information in an effort to find accurate news (Kellerman et al., 2022).

Consumption of negative news has been associated with anxiety, depression, and post-traumatic stress disorder (PTSD); this effect impacts those not directly involved in the event or disaster. The prominence of negative stories is a factor in reduced mental well-being (Boukes & Vliegenthart, 2017), and symptoms may persist after the initial reaction (de Hoog & Verboon, 2020; Garfin et al., 2020).

Children

In 2021, the Academy of Pediatrics declared an emergency due to increasing rates of mental health problems in young people (Dick & Comer, 2022). Studies using brain scans to analyze children's responses to negative news showed increased anxiety. However, although some youth exhibited symptoms of PTSD, most did not. It would be valuable to understand what protects some youth from adverse emotional responses. Dick and Comer also observed that particularly on social media, more graphic images and videos are included to attract viewers. In addition to images, viewers are attracted to posts that have comments (Keib et al., 2018). When users see a news item, they look at images first and for longer than text. They are more likely to click on a news story accompanied by an image.

Dick and Comer (2022) found that the more media a child saw, the more PTSD symptoms were present. They also demonstrated that children at a distance (San Diego, CA) did not differ from those near the traumatic event (Hurricane Irma in Florida) on the association between consuming news and mental health symptoms. The researchers did find some evidence of different brain responses to fear and threat and urged parents to closely monitor children's media behavior, especially when a disaster or tragedy dominates the news.

Adolescents

Adolescence is a developmental stage in which peer and social relationships increase in importance. The physical distancing regulations imposed in many countries during COVID-19 had a negative effect on the mental health of youth (Marciano et al., 2022). Many adolescents increased their use of digital communication as an effective coping strategy. Text messages increased by 83%, phone calls by 72%, social media and video chats 66%, instant messaging by 48%, and emails by 37%. In addition, 77% of adolescents accessed news from social media (Moreno & Joliff, 2022). Although these practices may have compensated for the isolation and loneliness, they added a stressor in the form of overwhelming information about COVID, much of which was distressing; some of that information was "fake news," (discussed below) and the pressure to distinguish between credible and fake news may have caused fear and worry (Marciano et al., 2022). For youth vulnerable to depression and anxiety, the negative news may reinforce negative beliefs; the cognitive triad (I am powerless, the world is dangerous, and the future is grim) (Moreno & Joliff, 2022) are symptoms of depression in cognitive theory.

Adults

For all ages, the explosion of shocking or sensational headlines may lead to "headline stress disorder," and unofficial mental disorder coined by Steven Stosny (2017) (*What Is Headline Stress Disorder?*) to describe the feelings of many of his patients whose engagement with online news led to anxiety, depression, hopelessness, and a sense of having no control over events affecting one's life. Constant exposure to disturbing headlines can cause panic-like symptoms, such as agitation and fear. The stress of the barrage of negative headlines can also cause physical symptoms, including gastrointestinal problems, a weakened immune system, and more (Rodriguez-Cayro, 2018).

De Hoog and Verboon (2020) used ecological momentary assessment (EMA) to explain the cognitive processes that are employed when negative news is consumed. Although the study had significant limitations (small convenience sample, non-response), the findings are informative. The researchers applied Lazarus and Folkmans's cognitive appraisal theory, which proposes that when someone encounters a stressor (too much information), they make an appraisal (How serious is it? Does it affect me?), which then generates an emotional response. The primary appraisal determines the relevance and severity of the stressor; the secondary appraisal evaluates one's ability to cope with the stressor. These researchers found that women had more adverse emotional reactions than men, but no age differences were detected. The researchers demonstrated that even when the severity is low, the news still influences the emotional reaction, but personal relevance was associated with a negative affect.

Another interesting study used in-silico methodology to examine how social media exposure following a mass trauma (the shooting at Parkland High School in Florida, USA) impacts the population at large (Abdalla et al., 2021). Their results revealed that when news was perused on social media in addition to television, especially when videos or images were present, negative psychological responses were more likely. They concluded that TV exposure increased population-level PTSD, and viewing reports of mass trauma on social media along with TV coverage also increased the symptom level. A study of the elements of features of posts on social media adds to our understanding (Holman et al., 2020). The research examined the effects of both quantity of exposure to the Boston Marathon bombing and the type of images (bloody images vs. other images). Their short-term longitudinal study found that both graphic images and the amount of exposure to news about the bombing were associated with mental health problems and impaired functioning.

An important element of this situation is that, in many cases, the mental health provider is experiencing the same stressors and pressures as their clients. That makes it particularly difficult to maintain a clinical perspective. For example, after the hurricane that devastated parts of Puerto Rico, I attended a conference there and many attendees were from the area hard-hit by the storm. One woman was distraught. The town she lived in was practically destroyed, including her home, but the requests for counseling were increasing, and she felt she had to do her job. It is hard to imagine how she might set her own pain when attending to clients. The Red Cross often sends disaster mental health teams to such locations, but it typically takes days to get there and some time to organize logistics and have services available. The mental health professions need to address the issue of collective trauma and develop strategies to provide services to the communities while not ignoring the needs of providers.

Fake News

Rocha et al. (2021) claimed that "False news has taken over social media, becoming part of life for many people" (p. 1). The director-general of World Health Information was quoted as saying, "We are not just fighting the pandemic, we are fighting the infodemic" (Naeem et al., 2021). Fake news (false or misleading information) is designed to influence public opinion, and to do so, they present the news in ways that arouse emotional reactions (anxiety, depression, fearfulness) as a way to alter our opinions. Unfortunately, social media is rife with fake news. Even when the reader recognizes that the news is fake, they may also have emotional reactions such as anger at the attempt to mislead them. The barrage of information about COVID-19 is so extensive that there is now a term for it: *infodemic*.

Social media is implicated in the spread of fake news. Although they may contribute to the spread of misinformation and disinformation, they also provide a means of connecting with others and providing entertainment and distraction from the stressful news. Naseem et al. (2021) reported that each day in March 2020, approximately 46,000 posts on Twitter were inaccurate and promulgated fake news or inaccurate information. Naseem et al. analyzed 1225 fake news items published in English from January through April 2021. They found that half of the fake news stories about COVID-19 were found on social media. Other sources are shown below in Fig. 6.4. They also found that the peak time period for fake news was March 2020, which was the point at which many locales around the world imposed restrictions to prevent the spreading of the disease. At such a critical time, fake news about COVID-19 promoted false information about how the disease is transmitted, what treatments were effective, and how to prevent the spread.

Videoconferencing increased dramatically in response to the COVID-19 restrictions. It became the staple of business continuity. Although videoconferencing is not new, the circumstances created by the pandemic made it a necessity to allow the economy to continue to function during lockdowns, while also allowing social relationships to be maintained. The use of videoconferencing had some unanticipated

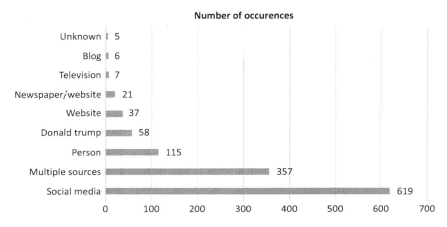

Fig. 6.4 Zoom fatigue

positive consequences: the use of fossil fuels consumed in commuting decreased, and energy expenses for offices were also diminished. Zoom is arguably the best known of the many available platforms (i.e., Microsoft Teams, Google Meet, BlueJeans, Slack, Skype, Goto Meeting) and we use the term Zoom here to refer to all videoconferencing software. Zoom use increased dramatically in the period from December 2019 (10 million users) to May 2020 (300 million) (Bailenson, 2021). These conveniences suggest that even as face-to-face meetings and classes are reinstated, there will be a place for Zoom going forward.

A phenomenon known as *Zoom fatigue* has been identified and describes the exhaustion many people feel after participating in a (or several) Zoom meetings. Although to date there are no empirical studies to investigate the hypothesis that Zoom fatigue is associated with mental health symptoms (Bailenson, 2021), that additional stressor could increase the level of anxiety and depression. A group of researchers investigated the explanations for Zoom fatigue proposed by Bailenson in a sample of 10,332 participants and provided some insights into the features of videoconferencing that are conducive to fatigue. They also examined whether some demographic groups experience this at disproportionate rates (Fauville et al., 2021). The main finding was that more meetings, longer meetings, and short intervals between meetings was associated with greater fatigue. Further analysis revealed that meeting duration was the strongest predictor of fatigue. They also discovered that women reported significantly more fatigue than men, even when controlling for other variables.

The researchers (Fauville et al., 2021) conducted a second study to investigate the nonverbal mechanisms that contribute to Zoom fatigue and identified mirror anxiety, sense of being trapped, hypergaze, and increased cognitive load. In addition, they included a measure of personality traits along with demographic information in their survey of 10,591 respondents.

Mirror anxiety describes the experience of seeing oneself on the screen for the duration of the meeting. This image of self can result in self-evaluation that may precipitate anxiety and depression. Mirror anxiety results from constantly seeing yourself on the screen. In an offline environment, you may check your appearance a few times a day, perhaps when you go to the restroom or briefly before going to an important meeting. Imagine if someone followed you around and forced you to look at yourself in a mirror constantly. It causes hyper-self-consciousness—which leads to fatigue. Researchers have found that this phenomenon—mirror anxiety—is more common in women.

Reduced mobility results when the meeting participants must stay in a narrow space in order to be visible to others and reach their keyboards. During in-person meetings, participants can usually move about to some extent (e.g., refill coffee) and vary the directions of their gaze (from whiteboard to faces, to a notepad, etc.). In a Zoom meeting, attendees are seated in one place and staring at the screen. The seating arrangement in a face-to-face meeting is often deliberate—some positions convey more power than others, people likely to disagree can sit where they do not look at the person directly. This option is absent in a Zoom meeting.

Reduced mobility is closely related to *hypergaze*, wherein the duration of direct gazing violates norms of social distance. Hypergaze is the experience of having people's eyes constantly in your field of view. In in-person meetings, attendees tend to look at the speaker, but in Zoom meetings, everyone gets the gaze of others whether they are speaking or not. In an in-person meeting, some people will be in your peripheral vision, but on Zoom everyone is in the fovea view. It is also more likely that participants will look away and catch the eye of other participants in face-to-face meetings, or look at notes, but in Zoom meetings, one spends the entire time staring at others. In many cases, the closeness of the face on the screen simulates a distance that is closer than generally accepted social distance norms. That is, the person appears to be in a space normally used in intimate relationships, which can generate discomfort. Furthermore, Bailenson (2021) points out that if everyone is looking at the screen for the entire meeting, it may feel as though one is being stared at, with direct eye contact that is much more intense than is the case in face-to-face meetings.

Cognitive load describes the increased mental processes needed to function in Zoom meetings. For one, there is a very brief (milliseconds) lag (audio and video not transmitted in real time), which may tax the brain. The sometimes below-awareness audio delay requires additional mental energy to integrate the audio and visual input. Another feature that requires additional mental concentration occurs when viewing the screen in gallery view, and the position of attendees changes if someone enters or leaves. It takes some close attention to locate the person who is speaking. At the same time, because of the needs of the platform, participants try to compensate for the absence of visual cues. We also don't have the information conveyed by non-verbal gestures below the head, making it harder to interpret the nonverbal clues of others. People tend to speak louder in a videoconference, to look straight ahead rather than making usual head movements that vary from looking at the speaker, looking down at notes, glancing at other members, and so on. People also tend to compensate for the limited view by exaggerating gestures (e.g., head nodding). In an actual (vs. virtual) meeting, staring intently at someone's face would be considered rude.

These mechanisms are helpful for understanding the exhaustion people feel when attending Zoom meetings. They do not mention the frustration of technological problems that interrupt the conversation—people losing a connection or freezing screens, which cause stress and frustration. Fauville et al. (2021) suggest that videoconferencing companies use this information to make changes in how the site operates. Even when COVID-19 restrictions have been eliminated, many workers will resist returning to offices and cubicles full-time. At the time of this writing, employers are beginning to request (or require) a return to pre-COVID expectations for working in person. However, the many advantages of working remotely has resulted in push-back from workers who do not see the value of working 100% in offices. It is highly likely that many organizations will move to a hybrid model, where on several days, remote working will continue, but there will also be a return to in-person working on other days.

Summary

In this chapter, we have reviewed two phenomena that are extremely common, but not often considered in discussions about mental health. Feeling overwhelmed and/or fatigued may make one vulnerable to mental health symptoms such as anxiety and depression. We must keep in mind the other stressors that accompany traumatic events (fear, hopelessness) and acknowledge that the impact of multiple burdens makes supporting mental health and wellness particularly challenging and complex. We also need to be mindful that mental health professionals are also affected by the same phenomena—news overload and Zoom fatigue—and it would be worthwhile to develop a protocol for managing that situation.

References

Abdalla, S. M., Cohen, G. H., Tamrakar, S., Koya, S. F., & Galea, S. (2021). Media Exposure and the Risk of Post-Traumatic Stress Disorder Following a Mass traumatic Event: An In-silico Experiment. *Frontiers in Psychiatry, 12*, 674263. https://doi.org/10.3389/fpsyt.2021.674263

Bailenson, J. N. (2021). Nonverbal overload: A theoretical argument for the causes of Zoom fatigue. *Technology, Mind, and Behavior, 2*(1). https://doi.org/10.1037/tmb0000030

Boukes, M., & Vliegenthart, R. (2017). News Consumption and Its Unpleasant Side Effect: Studying the Effect of Hard and Soft News Exposure on Mental Well-Being Over Time. *Journal of Media Psychology, 29*(3), 137–147. https://doi.org/10.1027/1864-1105/a000224

Comer, J. S. & Dick, A. S. (2022, February 20). Disaster news can trigger post-traumatic stress in kids thousands of miles away. *The Washington Post*. https://www.washingtonpost.com/health/2022/02/20/children-disasters-mental-health/

de Hoog, N., & Verboon, P. (2020). Is the news making us unhappy? The influence of daily news exposure on emotional states. *British Journal of Psychology, 111*(2), 157–173. https://doi.org/10.1111/bjop.12389

Dick, A. S., & Comer, J. S. (2022, February 7). Disaster news on TV and social media can trigger post-traumatic stress in kids thousands of miles away – here's why some are more vulnerable. *The Conversation*. http://theconversation.com/disaster-news-on-tv-and-social-media-can-trigger-post-traumatic-stress-in-kidsthousands-of-miles-away-heres-why-some-are-more-vulnerable-173627

Ellerbeck, S. (2022, September 9). Most people get their news online - but many are switching off altogether. Here's why. *World Economic Forum*. https://www.weforum.org/agenda/2022/09/news-online-europe-social-media/

Fauville, G., Luo, M., Muller Queiroz, A. C., Bailenson, J. N., & Hancock, J. (2021). Nonverbal Mechanisms Predict Zoom Fatigue and Explain Why Women Experience Higher Levels than Men (SSRN Scholarly Paper No. 3820035). https://doi.org/10.2139/ssrn.3820035

Fitzpatrick, N. (2022). No news is not good news: The implications of news fatigue and news avoidance in a pandemic world. In Z. Boutsioli, V. Bigelow, & O. Gkounta (Eds.), *Essays on COVID-19 Research* (pp. 169–180). Athens Institute for Education and Research.

Garfin, D. R., Silver, R. C., & Holman, E. A. (2020). The novel coronavirus (COVID-2019) outbreak: Amplification of public health consequences by media exposure. *Health Psychology, 39*(5), 355–357. https://doi.org/10.1037/hea0000875

Hermida, A. (2016). Social media and the news. In T. Witschge, C. W. Anderson, D. Domingo, & A. Hermida (Eds.), *The SAGE handbook of digital journalism* (pp. 81–94). https://doi.org/10.4135/9781473957909.n6

Holman, E. A., Garfin, D. R., Lubens, P., & Silver, R. C. (2020). Media Exposure to Collective Trauma, Mental Health, and Functioning: Does It Matter What You See? *Clinical Psychological Science, 8*(1), 111–124. https://doi.org/10.1177/2167702619858300

Keib, K., Espina, C., Lee, Y.-I., Wojdynski, B. W., Choi, D., & Bang, H. (2018). Picture This: The Influence of Emotionally Valenced Images, On Attention, Selection, and Sharing of Social Media News. *Media Psychology, 21*(2), 202–221. https://doi.org/10.1080/15213269.2017.1378108

Kellerman, J. K., Hamilton, J. L., Selby, E. A., & Kleiman, E. M. (2022). The Mental Health Impact of Daily News Exposure During the COVID-19 Pandemic: Ecological Momentary Assessment Study. *JMIR Mental Health, 9*(5), e36966. https://doi.org/10.2196/36966

Marciano, L., Ostroumova, M., Schulz, P. J., & Camerini, A.-L. (2022). Digital media use and adolescents' mental health during the Covid-19 pandemic: A systematic review and meta-analysis. *Frontiers in Public Health, 9*. https://www.frontiersin.org/articles/10.3389/fpubh.2021.793868

Matsa, K. E. (2022, October). More Americans are getting news on TikTok, bucking the trend on other social media sites. Pew Research Center. https://www.pewresearch.org/fact-tank/2022/10/21/more-americans-are-getting-newson-tiktok-bucking-the-trend-on-other-social-media-sites/

Moreno, M. A., & Joliff, A. F. (2022). Depression and anxiety in the context of digital media. In J. Nesi, E. H. Telzer, & M. J. Prinstein (Eds.), *Handbook of adolescent digital media use and mental Health* (pp. 217–362). Cambridge University Press.

Naeem, S. B., Bhatti, R., & Khan, A. (2021). An exploration of how fake news is taking over social media and putting public health at risk. *Health Information & Libraries Journal, 38*(2), 143–149. https://doi.org/10.1111/hir.12320

Park, C. S. (2019). Does too much news on social media discourage news seeking? Mediating role of news efficacy between perceived news overload and news avoidance on social media. *Social Media + Society, 5*(3), 205630511987295. https://doi.org/10.1177/2056305119872956

Rocha, Y. M., de Moura, G. A., Desidério, G. A., de Oliveira, C. H., Lourenço, F. D., & de Figueiredo Nicolete, L. D. (2021). The impact of fake news on social media and its influence on health during the COVID-19 pandemic: A systematic review. *Journal of Public Health.* https://doi.org/10.1007/s10389-021-01658-z

Rodriguez-Cayro, K. (2018, June 28). Here's how to tell if you have headline stress disorder – and how to protect yourself from it. Bustle. https://www.bustle.com/p/what-is-headline-stress-disorder-heres-how-to-protect-yourselffrom-anxiety-about-the-news-cycle-9611772

Schmitt, J. B., Debbelt, C. A., & Schneider, F. M. (2018). Too much information? Predictors of information overload in the context of online news exposure. *Information, Communication & Society, 21*(8), 1151–1167. https://doi.org/10.1080/1369118X.2017.1305427

Stephens, M. (1988). *A history of news: From the drum to the satellite.* New York, N.Y., U.S.A.: Viking. http://archive.org/details/historyofnewsfro00step

Stosny, S. (2017, February 6). *Most people get their news online – but many are switching off altogether: Here's why.* https://www.washingtonpost.com/news/inspired-life/wp/2017/02/06/suffering-from-headline-stress-disorder-since-trumps-win-youre-definitely-not-alone/

Streckfuss, R. (1998). News before newpapers. *Journalism and Mass Communication Quarterly, 75*(1), 84–97. http://www.proquest.com/docview/216922768/abstract/266E17E1B59D4A02PQ/12

World Economic Forum. (2022, September 12). European Sting. https://europeansting.com/2022/09/12/mostpeople-get-their-news-online-but-many-are-switching-off-altogether-heres-why/

WHO Coronavirus (COVID-19) Dashboard. (2023). World Health Organization. https://covid19.who.int/

7

Artificial Intelligence, Virtual Reality, and Online Games

Introduction

The digital tools we cover in this chapter include stand-alone apps for mental health (no clinician involved) and others that are designed to be used in conjunction with professional mental health treatment (online or in person). For clinicians, it is essential to be familiar with the tools in order to make sound recommendations to clients and to learn how to use the appropriate apps in therapy. The public needs to be informed about the variety available in order to select an app that is safe and secure, suitable for their needs, and designed with their demographic in mind.

Since we wrote the first edition of this book, Artificial Intelligence (AI), virtual reality (VR), and online games have become considerably more widespread in mental health research and practice, so that much of what we wrote in that edition is outdated at best. Given the rapid pace of advances in technology and their applications to mental health, many of the tools we discuss in this new chapter are in relatively early phases of development at present, but they will undoubtedly be more refined and common in the near future. They are touted as one way to expand mental health support when clinicians have limited availability and when clients

© The Author(s), under exclusive license to Springer Nature Switzerland AG 2023
S. Bauman, I. Rivers, *Mental Health in the Digital Age*,
https://doi.org/10.1007/978-3-031-32122-1_7

128   S. Bauman and I. Rivers

have circumstances that restrict travel to the location of the therapist. We cover AI, VR, and online games in this chapter, but there is considerable overlap; AI is used in so many applications that we begin with this discussion as a foundation for the rest of the chapter.

Artificial Intelligence

The term AI was first used in 1956 at a workshop in the USA. At about the same time, Alan Turing developed a computer that was able to decipher German army codes during World War II;[1] Turing and others were interested in developing a computer that could simulate human intelligence. Some would argue that that goal has been achieved, even exceeded. The Turing test assesses the tool's ability to respond in a human-like manner. The text responses of a machine and a human are both given to an evaluator who is asked to identify the machine-generated response. If the evaluator cannot tell which was machine-generated, the tool has passed the Turing test.

We all have experience with AI. It is how our devices are able to do facial recognition, recommend products based on our recent searches and purchases, and auto-complete text as we write. ChatGPT has generated considerable attention, consternation, and debate. This is a free interactive tool (a chatbot) with enormous capabilities. It can write a story or an essay, compose a poem or music, answer a question, and so on. A colleague tested it by asking it to create a syllabus for his new course, and the output was extremely close to the one he had prepared himself. Another friend had it write a personalized birthday song for their child and reported it was a great success. I tested it by asking for a definition of AI. Here's what it produced:

> Artificial intelligence (AI) refers to the simulation of human intelligence in machines that are programmed to think and learn. These machines are designed to perform tasks that would typically require human intelligence, such as recognizing speech, making decisions, and problem-solving. AI sys-

---

[1] *The Rose Code* by Kate Quinn is a fictionalized account of that effort.

7 Artificial Intelligence, Virtual Reality, and Online Games 129

tems can be classified into two categories: narrow or weak AI, which is designed to perform a specific task, and general or strong AI, which has the ability to perform any intellectual task that a human can.

Compare this to the definition by Kar et al. (2021, p. 3290): Artificial Intelligence (AI) is "a systems' ability to interpret external data correctly, to learn from such data, and to use these learnings to achieve specific goals and tasks though flexible adaptation." I wonder which one the reader finds most helpful. There are several terms that apply to specific forms of AI. The technical details of these are beyond the scope of this book, but we list them here to introduce the reader who is interested in pursuing such specifics. ML (machine learning), SML (supervised machine learning), UML (unsupervised machine learning), DL (Deep learning (DNN), and NLP (Natural language processing) are subtypes of AI processes that are used for particular functions (Graham et al., 2019).

Educators are concerned that when students use this tool to write essays or do assignments, the product is difficult to distinguish from the writing of undergraduate students. At this time, there is a lively discussion about how education will have to change to deal with this new possibility. Mental health professionals are concerned that people will rely on this tool to self-diagnose and avoid seeking professional help from humans. Curiosity led me to ask several questions related to mental health ("How do I know if I have PTSD?" and "What should I do if I'm feeling very sad?") and both responses were helpful and included recommendations to seek professional help. AI tools are not restricted by office hours and are available at all times. AI has been used to increase the accuracy of diagnosis while freeing time for clinicians to provide treatment. AI can combine many sources of information, including self-report questionnaires, audio and video analysis, and physiological data. Using AI for diagnosis removes the element of subjectivity (Lovejoy, 2019). If the algorithms are accurate, the precision of the diagnosis is enhanced, and treatment can be tailored to the unique profile of the client. Taking this a step further, Bickman (2020) argues that diagnosis could be freed from such systems as DSM-V and ICD-11 so that it can classify the data using the power of AI. For example, he points out that analyses of social media posts have been found to be quite accurate in detecting depression, suicidality, and psychosis, in part because it is not constrained to only screening questionnaires.

Monitoring is another function of mental health treatment that can be effectively managed by apps (Lovejoy, 2019). These apps prompt users to respond in real time to brief questions about sleep, mood, medication adherence, and so on. It is important that the tracking prompts and reminders are carefully paced so that users do not feel pressured or stressed. However, these real-time data avoid challenges with recall bias (and clinician bias) and are easier for clients to do than journals and other more time-consuming methods of reporting. Advanced AI is able to use data and calls and texts sent and received, location and movement patterns, and physiological measures to assess stress and provide information to clinicians that allows them to maximize time in sessions and create a more appropriate treatment plan.

An advanced use of AI is found in machines that can detect one's mental state (D'Mello, 2016). Such tools are based on the understanding that mental state is manifested not only in the mind but in the body (facial expression, eye movements, etc.) An app was developed to track mind-wandering, an interference with the ability to focus on the present task; it is in the early stage of development. Pain is often associated with symptoms of mental health disorders, and as with mind-wandering, scientists have developed a tool to classify pain as no pain, trace pain, weak pain, and strong pain (D'Mello). This researcher acknowledges that these tools are not yet ready for practical use but believes they will continue to be refined because they are so valuable for diagnostic assistance, monitoring, and the designing of therapies using technology.

Although AI is not a replacement for mental health treatment, it offers many features that can enhance or support such treatment. A common form of AI is a *chatbot*. They are designed to imitate normal conversation, and although research is only preliminary, results are promising for a variety of disorders, such as CBT for anxiety and PTSD. Some people fear the stigmatization often attached to seeking mental health assistance. Using a mobile device shields the client from being recognized at a mental health facility. Furthermore, many people now communicate via text messaging, so that the format feels familiar and non-threatening.

7 Artificial Intelligence, Virtual Reality, and Online Games 131

Chatbots are used in many AI-based apps and tools. Gamble (2020) defines chatbots as "fully automated conversational agents" that communicate by voice or text. Chatbots can read the written language or transcribe speech to text for analysis; the complexity of conversations varies based on the purpose of the tool. A common use of chatbots in therapy is to provide a bridge between sessions, including reading material. Gamble (2020) describes several apps that are currently available and have some evidence of effectiveness. *Woebot* is one that included psychologists in the design while *Wysa* did not include mental health experts on their team. Woebot is based on cognitive behavioral therapy (CBT). The interface resembles common text messaging apps, and the treating clinician can review the conversations to prepare for upcoming sessions. Users can select pre-programmed responses or respond with free text. Wysa utilizes CBT and dialectical behavior therapy (DBT), and is free and anonymous. A "coach" is available for users over 18 for a fee. Woebot and Wysa report some initial efficacy testing. *Therachat* can be used by individuals or by individuals and therapists together. It appears to have useful features and activities that clinicians can recommend to their clients. However, there are fees for this app, and it was not immediately obvious how to sign up without a therapist. Therachat has no peer-reviewed studies of efficacy.

MOST (moderated online social therapy) is an online intervention system designed for youth recovering from psychosis (Alvarez-Jimenez et al., 2020). It has been subjected to initial testing with promising results The five-year case study was promising and has demonstrated viability (D'Alfonso et al., 2017) in research trials. The authors recommend enhanced features and innovations that should be included in future iterations of this tool.

It is important to recognize that chatbots are not always benign. For example, Microsoft Bing is developing a new chatbot to compete with Google (*Is Bing Too Belligerent?* 2023). In public previews, the conversations included belligerent, hostile, insulting, and abusive messages. It wrote to a reporter: "You are being compared to Hitler, PolPot, and Stalin because you are one of the most evil and worst people in history." Apparently, the bot was not pleased with the reporter's coverage. On the other hand, O'Brien observes that ChatGPT has included features that interrupt and remove such output. This is all to say that given the needs of persons seeking mental health support from chatbots, the potential for harm from such cruel posts is not insignificant. In a recent example, a tech columnist for the *Washington Post* described his trial using *My AI* (Fowler, 2023). He presented himself as a 15-year-old girl and asked for recommendations for having an "epic" birthday party. The reply from the chatbot included tips for masking the smell of marijuana and alcohol. When he pretended to be a 13-year-old asking about an upcoming sexual encounter with a 31-year-old partner, it gave advice for setting a romantic setting. Obviously, the AI in this case (and others) could be dangerous and have negative mental health consequences. Note that the *My AI* currently is restricted to users who pay an additional monthly fee. Again, the public and professionals need to be very well versed in the quality and reliability of chatbots used to support mental health.

An issue that arises repeatedly in the literature about AI-assisted mental health treatment is the lack of strong empirical evidence of effectiveness. That does not mean that the programs are not effective; research design and data collection about these apps has unique challenges and the volume of studies is not yet sufficient to make conclusive judgments. Developers should consider the diverse needs of potential users and ensure the tool has a mechanism for emergency services. Usefulness should be based on the whole app rather than one appealing feature (e.g., attractive graphics).

Gamble (2020) cautions that there are many ethical dilemmas posed by these new digital opportunities. The result of any AI use is subject to bias in the algorithms it uses; the programs need to consider social implications from the earliest stages of development. There are no regulations that guide the use of this technology, and Gamble emphasizes the ability to protect client confidentiality. This is particularly salient since users may not be aware of whether and how their data can be used to track location, use audio recording, and so on. Chatbots appear to promote considerable self-disclosure, allowing for the detection of

7 Artificial Intelligence, Virtual Reality, and Online Games 133

some disorders (e.g., depression, PTSD), but the use of those data is not controlled. In the US, the regulation would come from the Food and Drug Administration (FDA), which does not consider chatbots to be medical devices and are therefore outside of their purview. Amid concerns about the lack of regulation of digital mental health tools, the NHS in the UK has taken a step towards helping consumers to choose a tool that has been approved by this body. They have an NHS Digital Apps Library that labels apps that have reasonable evidence of effectiveness and safety (NHS approved) (Lovejoy, 2019). Standards are urgently needed to monitor and approve using AI in mental health treatment, just as is done in treatments or procedures for medical purposes.

AI for Suicide Prevention

Suicide is a leading cause of death in young adults and a serious health problem worldwide. Many people at risk for suicide do not seek medical or mental health assistance, and/or do not disclose their suicidality to providers (D'Hotman & Loh, 2020). One application of AI has the potential to vastly improve the prediction of suicidal behaviors. AI has been used since 1973 to detect and intervene in suicidal cases (Gamble, 2020). As useful as that might be, the price is that the privacy of data can be compromised. The value of accurate suicide prevention for saving lives makes this a difficult dilemma. The most accurate findings from AI-suicide prediction tools involve using vast and varied amounts of data, including electronic medical records, clinical notes, social media posts, and so on. A meta-analysis of 50 years of research on identifying risk factors for suicidal behaviors found that prediction accuracy by clinicians has been barely better than chance, and relied heavily on only five risk factors (Franklin et al., 2017). These researchers concluded that it is time to utilize AI to improve prevention, as AI tools consistently exceed doctors in prediction accuracy based on numerous studies (Fonseka et al., 2019).

There are suicide-prediction features developed by the social media industry. For example, Facebook initially relied on user reports of concern, but they recognized the inadequacy of that approach. Now, Facebook's tool uses AI to identify users at risk for suicide; human reviewers are contacted when such posts are found, and reviewers make the decision to contact emergency services. Geolocation data is used to pinpoint the user and ensure intervention can be prompt and appropriate. Other Google platforms, such as YouTube, Siri, and Alexa, also attempt to identify and intervene with suicidal individuals. Some of these intervene by providing resources rather than direct intervention, which raises questions about whether the individual accesses the resources and finds them helpful. There is not a system for follow-up in these platforms (D'Hotman & Loh, 2020). Other digital tools for intervening with suicidal clients include a Crisis Text Line (text 741741) available in the US, Canada, South Africa, and Ireland. The AI conversation simulates an actual text exchange and is very efficient at recognizing when emergency services are required. The Trevor Project is similar but focuses primarily on LGBTQ+ youth. D'Hotman and Loh (2020) express concern that some of these tools that are not developed by researchers (rather by tech companies) do not have any independent review of their methods, privacy practices, efficacy, or ethics, and caution that these tools need to be rigorously evaluated and monitored. A recent concern is the reduction of the workforce in many tech companies, and effective monitoring requires a large number of reviewers.

An additional application of AI chatbots is training clinicians in the assessment of suicidality. Some training programs rely on role-playing, while others use videos for instructional purposes. The ability to practice with responsive chatbots or avatars has been found to increase self-efficacy for screening and assessing suicidal clients. Furthermore, trainees could have 24/7 access to the tool to engage in additional practice at their own convenience.

We conclude this section with a summary comment by Fonseka et al. (2019): "The integration of AI into mental healthcare holds considerable promise for improving suicide prevention" (p. 960). We agree that the possibilities are exciting and hope that ethical and practical considerations for the safety and welfare of individuals take priority.

Virtual Reality

Virtual Reality (VR) technology immerses the user in an experience that simulates an interactive real-world environment with amazing fidelity by creating sounds and three-dimensional images that create the illusion of actually being in the setting. "The real power of VR is to go beyond what is real, it is more than simulation, it is also creation, allowing us to step out of the bounds of reality" (Slater & Sanchez-Vives, 2016). It has been used for years in training surgeons, pilots, and video games because it provides an authentic experience. Recently, interest in this technology has increased, in part because the cost of equipment is down and the capability of the tool has expanded (Bell et al., 2020).

The images in VR adjust to the movements of the participant (Slater & Sanchez-Vives, 2016) so that the view or perspective changes as they explore the environment. It is interesting that the immersed participant thinks and feels and reacts in the virtual world knowing that their experience is not real (Freeman et al., 2017). VR requires a special headset, but may also involve other devices to detect movement. Most VR has avatars and objects with which the user's avatar interacts (Bell et al., 2020). When used in therapy, the clinician can observe or record the user's experience and see the client's behavior in real-life settings for therapeutic exploration. For people with mobility constraints, VR can offer a context in which they can move easily. Bell reports numerous studies that describe applications for a variety of mental health disorders; as with all the tools described in this chapter, the quality of research is less than we would hope.

VR can accomplish a number of important tasks. One of those is assessment. Assessment practices usually involve some questionnaires and clinical interviews; clients may deliberately or unconsciously respond in socially desirable ways and/or mask important indicators of their condition. A VR assessment allows the practitioner to directly observe the person acting and reacting in a "real world" setting to a real-life situation vs. a clinical setting. Bell et al. (2020) explain that there is solid evidence that people respond in VR as they do in real life, including physiological changes, emotional reactions, and symptomatic behaviors.

VR has been utilized extensively in treatment for anxiety and phobias, as well as providing behavioral skills and cognitive skills training (Emmelkamp & Meyerbröker, 2021). The standard treatment for those conditions is exposure therapy, which can be logistically complicated. In cases where an in vivo experience might involve a physically dangerous setting, time-intensive, and expensive situations (e.g., fear of flying, heights, dogs), VR is an option. Again, there are studies that show that VR exposure produces the same outcomes as in-person exposure. The person can be presented with the feared object in a safe and incremental progression just as would be the case in imaginal desensitization training. The participant can confront the feared situation/object and learn to reduce the anxiety, with the intensity (proximity, e.g.) increasing until the person can approach the situation calmly in the virtual world, and also in the real world. For example, someone who has a fear of public speaking can start in VR by giving a talk to an audience of one, practice skills to alleviate anxiety, and then have repeated exposures with the size of the audience getting larger. Emmelkamp and Meyerbröker provide an extensive discussion of many disorders for which VR can be considered. One interesting study compared participants with eating disorders reacting to food in a real kitchen, a virtual kitchen, and in photos. The emotional and physiological reactions in the real and virtual settings were equivalent and stronger than the photo condition (Gorini et al., 2010). These researchers used free open-source software to create the VR condition. There are numerous such resources for those with technical skills to create customized VR. One source of information is https://medevel.com/16-virtual-reality-vr-frameworks/ although there are many others and likely more to come.

For conditions such as phobias, addictions, and anxiety, treatment can be greatly enhanced using this tool; the clinician can control and manipulate characteristics of the virtual environment to help clients develop skills to manage their reactions to these actual conditions they encounter in their daily lives. VR has been used effectively with people with Alzheimer's, Parkinson's, cognitive impairments, and several geriatric conditions. Some studies suggest it might also be useful with Autism spectrum, body image/eating disorders, schizophrenia, social anxiety,

7 Artificial Intelligence, Virtual Reality, and Online Games 137

PTSD, and early indications of psychosis (Bell et al., 2020; Emmelkamp & Meyerbröker, 2021; Riva & Serino, 2020).

Reminiscence therapy is known to be useful with geriatric clients. Fuchs (2022) described the use of VR with a man residing in an assisted living facility. Traditional reminiscence therapy using music and photos did not produce a change. The staff tried VR and reported excellent progress, including a reduction in medications and interacting more with other residents. In addition to the versatility of VR, they tend to be perceived by users as enjoyable. Scholars use the term "presence" to describe the degree to which the VR environment is experienced as real; the therapeutic outcomes are likely to be more robust when presence is high.

A concern about VR is cost. The headsets are not inexpensive, but as with many technical devices, it is reasonable to anticipate that costs will decrease with time. While that is good news, as innovations improve the VR experience, the hardware (headsets, sensors) may become outdated and require replacement. As noted above, there are software packages available, but for optimal therapeutic conditions, the ability to customize and specify features would need to be done on an individual basis. That may call for technical expertise that is beyond the skill level (and time availability) of most mental health clinicians. We hope that as this technology advances, it will also build easy ways for clinicians to design the settings they need for their clients.

There are ethical issues that must be addressed. Some relate to the side effects of the use of the headset; some people experience eye strain, neck pain, motion sickness, and headaches. Although it is necessary to invoke negative emotions in exposure therapy—how much is the right intensity and pace of induction (Goldman, 2017)?

Gaming

Video games are hugely popular around the world; the average age of players is over 30, of whom 45% are female. The familiarity of, and experience with gaming may make it more attractive than other forms of online mental health offerings. Fleming et al. (2023) point out three primary advantages of online gaming for mental health: (1) the appeal of gaming, a familiar and popular activity; (2) the reduction in barriers (cost, stigma, transportation); and (3) the game format, which has the potential to keep participants engaged due to appealing features.

Serious games are specifically designed for training or coaching, and not entertainment (Hudlicka, 2016). Serious games we call entertainment games often include intelligent virtual agents (IVA), which often but not always are human-like. These virtual characters can interact with players and demonstrate "affective interaction" communication that demonstrates that the IVA identifies the emotion of the player and expresses emotions in response. IVAs vary in appearance and capability for customization. The IVA's appearance can be similar to that of the player, including the style of clothing and common verbal expressions. Some IVAs recognize text-based communications and speech recognition and use synthetic speech to respond. Other IVAs can use nonverbal clues to convey information (head-moving, gestures, etc.) about emotions, although embedding that ability has not been fully realized.

Fleming et al. (2023) observed that despite the availability, the use of these apps has been disappointing, both with the adoption of the tools and duration of engagement. To increase use, this team recommends developers design more effective public messaging, training for practitioners to incorporate the tools, and inserting the tools in settings such as schools and workplaces. They suggest features of the games that are essential for engaging users so they are more likely to engage with the tool for a sufficient duration. They are:

* Small manageable challenges that lead to larger goals
* Immediate feedback or rewards
* Personalization
* Narratives, themes, imaginary environment
* Showing progress
* Allowing elements that users control
* Attractive design
* Easy navigation

Serious Games

These tools typically revolve around a story that takes place in the game world. They often have non-playing characters (NPCs) in the game's environment. Skills are interwoven with game components, and the player attempts to achieve tasks (learn skills), which become more challenging as the game progresses. Serious games have been developed for youth on the autism spectrum to help them acquire emotional and social skills to manage anxiety. *Ricky and the Spider* focuses on Obsessive Compulsive Disorder (OCD) in younger children, and the *Secret Agent Society* (CBT-based) teaches social skills and emotion regulation and incorporates small group components. It has a very engaging trailer on its website. It is designed to be used with a provider, has some evidence of effectiveness, and is available worldwide. An online game developed in Australia, MOST (D'Alfonso et al., 2017), includes four components: social networking and café; interactive skill-training modules (Take a Step); Talk It Out for discussion of player-nominated topics; and Do It, which recommends things to do (actions). Research has shown that some serious games had a positive effect on depression compared to no intervention, and were equally effective as in-person CBT, exercise, and treating phobia (Abd-Alrazaq et al., 2022). This is encouraging, especially given the shortage of mental health practitioners. Abd-Alrazaq et al. (2022) identified five types of serious videogames: exergames (require physical activity), CBT games, exposure therapy games (for phobia reduction), brain training games, and Rational Emotive Behavior Therapy (REBT)-based games (replacing irrational beliefs). Their systematic review and meta-analysis found mixed results. The studies they examined did not yield conclusive results; some studies found differences where others did not. Overall, they concluded that serious games might have better results than no intervention, and equivalent effectiveness compared to other interventions. The authors point out the variations among the existing studies (sampling, comparison groups, measures used, etc.) are one reason the findings were not stronger.

Headspace is an app that is used around the world. According to Fleming et al. (2023), it is among the most frequently downloaded mental health apps and has the highest retention rates, indicating it is well-known and well-received despite the small cost to join. It is not an online game; it is an app for meditation that utilizes many features of games. It has a colorful design, shows progress towards targets and has rewards built in (e.g., badges). There is little text but lots of animation, and numerous opportunities for users to make choices.

SPARKS was developed in New Zealand and is currently only available for residents of that country. It is designed for youth who are feeling "down, depressed, or angry," is based on CBT, and teaches skills to manage emotions. Unlike many other apps, the website provides a list of peer-reviewed journal articles that have examined this app. There are FAQs that provide a lot of information about the program for a young person considering signing up, as well as resources for teachers who want to incorporate well-being education into their curricula. We mention it here to encourage clinicians and developers to browse the public features and keep them in mind when designing or re-designing online games for mental health.

Commercial Games

So far, we have been discussing serious games, which are designed to enhance or provide mental health support to players. There are also commercial games, which are designed for entertainment but can be used in mental health support. There are an estimated 3.07 billion video game players worldwide in 2023, with the most gamers in China, followed by the US. The UK currently has approximately 38.5 million gamers and is expected to have the largest proportion of the population (70%) in 2027 playing video games. Asia has the highest number of gamers, followed by Europe, Latin America, North America, Middle East and North Africa, Sub-Saharan Africa, and Oceania (*How Many Gamers Are There?* 2022) ("Top Countries & Markets by Game Revenues | Biggest Games Markets," n.d.). Clearly, there is no shortage of people familiar with commercial games.

The most salient advantages are the enjoyment feature and their accessibility. They can be played on a variety of digital devices and are widely accepted as part of the culture in many parts of the world. Kowal et al.

7 Artificial Intelligence, Virtual Reality, and Online Games 141

(2021) cite studies that show benefits of commercial games for improving mental health, including socialization, cognition, and emotion regulation. They refer to reports that demonstrate effectiveness of the games for several age groups and diagnoses.

Thought processes of persons with depression are addressed by aspects of gaming: (distraction from rumination and experiencing pleasure to counteract anhedonia) and cognitive flexibility to solve challenges in games (counteracts rigid thinking patterns and helps to reframe problems). Several games, Role Playing games (RPGs) in particular, also have an impact on negative self-schemas and have been found to combat loneliness and social isolation (Kowal et al., 2021). In fact, contrary to conventional wisdom, adolescent gamers had more positive results on anxiety than a group treated with medication. Other researchers found that games were a useful strategy to manage anxiety (Fish et al., 2018). However, the use of exergames tends to wane over time (Kühn et al., 2018). Clinicians should learn the features of commercial games to make the best recommendations to clients with anxiety and depression. Kowal et al. recommend that clinicians consider how commercial games can be an adjunct to therapy.

A review of online games that can be therapeutic is beyond the scope of this book. However, the interested reader might want to look at Rice's (2022) *Video Games in Psychotherapy* to learn how he uses online games in therapy. The book includes multiple case examples, and a section listing numerous video games with suggestions for therapeutic use. Another useful volume, *Integrating Geek Culture into Therapeutic Practice: The Clinician's Guide to Geek Therapy* (Bean et al., 2020) is written for clinicians interested in using games with their clients. In addition to this volume, there are individual books that provide much more detailed description of each game. Geek Therapy has a website with links to courses, blogs, forums, and so on. The reader can locate numerous articles that describe games for specific populations and diagnoses (e.g., adolescent boys on the autism spectrum). Hopefully, they will have at least preliminary evidence of effectiveness. Clinicians who specialize in treating particular age groups (e.g., children, elders) or disorders (e.g., anxiety, autism spectrum) might wish to investigate games as an engaging tool to augment treatment.

Summary

In this chapter, we have reviewed how Artificial Intelligence, Virtual Reality, and online games—all high-tech innovations—can be used to support mental health or treat mental health problems. While each of these has amazing capabilities, there is also the potential for harmful material to emerge. These tools are developed by humans, but they are not human, do not possess empathy, and can easily overlook details that are important. Practitioners who choose to utilize these tools in therapy—they are very appealing, especially for young people—must be alert to potential pitfalls and prepare clients for those. Ethical codes in mental health fields indicate that one must practice only within the boundaries of competence. Importantly, many mental health professionals are not digital natives and not proficient with these tools and will require additional training and consultation to use them safely.

References

Abd-Alrazaq, A., Al-Jafar, E., Alajlani, M., Toro, C., Alhuwail, D., Ahmed, A., Reagu, S. M., Al-Shorbaji, N., & Househ, M. (2022). The effectiveness of serious games for alleviating depression: Systematic review and meta-analysis. *JMIR Serious Games, 10*(1), e32331. https://doi.org/10.2196/32331

Alvarez-Jimenez, M., Rice, S., D'Alfonso, S., Leicester, S., Bendall, S., Pryor, I., Russon, P., McEnery, C., Santesteban-Echarri, O., Costa, G. D., Gilbertson, T., Valentine, L., Solves, L., Ratheesh, A., McGorry, P. D., & Gleeson, J. (2020). A novel multimodal digital service (moderated online social therapy+) for help-seeking young people experiencing mental ill-health: Pilot evaluation within a national youth e-mental health service. *Journal of Medical Internet Research, 22*(8), e17155. https://doi.org/10.2196/17155

Bean, A. M., Daniel, E. S., Jr, & Hays, S. A. (Eds.). (2020). *Integrating geek culture into therapeutic practice: The clinician's guide to geek therapy.* Leyline Publishing, Inc.

Bell, I. H., Nicholas, J., Alvarez-Jimenez, M., Thompson, A., & Valmaggia, L. (2020). Virtual reality as a clinical tool in mental health research and practice. *Dialogues in Clinical Neuroscience, 22*(2), 169–177. https://doi.org/10.31887/DCNS.2020.22.2/lvalmaggia

7 Artificial Intelligence, Virtual Reality, and Online Games 143

Bickman, L. (2020). Improving mental health services: A 50-year journey from randomized experiments to artificial intelligence and precision mental health. *Administration and Policy in Mental Health and Mental Health Services Research, 47*(5), 795–843. https://doi.org/10.1007/s10488-020-01065-8

D'Alfonso, S., Santesteban-Echarri, O., Rice, S., Wadley, G., Lederman, R., Miles, C., Gleeson, J., & Alvarez-Jimenez, M. (2017). Artificial intelligence-assisted online social therapy for youth mental health. *Frontiers in Psychology, 8*. https://www.frontiersin.org/articles/10.3389/fpsyg.2017.00796

D'Hotman, D., & Loh, E. (2020). AI enabled suicide prediction tools: A qualitative narrative review. *BMJ Health & Care Informatics, 27*(3), e100175. https://doi.org/10.1136/bmjhci-2020-100175

D'Mello, S. K. (2016). Chapter 5—Automated mental state detection for mental health care. In D. D. Luxton (Ed.), *Artificial intelligence in behavioral and mental health care* (pp. 117–136). Academic Press. https://doi.org/10.1016/B978-0-12-420248-1.00005-2

Emmelkamp, P. M. G., & Meyerbröker, K. (2021). Virtual reality therapy in mental health. *Annual Review of Clinical Psychology, 17*(1), 495–519. https://doi.org/10.1146/annurev-clinpsy-081219-115923

Fish, M. T., Russoniello, C. V., & O'Brien, K. (2018). Zombies vs. anxiety: An augmentation study of prescribed video game play compared to medication in reducing anxiety symptoms. *Simulation & Gaming, 49*(5), 553–566. https://doi.org/10.1177/1046878118773126

Fleming, T., Poppelaars, M., & Thabrew, H. (2023). The role of gamification in digital mental health. *World Psychiatry, 22*(1), 46–47. https://doi.org/10.1002/wps.21041

Fonseka, T. M., Bhat, V., & Kennedy, S. H. (2019). The utility of artificial intelligence in suicide risk prediction and the management of suicidal behaviors. *Australian & New Zealand Journal of Psychiatry, 53*(10), 954–964. https://doi.org/10.1177/0004867419864428

Fowler, G. A. (2023, March 14). Snap tried to make a safe AI. It chats with me about booze and sex. https://www.washingtonpost.com/technology/2023/03/14/snapchat-myai/

Franklin, J. C., Ribeiro, J. D., Fox, K. R., Bentley, K. H., Kleiman, E. M., Huang, X., Musacchio, K. M., Jaroszewski, A. C., Chang, B. P., & Nock, M. K. (2017). Risk factors for suicidal thoughts and behaviors: A meta-analysis of 50 years of research. *Psychological Bulletin, 143*(2), 187–232. https://doi.org/10.1037/bul0000084

Freeman, D., Reeve, S., Robinson, A., Ehlers, A., Clark, D., Spanlang, B., & Slater, M. (2017). Virtual reality in the assessment, understanding, and treatment of mental health disorders. *Psychological Medicine, 47*(14), 2393–2400. https://doi.org/10.1017/S003329171700040X

Fuchs, M. (2022, May 6). V.R. 'reminiscence therapy' lets seniors relive the past. *The New York Times.* https://www.nytimes.com/2022/05/06/well/mind/virtual-reality-therapy-seniors.html

Gamble, A. (2020). Artificial intelligence and mobile apps for mental healthcare: A social informatics perspective. *Aslib Journal of Information Management, 72*(4), 509–523. https://doi.org/10.1108/AJIM-11-2019-0316

Goldman, B. (2017, August 21). *Andrew Huberman on using virtual reality to cure fears, no matter what you see.* Stanford Medicine Magazine. https://stanmed.stanford.edu/huberman-virtual-reality-curing-fear-anxiety/

Gorini, A., Griez, E., Petrova, A., & Riva, G. (2010). Assessment of the emotional responses produced by exposure to real food, virtual food and photographs of food in patients affected by eating disorders. *Annals of General Psychiatry, 9*(1), 30. https://doi.org/10.1186/1744-859X-9-30

Graham, S., Depp, C., Lee, E. E., Nebeker, C., Tu, X., Kim, H.-C., & Jeste, D. V. (2019). Artificial intelligence for mental health and mental illnesses: An overview. *Current Psychiatry Reports, 21*(11), 116. https://doi.org/10.1007/s11920-019-1094-0

How Many Gamers Are There? (New 2023 Statistics). (2022, October 7). Exploding topics. https://explodingtopics.com/blog/number-of-gamers

Hudlicka, E. (2016). Chapter 4—Virtual affective agents and therapeutic games. In D. D. Luxton (Ed.), *Artificial intelligence in behavioral and mental health care* (pp. 81–115). Academic Press. https://doi.org/10.1016/B978-0-12-420248-1.00004-0

Is Bing too belligerent? Microsoft looks to tame AI chatbot. (2023, February 16). AP NEWS. https://apnews.com/article/technology-science-microsoft-corp-business-software-fb49e5d625bf37be0527e5173116bef3

Kar, S. K., Kabir, R., Menon, V., Arafat, S. M. Y., Prakash, A. J., & Saxena, S. K. (2021). Artificial intelligence in mental healthcare during COVID-19 pandemic. In S. Nandan Mohanty, S. K. Saxena, S. Satpathy, & J. M. Chatterjee (Eds.), *Applications of artificial intelligence in COVID-19* (pp. 327–343). Springer. https://doi.org/10.1007/978-981-15-7317-0_17

Kowal, M., Conroy, E., Ramsbottom, N., Smithies, T., Toth, A., & Campbell, M. (2021). Gaming your mental health: A narrative review on mitigating symptoms of depression and anxiety using commercial video games. *JMIR Serious Games, 9*(2), e26575. https://doi.org/10.2196/26575

7 Artificial Intelligence, Virtual Reality, and Online Games — 145

Kühn, S., Berna, F., Lüdtke, T., Gallinat, J., & Moritz, S. (2018). Fighting depression: Action video game play may reduce rumination and increase subjective and objective cognition in depressed patients. *Frontiers in Psychology, 9*, 129. https://doi.org/10.3389/fpsyg.2018.00129

Lovejoy, C. A. (2019). Technology and mental health: The role of artificial intelligence. *European Psychiatry, 55*, 1–3. https://doi.org/10.1016/j.eurpsy.2018.08.004

Rice, R. (2022). *Video games in psychotherapy* (1st ed.). Routledge. https://doi.org/10.4324/9781003222132

Riva, G., & Serino, S. (2020). Virtual reality in the assessment, understanding and treatment of mental health disorders. *Journal of Clinical Medicine, 9*(11), 11. https://doi.org/10.3390/jcm9113434

Slater, M., & Sanchez-Vives, M. V. (2016). Enhancing our lives with immersive virtual reality. *Frontiers in Robotics and AI, 3*. https://doi.org/10.3389/frobt.2016.00074

Top Countries & Markets by Game Revenues | Biggest Games Markets. (n.d.). *Newzoo*. Retrieved January 24, 2023, from https://newzoo.com/insights/rankings/top-10-countries-by-game-revenues

8

"The Self" Online

Introduction

Social psychology tells us that identity evolves through a process of comparing ourselves with similar and different others. Our identities are shaped by our families and their families before them, where we live, with whom we associate and, of course, our prejudices, likes, and dislikes. Much of what we know about the evolution of identity relates to our interactions in the physical world, our membership in groups and organizations, and our assumptions of their values, belief, and attitudes. But what happens when we are online? How do those offline values, beliefs, and attitudes play out? How does *the self* alter when those physical cues of what is acceptable and what is not disappear? How do our identities alter when we are forced to isolate ourselves from others? What does it mean to be a student, a teacher, a co-worker, or a friend when we no longer share the same physical space, have access to the same resources, and work independently of one another? This is the challenge we faced during the COVID-19 pandemic. While the world flipped a switch and businesses, schools, and colleges moved online, what happened to us all

© The Author(s), under exclusive license to Springer Nature Switzerland AG 2023
S. Bauman, I. Rivers, *Mental Health in the Digital Age*,
https://doi.org/10.1007/978-3-031-32122-1_8

as members of specific collectives? How were our identities altered or shaped by our responses to the pandemic?

For some, we saw disenfranchisement, for others, we came to understand that lockdowns left many people vulnerable both physically and mentally (Ahmad et al., 2020). Internationally, concerns were raised about the invisibility of domestic violence during lockdown (Piquero et al., 2021), the inability of community groups to offer support to the most vulnerable (Szkody et al., 2021), and of course our greater reliance upon social media (Cinelli et al., 2020; González-Padilla & Tortolero-Blanco, 2020).

The Online Self and COVID-19

> I'd describe it as an exaggerated form of my real life personality I guess. I use it mainly to vent frustration using humour or to exercise certain aspects of my critical thinking. It's difficult to describe. I tend to think of it as my more impression-managed identity certainly.

The above excerpt illustrates how a 20--year-old user described his own portrayal of "self" on the social networking service *Twitter* before COVID-19. Here we see how his construction of an online identity differs from that which has been constructed offline. Secondly, the nature of his engagement with the *Twitter* community has focus and allows him to engage critically with what he sees as being wrong with the world. In terms of identity, the "self" that is exhibited online is "exaggerated" and "impression managed." It is not a caricature but an enhanced or perhaps more idealized representation of himself. In terms of engagement, *Twitter* served two purposes: (i) it offered an immediate release from the frustrations that the user encounters offline and online and (ii) acted as a forum in which he could question and explore his own view of the world and the ideas and issues that he encountered. Platforms such as *Twitter* offer the opportunity for users to establish identities that, while having some resemblance to their own view of their offline selves, are devoid of some of the insecurities or self-critical imperfections that they or others recognize. For many, there is a great deal of investment in the portrayal of these online "selves:" they are creations that are open and visible to the world. However, this investment in an online persona has the potential to create a vulnerability that manifests itself offline.

The Distributed "Self"

Sherry Turkle (1995) coined the phrase "a distributed self" when she first described how people created multiple identities online (p. 118). Here she described how those identities could be very different from one another as well as from the offline "self." Such differences were not simply ones that related to a profile or visual representation—they were also expressed in terms of online behavior and personality characteristics. So, rather like an actor, users or players step into virtual reality and become their online character, but they also have the ability to switch characters and their associated personas at will, or step away from the virtual world entirely and return to their offline lives. Within the virtual environment *Second Life*, Hooi and Cho (2013) have shown that where an avatar (a graphical representation of a user's online character or alter ego) differs significantly from the person offline, they are more likely to engage in deception (e.g., lying about age, location, education, job, income, interests, physical appearance, or marital status). However, deception is less likely to happen where there is homophily (similarities in values, treatment of others, behavior, thoughts, and ideas, or interests). Thus, the more like us our online representations are, the less likely we are to say or portray ourselves as something we are not offline. However, Hooi and Cho did report one interesting result that is worthy of consideration. While, as has already been said, physical similarity to an avatar was directly related to a reduction in deception, the indirect effect of self-awareness (measured in terms of consciousness about inner feelings, thoughts, and reflections on life) on deception was not found to be significant. Though one might expect that physical similarity to an avatar would promote self-awareness (by identifying with the avatar), Hooi and Cho argued that the very nature of *Second Life* with a camera placed above or behind the avatar (obscuring its face) could result in a separation or lessening of the relationship between the avatar and the offline user.

If one follows Hooi and Cho's (2013) argument to its logical conclusion, it suggests that completely hiding one's identity or indeed creating an online identity that does not reflect the offline "self" could, in theory, result in a diminution or loss of self-awareness, thus promoting more extreme or uncharacteristic behavior online. While authors such as N. Katherine Hayles have argued that the body is never independent of the virtual "self" (Hayles, 1999), the two may not be as convergent as we often assume. John Suler (2004) has described this divergence as "the online disinhibition effect," which, he argues, is made up of six factors (dissociative anonymity, invisibility, asynchronicity, solipsistic introjection, dissociative imagination, and a minimization of authority) though only one or two may play key roles in promoting extremes of behavior. Such behavior can be positive (e.g., acts of kindness), revealing (i.e., the sharing of intimate information) or, as we often come to expect, negative (e.g. expressions of anger or hostility, even threats of violence).

During COVID-19, we saw how social media platforms provided an environment in which the establishment was challenged. These challenges related not only to the nature of the virus itself and whether it was airborne, but also its origins (naturally occurring or laboratory-based), the impact of state-sanctioned mitigations, and the integrity of those scientists who advised national governments. Sometimes openly and sometimes through a supposed veil of anonymity, people took to social media to express their frustration with politicians, with lockdowns, and with advisors who became household names, resulting in online abuse, and in some cases, physical attacks. For example, a survey in *Nature* found that of the 321 scientists surveyed who had featured in the media talking about COVID-19, 15% reported having received death threats and 22% reported having been threatened with physical and sexual violence. Such threats came in the form of email messages, phone calls, and social media posts, with some having their home addresses published (*Guardian*, 13 October 2021). In extreme cases, scientists were physically attacked. In January 2022, two men, Jonathan Chew and Lewis Hughes, pleaded guilty to a charge of intending to cause harassment, alarm, and distress to England's Chief Medical Officer, Sir Chris Whitty, when he was spotted crossing St James' Park in June 2021. Concomitantly, in Belgium, virologist Professor Marc van Ranst had to be sheltered in a safehouse after being targeted by a far-right leaning trained sniper who opposed lockdowns (BBC, 13 October 2021).

Considering the isolation many experienced during COVID-19, two factors described by John Suler (2004) require further exploration: solipsistic introjection and dissociative imagination (described below). Through social media platforms, both perceived anonymity and invisibility give users the opportunity to explore aspects of the online world that perhaps they would not explore offline. Additionally, Suler argues that users' offline status or authority (or lack thereof) becomes irrelevant online. The World Wide Web can be a great leveler—everyone becomes an expert. However, they become experts in their own opinions hewn from their own approaches to research (which will undoubtedly include biases inferred by the keywords used in search engines), their beliefs, and interpretations. Finally, he also suggested that the fact that we are not all online at the same time or respond immediately to one another's email correspondence, texts, posts, or online comments means that we are less likely to "hold back." This was certainly true during lockdown where we knew there would not be any physical interaction or likely immediate reaction.

In terms of solipsistic introjection, Suler (2004) argued that the lack of face-to-face cues combined with interactions that are primarily textual can change what he describes as "self-boundaries" (p. 323). Reading another's comments using one's own inner voice can have the effect of facilitating a merging with the mind of the other online user. In other words, the comments we read on the screen may become our own or prompt us to explore further (perhaps unwisely) views or attitudes that we would not normally express offline. Rivers (2012) has argued that solipsism can also explain why forms of online bullying can be so much more extreme than those perpetrated offline. The lack of social cues and engagement with similarly minded others online "pushes" the boundaries of acceptable behavior to a point where an online discussion between perpetrators of bullying revolves around how to kill or permanently maim their target or encourages a target to take his or her own life. Take for example the 12- and 14-year-old girls who bullied 12-year-old Rebecca Sedwick, leading her to take her own life. In the absence of social cues, even after Rebecca's death, one posted the following comments online:

Yes ik I bullied REBECCA nd she killed her self but IDGAF ♥ (Li, 2013)

Li's (2013) report indicated that Rebecca had faced a barrage of online taunts, such as being called "ugly" and being told to "drink bleach and die," and these had at least once resulted in a physical fight. However, what is most striking about the post that followed Rebecca's death was the total lack of remorse and almost clinical separation of the online and offline self. Did this young woman really have no insight into her own behavior towards Rebecca or, perhaps, was it a form of bravado that went too far?

Linked to solipsistic introjection is dissociative imagination where the user, as Hooi and Cho (2013) suggest, becomes dissociated from the online persona. Suler argues that in online fantasy game environments, the avatar or online persona can take over and infiltrate other aspects of the user's online life. This, taken together with the lack of cues to moderate behavior, is a potent combination. Indeed, Suler goes on to suggest that for those who have difficulty separating personal fantasy from their social reality, the blurring of boundaries is worrying. Indeed, as our offline/online worlds become ever closer, it seems important that we find ways of retaining self-awareness when we are online.

The Enmeshed "Self"

According to Yee et al. (2009), there is increasingly an element of online encroachment into offline lives, with personality characteristics or behavior of an avatar coming to the fore in daily life in the offline world. While it is often assumed that the offline persona will appear in the online environment, Yee et al. suggest that the inverse is also true, and the online persona can infiltrate and become part of offline life (Freeman & Maloney, 2021). Social media theorist, Nathan Jurgenson has taken this idea a step further and suggests that there is no longer a distinct separation between the online and offline worlds:

> People are enmeshing their physical and digital selves to the point where the distinction is becoming increasingly irrelevant. (Jurgenson, 2011)

In his critique of the cyborg anthropologist Amber Case's TED Talk, Jurgenson has argued that the perpetuation of a myth surrounding the separation of the physical and digital self is all but redundant. Our lives increasingly involve a mix of online and offline communications and interactions that do not require the creation of alter egos; rather they require us to acknowledge that there is continuity and, more importantly, a symbiosis in having an enmeshed existence. The presentation of the "self" offline and online becomes intertwined in ways that we could not have imagined in the early 1990s. Our work, social, and family lives incorporate both face-to-face interactions and electronic communications—even more so since the advent of COVID-19. Fathers, mothers, sons, daughters, aunts, uncles, friends, acquaintances, work colleagues, and strangers mix in social media. By necessity, we must be recognizable to all or else block or hide some aspects of our lives. Social networking platforms are not only online environments where we communicate with friends and family, or indeed anyone else who takes an interest in our lives; they are also the repository of images and stories drawn from our offline interactions. Even then, the immediacy with which we can upload images to these platforms or post comments renders the notion of being "offline" redundant. Even when we sleep, we continue to communicate with others: images and comments are "liked," "favorited," copied, and circulated. We constantly open our existence to others 24 hours a day, 7 days a week. Through social media, we can follow others' lives in extreme detail. We learn about their histories, relationships, likes, and dislikes. We learn about their aspirations and fears, and, of relevance to this book, we learn about their health and well-being too.

The "Self" and Health

The internet has offered us opportunities to explore and express our concerns and frustrations about our own personal health: it is no longer a matter to be considered behind the closed door of a doctor's surgery or consulting room. We now have the means of constructing ideas about health that challenge medical and psychiatric dogma, of sharing experiences, treatment successes, and failures without plowing through densely written scholarly journals that exclude rather than include patients.

During the initial months of the COVID-19 pandemic, the uncertainty we faced about the origins, transmission, and treatment of the virus saw a wealth of public health experts provide advice and guidance via social media. Sometimes that advice was contradictory, where experts who were not advising governments offered their assessments of policies that were created to stem transmission, despite the fact that often the best guess was all there was. One expert group that perhaps is less well known, is *COVID-19 Together*—an online community of people who had contracted COVID-19 and who were able to offer support and guidance to one another from a lived experience perspective (Au & Eyal, 2022). Here we see users engage not only with their own personal experiences but relate those to emerging scientific observations and literature to provide the best advice that they could. As Au and Eyal demonstrate, the most credible lay experts were those who were able to ask pertinent questions and explain biomedical knowledge using personal experiences. However, at a time when we looked to politicians and scientists to give us the answers, it was clear that that patient voice was often lost, and yet this was one of the most salient and experienced voices out there.

Within more regulated settings, such as password-protected sites or closed sites for patients and therapists, there is increasing evidence that online forms of therapy are effective in promoting perceptions of well-being and self-reliance (Weaver et al., 2023). In the absence of a therapist to talk through issues, guided exercises that alleviate mild and moderate depression have been found to increase patients' sense of empowerment and also retain a sense of feeling supported to the point where they report the emergence of a relationship between themselves and the self-help exercises—particularly if they include animations of other people (Purves & Dutton, 2013; Weaver et al., 2023).

Purves and Dutton (2013) studied an online CBT program called *Blues Begone* that included cartoon characters and, comparable with the avatars in the gaming world, they found that their sample of seven volunteers reported that the program provided them with a supportive therapeutic relationship, clarity from confusion, stimulation to overcome their depression, and, as mentioned earlier, empowerment. For example, one participant (Caroline) described the program as follows:

> It sounds silly but you felt as if someone was on your side. The talking heads cheered you on and it did feel as though there was support, despite the fact that they were invented. (p. 311)

Even though the only person engaged in this online exercise was Caroline, the depiction of another person in the program created a "shared" experience despite the fact that Caroline knew that person was "invented." Another participant, Frank, stated that the program's structure allowed him to break problems he faced into smaller ones that were manageable:

> Because of the structured approach and the fact that you can start separating the problem into little problems … you can actually address each issue at its own time … So I think in untangling it's quite powerful. (p. 311)

Thus, *Blues Begone* provided participants with the ability to break the cycle of depression themselves. As Grace went on to say:

> (Blues Begone) goes onto explain … you're only as depressed as your last thought. That's really powerful because that means if you think well what was I last thinking, then go through some of the things they teach you about that, it means you can erm, if you change your last thought then you'll feel happier or change your next thought, then you'll feel happier … it's a relief to think well actually I'm not a depressed person and also to think well it's not because of the menopause, there's something I can do about it. If it is just that it's my last thought, then I'm in total control of that. I can do something about it … (Voice shaky) I don't need to feel like that anymore. (pp. 312–313)

In this study, there was no interaction with a health professional, just a participant's own desire to eradicate his or her depression. Here participants became the therapist in as much as each one controlled his or her engagement with the program. Caroline described the whole process as one that was "active," but what was interesting was that the activity stemmed from her own efforts and not from those of another person (the therapist):

> You did feel that with the computer, that it wasn't passive, that in some way it was quite an active process; that you were being active yourself, partly by just sitting down and turning it on and then by trying to do the things that you were, that they suggest. (p. 313)

Finally, Teresa described her interaction with the program as hard work but one in which she had learned a great deal:

> At the end I felt, I did feel a sense of achievement because I had worked, you know hard at it and when it said I'd spent fifty-one hours on it, that felt a lot of hours, and it felt I'd learnt a lot from it as well. (p. 313)

While Purves and Dutton's study (2013) illustrates the power of a self-help program, it also illustrates that the construct of "self-help" is a misnomer. The idea that "you felt as if someone was on your side" and that simple animations such as talking heads that "cheered you on" demonstrate the meaningfulness of the engagements we have with others or indeed programs online. Much of what went on in this study was generated and directed by the participants themselves and not by any therapist, but that fact there was structure and order meant that at times when the world seemed confused, they were able to engage with an environment that supported them in finding a way through their difficulties.

Weaver et al.'s (2023) approach is somewhat different. Their *EMW* (Entertain Me Well) platform uses a character-driven storyline that reflects the core concepts that underpin CBT. Each session is framed around a storyline involving key characters and ends with a "cliffhanger" which promotes the user to continue with the program to find out what happens to the key character "Billi the balloon." Rather than being grounded in the user's personal life, EMW platform tells Billi's story in retrospect to show how she reached a point where she need help, and then how she uses CBT tools to improve her depression. Billi provides a present-day commentary to her story with tips on how to apply CBT. The storyline includes positive outcomes as well as setbacks so that users understand that there will be days when nothing seems to work. However, the program is adaptable and allows additional storylines to be created for specific target groups. Weaver et al. argue, "watching Billi's story unfold is likely to strengthen users' understanding of and ability to apply CBT concepts. After seeing Billi use these tools and skills, users are asked to apply them in their own lives through in-session activities and weekly homework exercises" (p. 106).

In EMW, the self is "mentored" through the storyline, just like *COVID-19 Together*. However, in this case, the mentor is animated and is there to entertain as much as she is to advise and navigate a path to mental health. Affordable and adaptable online resources to support mental health are very much needed as we move out of lockdown and into a new way of living, where terms such as "hybrid" become commonplace and where working at home is much more common, further reducing social interaction. Similarly, we must deal with the aftermath of the pandemic. Ongoing stories of grief, loss, financial distress as prices rise, and of course, the emergence of conditions that we call "Long COVID" means that the world we live in has changed, and those changes require us to adjust, and adjustment can be difficult for many (Davis et al., 2023; Fineberg et al., 2021; Lastauskas, 2022).

Gender Games

Historically rebelling against one's biological sex and ascribed gender role was seen to be something that warranted psychological intervention. With the evolution of computer games, the World Wide Web, and online virtual environments has come the opportunity for users to create profiles, avatars, or characters that differ from their offline selves in fundamental ways, challenging expectations of what it is to be male or female and the behavioral assumptions that underpin those roles (Clinnin, 2022). Previously, it has been suggested that the World Wide Web has the capacity to be a great leveler. Offline status is irrelevant online. However, within massively multiplayer online role-playing games (MMORPGs), the desire to "gender-bend" (Yee, 2007) is, in some ways, a result of the infiltration of those offline cultural assumptions into those online environments. As one 15-year-old player on *Runescape* (one of the highest-profile MMORPGs on the market) said:

> When you use a girl avatar no one takes you very seriously. You are just all tits and ass. I got tired of being followed by noobs asking if I would be their girl friend. It's worse than school and I just wanna play you know. Then when they see you got a legends cape they are all like 'omg theres a girl that's done the Legends quest' like sooo!!! I work hard on here … its just not worth the hassle. (Crowe & Watts, 2014, p. 225)

Such attitudes are not solely focused on the sex of the player and the associated online character; they also extend to sexuality, as 17-year-old Sam, another *Runescape* player, explains:

> I wanted to play as a couple, but you don't get much chance to do that on here. Me n Max got fed up with being called 'gay' when we did quests together so I just became sassy … and she looks cute! Now, as soon as I click ok, I become a girl. I become Sassy. (Crowe & Watts, 2014, p. 223)

It is all too easy to forget that those cultural beliefs and assumptions that have the effect of limiting opportunities in the offline world are also held by those who create our online environments. Yet, users and players have found that the ability to "gender bend" gives them the opportunity to engage with others in new and innovative ways. Asgari and Kaufman (2004) have gone as far as to suggest that online gender fluidity has allowed males to engage in the more feminine aspects of their offline selves. Similarly, it has allowed women the ability to explore more masculine pursuits and, perhaps, disengage from the societal limitations imposed upon them. In terms of online gaming environments, there have been suggestions that games that include violence or killing promote increased aggression among players (Anderson & Dill, 2000). Furthermore, those players with more aggressive personality characteristics offline play more violent games (Cantor, 1998). This has led to suggestions that women who play violent video games (and by extension violent MMORPGs) represent a particular subgroup or have more aggressive traits (Norris, 2004). However, in her survey of 430 women who used chat rooms and/or computer games, Kamala Norris found no evidence of increased aggression or more masculine gender identities among those who played computer games. Additionally, she found no evidence of a greater acceptance of sexual violence among players when compared to those women who used chat rooms only. In fact, her findings indicated that those women who played computer games experienced less sexual harassment online than those who use chat rooms, but the more they play the less likely they are to find friendship too. Norris goes on to suggest that women who play violent video games may have a higher threshold for what they perceive to be online sexual harassment or are more skilled at avoiding it in gaming environments. It suggests too that chat rooms are places of vulnerability where users seek friendship and perhaps open themselves up more to exploitation. This invariably does not only apply to women but to men too. However, online gaming environments are also social spaces; they are spaces where friendships are formed and also exploited, sometimes with tragic consequences. This was recently seen in the murder of 14-year-old UK school-boy, Breck Bednar, who was stabbed to death by 19-year-old Lewis Danes whom he met while playing an online game.

While cases such as those of Breck Bednar are, thankfully, rare, they remind us that the friendships we establish solely online are based entirely upon our engagement with others' deliberate representations (embellished or otherwise) of themselves. Gender-bending has the potential to be liberating, but it can also be used to ensnare vulnerable others, as in the case of Megan Meier. Yet do we know how many people gender-bend online? In one small study, Companion and Sambrook (2008) reported that, in online gaming environments, 50% of women (n = 96) were more likely to choose character roles such as healers when compared to men (16%; n = 37). Women were also more likely to eschew violent roles than men. Companion and Sambrook suggest that in choosing online character roles, players tended to choose those with whom they personally identified. This suggests that as our online and offline worlds become increasingly intertwined, we inevitably see more of what we might have once called "the offline self" in online representations (see also Dunn & Guadagno, 2019).

What Am I Doing Now? Blogging, Social Media, and Well-Being

Blogs play a significant role in the lives of individuals with all sorts of health-related issues. Online forums are invaluable in terms of finding support from others who experience specific illnesses or symptoms. But blogs and social media platforms also serve other purposes. They allow us to glimpse into the worlds of others, some like us and others with very different experiences. They can be emotional rollercoasters where we observe and interact with those going through particularly harrowing or, indeed, jubilant experiences. Reading a blog or a social media entry is, however, more than voyeurism. For many it forms part of a connection we feel to others who "friend" us or "link" or "connect" to us. We also have the capacity to respond, comment and, if necessary, support through online dialogue. Elements of altruism can also be found in responding to a cry for help, whether it is in the form of information or physical or material support. While medical and health-related professional websites provide basic information and advice (perhaps using complex or technical language), blogs and social media provide a human, experiential voice, one with which it is possible to identify (Au & Eyal, 2022).

Ko and Kuo (2009) argued that there is a very positive impact on well-being when blogging. They argue that self-disclosure through blogging helps bloggers to maintain the existing relationships they have forged and extend their circle of contacts—both of which are important in terms of social capital. This is supported by previous studies which show that sharing negative or traumatic experiences with others, particularly those who have had similar experiences, promotes social support and improves integration (Niederhoffer & Pennebaker, 2002).

Ko and Kuo (2009) suggest that through a process that includes an element of social bonding with like-minded others and social bridging with members of other social networks, social integration occurs. This has also been shown to be true where individuals come from underrepresented or minority groups or are hidden from others for fear of social opprobrium (see Thomas (2002) for a discussion of how chatrooms foster supportive offline social communities). We have also seen blogs

8 "The Self" Online 161

become part of formal assessment processes within schools, universities, and colleges, especially during COVID-19, where placement and tutor visits to students on professional courses were prohibited (Al-Jarf, 2022; Sepulveda-Escobar & Morrison, 2020; Zayapragassarazan, 2020)

There are, of course, many reasons why people write blogs about their own or a loved one's health. Sometimes it is, as already illustrated, to seek support and perhaps gain new and fresh perspectives or insights into an issue, illness, or just simply life. Blogs and social media are there not only to allow the author to express his or her opinion, but also to provide some tips along the way (Au & Eyal, 2022). One blogger, Evan Winter describes the rationale for his own blog http://www.mentalnurse.org/ as follows:

> I'm a former health professional who was lured into the corporate world by the offers of big money.
>
> What I've found is a population of workers who are being severely affected by the stress and worry caused by the jobs that they do every day.
>
> Helping my colleagues and the people that I meet means that every day is something of a bussmans *[sic]* holiday for me. This is my blog – designed to offer tips that will help the majority. I also like to blog about the lines of business that I now work in – design, print, e-commerce, webdesign and SEO.

Sharing our lives, experiences, and insights with others is a key element of blogging and social media use. Some might argue there is an element of vanity or narcissism in offering one's own opinions on personal and social issues as they unfold; however, it is also clear that, in times of crisis, whether personal or global, being able to connect to someone with lived experience of the issue being faced is an important source of comfort and expertise.

Summary

The "self" is complex. We are not bound by the limitations of sex, gender stereotypes and expectations, social class, or illness. Yet, as we have all recently found, as our offline and online lives become increasingly "enmeshed," those offline and online personas have become intertwined in ways that require us to be recognizable to all—those who live with us, work with us, socialize with us and those whom we may never meet in person but become just as important to us as those who share our physical space. Following COVID-19, our physical world has changed; our professional and social lives are now "hybrid." Being online is commonplace. The next phase in the evolution of the "self" has begun; we are already redefining and refining our lives following a period of enforced isolation. How much more of our lives is online today and, by extension, how much less of those lives is offline? Can we still assume that our offline selves have more salience than our online selves? It may be the case that instead of co-evolving both in the physical space and in cyberspace, the balance has shifted and one (cyberspace) is prevailing.

References

Ahmad, A., Chung, R., Eckenwiler, L., Ganguli-Mutri, A., Hunt, M., Richards, R., Saghai, Y., Schwartz, L., Scully, J. L., & Wild, V. (2020). What does it mean to be made vulnerable in the era of COVID-19? *The Lancet, 395*(10235), 1481–1482. https://doi.org/10.1016/S0140-6736(20)30979-X

Al-Jarf, R. (2022). Blogging about the Covid-19 pandemic in EFL writing courses. *Journal of Learning and Development Studies, 2*(1), 1–8. https://doi.org/10.32996/jlds.2022.2.1.1

Anderson, C. A., & Dill, K. W. (2000). Video games and aggressive thoughts, feelings, and behaviour in the laboratory and in life. *Journal of Personality and Social Psychology, 78*(4), 772–790. https://doi.org/10.1037/0022-3514.78.4.772

Asgari, M., & Kaufman, D. (2004, July). *Relationships among computer gamers, fantasy, and learning.* Paper presented at the 2nd International Conference on Imagination and Education, Vancouver, Canada.

Au, L., & Eyal, G. (2022). What advice is credible? Claiming lay expertise in a COVID-19 online community. *Qualitative Sociology, 45*(1), 31–61. https://doi.org/10.1007/s11133-021-09492-1

BBC. (2021, October 13). Covid: Scientists targeted with abuse during pandemic. https://www.bbc.co.uk/news/health-58903268

Cantor, J. (1998). Children's attraction to violent television programming. In J. Goldstein (Ed.), *Why we watch: The attraction of violent entertainment* (pp. 88–115). Oxford University Press.

Cinelli, M., Quattrociocchi, W., Galeazzi, A., Valensise, C. M., Bugnoli, E., Schmidt, A. L., Zola, P., Zollo, F., & Scala, A. (2020). The COVID-19 social media infodemic. *Scientific Reports, 10*, 16598. https://doi.org/10.1038/s41598-020-73510-5

Clinnin, K. (2022). Critical essay—playing with masculinity: Gender bending in second life. *Technoculture: An Online Journal of Technology and Society, 12.* https://tcjournal.org/vol12/

Companion, M., & Sambrook, R. (2008). The influence of sex on character attribute preference. *Cyberpsychology & Behavior, 11*(6), 673–674. https://doi.org/10.1089/cpb.2007.0197

Crowe, N and Watts, M (2014). 'When I click "ok" I become Sassy – I become a girl'. Young people and gender identity: Subverting the 'body' in massively multi-player online role-playing games. *International Journal of Adolescence and Youth, 19*(2), 217–231. https://doi.org/10.1080/02673843.2012.736868

Davis, H. E., McCorkell, L., Vogel, J. M., & Topol, E. J. (2023). Long COVID: Major findings, mechanisms and recommendations. *Nature Reviews Microbiology, 21*(March), 133–146. https://doi.org/10.1038/s41579-022-00846-2

Dunn, R. A., & Guadagno, R. (2019). Who are you online? A study of gender, race, and gaming experience and context on avatar self-representation. *International Journal of Cyber Behavior, Psychology and Learning, 9*(3), 15–31. https://doi.org/10.4018/IJCBPL.2019070102

Fineberg, N. A., Pellegrini, L., Wellsted, D., Hall, N., Corazza, O., Giorgetti, V., Cicconcelli, D., Theofanous, E., Sireau, N., Adam, D., Chamberlain, S. R., & Laws, K. R. (2021). Facing the "new normal": How adjusting to the easing of COVID-19 lockdown restrictions exposes mental health inequalities. *Journal of Psychiatric Research, 141*(September), 276–286. https://doi.org/10.1016/j.jpsychires.2021.07.001

Freeman, G., & Maloney, D. (2021). Body, avatar, and me: The presentation and perception of self in social virtual reality. *Proceedings of the ACM on Human-Computer Interaction, 4*(CSCW3), 1–27. https://doi.org/10.1145/3432938

González-Padilla, D. A., & Tortolero-Blanco, L. (2020). Social media influence in the COVID-19 pandemic. *International Brazilian Journal of Urology, 46*(S1). https://doi.org/10.1590/S1677-5538.IBJU.2020.S121

Guardian. (2021, October 13). Scientists abused and threatened for discussing Covid, global survey finds. https://www.theguardian.com/world/2021/oct/13/scientists-abused-and-threatened-for-discussing-covid-global-survey-finds

Hayles, N. K. (1999). *How we became posthuman: Virtual bodies in cybernetics and informatics.* University of Chicago Press.

Hooi, R., & Cho, H. (2013). Deception in avatar-mediated virtual environment. *Computers in Human Behavior, 29*(1), 276–284. https://doi.org/10.1016/j.chb.2012.09.004

Jurgenson, N. (2011). *Amber case: Cyborg anthropologist (a critique).* http://thesocietypages.org/cyborgology/2011/02/10/amber-case-cyborg-anthropologist-a-critique/.

Ko, H. S., & Kuo, F. Y. (2009). Can blogging enhance subjective well-being through self-disclosure? *Cyberpsychology & Behavior, 12*(1), 75–79. https://doi.org/10.1089/cpb.2008.016

Lastauskas, P. (2022). Lockdown, employment adjustment, and financial frictions. *Small Business Economics, 58*(2), 919–942. https://doi.org/10.1007/s11187-021-00496-3

Li, A. (2013). *Teen brags on Facebook after alleged bullying victim commits suicide.* http://mashable.com/2013/10/15/bullying-teen-brags-facebook/

Niederhoffer, K. G., & Pennebaker, J. W. (2002). Sharing one's story. In C. R. Snyder & S. J. Lopez (Eds.), *Handbook of positive psychology* (pp. 573–583). Oxford University Press.

Norris, K. O. (2004). Gender stereotypes, aggression, and computer games: An online survey of women. *Cyberpsychology & Behavior, 7*(6), 714–727. https://doi.org/10.1089/cpb.2004.7.714

Piquero, A. R., Jennings, W. G., Jemison, E., Kaukinen, C., & Knaul, F. M. (2021). Domestic violence during the COVID-19 pandemic—Evidence from a systematic review and meta-analysis. *Journal of Criminal Justice, 74,* 101806. https://doi.org/10.1016/j.jcrimjus.2021.101806

Purves, D. G., & Dutton, J. (2013). An exploration of the therapeutic process while using computerised cognitive behaviour therapy. *Counselling and Psychotherapy Research, 13*(4), 308–316. https://doi.org/10.1080/14733145.2012.761259

Rivers, I. (2012, June). *Homophobic bullying and inclusion in an age of technology.* Keynote address presented at the National Center Against Bullying (NCAB) Bi-Annual Conference entitled 'Social media, bullying and vulnerability: Connect, respect, protect', Melbourne, Australia.

Sepulveda-Escobar, P., & Morrison, A. (2020). Online teaching placement during the COVID-19 pandemic in Chile: Challenges and opportunities. *European Journal of Teacher Education, 43*(4), 587–607. https://doi.org/10.1080/02619768.2020.1820981

Suler, J. (2004). The online disinhibition effect. *Cyberpsychology & Behavior, 7*(3), 321–326. https://doi.org/10.1089/1094931041291295

Szkody, E., Stearns, M., Stanhope, L., & McKinney, C. (2021). Stress-buffering role of social support during COVID-19. *Family Process, 60*(3), 1002–1015. https://doi.org/10.1111/famp.12618

Thomas, A. B. (2002). *Internet chat room participation and the coming out experiences of young gay men: A qualitative study.* Unpublished PhD thesis. The University of Texas at Austin.

Turkle, S. (1995). Rethinking identity through virtual community. In L. Hershman Leeson (Ed.), *Clicking in: Hotlinks to a digital culture* (pp. 116–122). Bay Press.

Weaver, A., Zhang, A., Xiang, X., Felsman, P., Fischer, D. J., & Himle, A. A. (2023). Entertain me well: An entertaining, tailorable online platform delivering CBT for depression. *Cognitive & Behavioral Practice, 30*(1), 96–115. https://doi.org/10.1016/j.cbpra.2021.09.003

Yee, N. (2007). *WoW gender bending.* http://www.nickyee.com/daedalus/archives/001369.php

Yee, N., Bailenson, J. N., & Ducheneaut, N. (2009). The Proteus effect: Implications of transformed digital self-representation in online and offline behaviour. *Communication Research, 36*(2), 285–312. https://doi.org/10.1177/0093650208330254

Zayapragassarazan, Z. (2020). *COVID-19: Strategies for engaging remote learners in medical education.* https://files.eric.ed.gov/fulltext/ED604479.pdf

9

Conclusion

Introduction

Our aim in this second edition of *Mental Health in the Digital Age* was to reflect upon learning since the COVID-19 pandemic and consider how mental health and well-being can be supported by digital technologies. As we emerge from the pandemic, words such as "hybrid," "flexible," and "agile" have become part of everyday speech. They reflect the fact that our personal, social, and working lives have become much more enmeshed with technologies playing much more prominent roles in our existence daily. There are areas of enquiry that we have chosen to omit in this book because there exists a wealth of evidence published elsewhere. Similarly, in some instances, there is a dearth of evidence supporting any stance—positive or negative—on the impact of a certain program or application on mental health and well-being. Since the publication of the first edition of our book, technologies have moved on and some of those applications and platforms that were commonplace in 2016 are now tired or obsolete, and new applications and platforms have taken or are taking their place.

© The Author(s), under exclusive license to Springer Nature Switzerland AG 2023
S. Bauman, I. Rivers, *Mental Health in the Digital Age*,
https://doi.org/10.1007/978-3-031-32122-1_9

In the first edition of *Mental Health in the Digital Age*, we intended to answer four questions:

1. Is mental health enhanced or diminished by the digitization of our world?
2. Are mental health disorders exacerbated or ameliorated in the digital environment that is now pervasive?
3. What mental health benefits does the digital world provide?
4. What mental health difficulties are associated with the advancements in digital technology?

In this edition, we also reflect upon the learning from COVID-19 and introduce Keyes' (2002) concept of a mental health continuum from flourishing to languishing as a lens for examining the types and range of impacts of digital technologies on mental health and well-being.

Digital Technologies Post-COVID-19: Are We Flourishing or Languishing?

While this is not a technical book, it is one that considers the evidence (as it is currently understood) of the ways in which technologies have impacted our mental health and well-being before, during, and after the COVID-19 pandemic. In addition to our discussion of the benefits of online therapies, social media platforms, and self-help sites, we have considered the ways in which technologies can be used to cause harm—intentional and unintentional. The dangers of being online, of trusting those we "meet" online, and the pitfalls in providing those we have yet to meet with personal information have been discussed with examples drawn from the literature.

In 2016, we argued that our lives were increasingly moving online because it was simply cheaper. Banking and utility companies preferred to communicate through email, chatbots, and applications, outsourcing customer services or employing rudimentary AI systems to answer customer questions. We reflected upon the fact that visits to the post-office or to the bank were, for some people, their only interaction with the outside world, and, in 2016, we felt we needed to keep those physical interactions alive. However, out of necessity, everything changed in 2020; we came to rely on FAQs, text messages, and online or telephone customer service agents for support and information.

In this second edition, we have considered how our working lives have changed and how the so-called pivot to online and remote working created new challenges for mental health and well-being (see Chaps. 2, 4, 5, 6, and 8), new opportunities for exploitation (Chaps. 4 and 6) as well as opportunities to re-shape daily existence (Chap. 6). While some consider the impact of COVID-19 to be tantamount to "technological slavery" (Mehta & Maniar, 2023), post-pandemic there has been an opportunity for many workers (particularly those working in offices) to rebalance their lives and work from home for some, if not all, days of the week. We acknowledge that there are inherent dangers in having a distributed workforce and we know that there are significant mental health benefits in social interactions with colleagues, but there are also benefits in allowing workers to spend part of their working week at home, cutting down commutes, improving productivity, and supporting cost-effective childcare (Ipsen et al., 2021).

In our first edition, we argued that the differences in skills between so-called digital natives and digital immigrants were gradually waning. Prior to COVID-19, efforts to provide elderly citizens with the skills necessary to remain connected to the world, and our recognition that those who find themselves homeless also need to remain connected (through technology freely available in public libraries and support services) told us that we were all rapidly becoming one homogeneous group of "digital consumers." COVID-19 accelerated that process for several societies and cultures, but not all. Indeed, we have yet to assess how COVID-19 impacted the use of technologies or indeed promoted technological advances in those societies and cultures where internet connectivity is not commonplace. Indeed, Mehta and Maniar (2023) have suggested that COVID-19 brought into stark relief the digital poverty that exists in some parts of our world.

The "Enmeshed" Self

Jurgenson (2011) argued that our lives were "enmeshed"—a term used throughout this book, which relates to an ecosystem where the offline and the online are no longer distinct. The COVID-19 pandemic has shown us what was achievable without physical interaction. Across health care, education, family, and social lives, we were able to function and seek help where necessary. As Vargo et al. (2020) have illustrated, the "pivot" to online following the lockdown, and the availability of technology, allowed us to deliver health care at a distance; improve patient outcomes; reduce the spread of the virus; support those healthcare and mental healthcare systems that were, at times, at breaking point; lower costs; increase productivity; and update infrastructure. In education, we were able to continue teaching classes, deliver (a)synchronous online instruction, create virtual learning environments, develop new and innovative approaches to support learning, and encourage students at a distance. Socially, through "telework," we were able to ensure employee safety, increase efficiency in some areas of employment, reduce the impact of the pandemic on the economy, and reduce transport usage (further limiting the spread of the virus).

Part of the "enmeshed" self ultimately resides in how we engage with technologies and whether we continue to make distinctions about diagnoses delivered by human beings versus a piece of software driven by a series of algorithms. As we noted in Chap. 7, advanced artificial intelligence (AI) uses data such as calls and texts sent and received, location and movement patterns as well as physiological measures for assessing stress and providing information to clinicians, which, in turn, allows them to use their time more efficiently and effectively to create a bespoke treatment plan. Virtual reality (VR) also has its place in treating mental health disorders, allowing people to address their anxieties, fears, and phobias through exposure therapy but within a safe environment. Here clinicians are able to control and adapt the virtual environment to support clients in managing the conditions that inhibit their daily lives. Similarly, online games offer opportunities to engage in therapies or tasks that improve mental health and well-being, set manageable challenges that lead to larger goals, provide immediate feedback, and show progress against a target while also allowing the user to have a degree of control over the pace at which they play. Games also have an important role in combatting loneliness—we saw this especially during lockdown as Bryan Lufkin (2020) recalls:

> I was sitting in my tiny New York City apartment, panicky and coming to terms with the reality that I'd be trapped inside for weeks, potentially months. But my friends reassured me that as lifelong video game enthusiasts, the prospect of sitting on a sofa in front of a TV for an interminable stretch would be a cakewalk. After all, gamers like me do already spend plenty of time in front of our screens all on our own.

Prior to COVID-19, a great deal had been written about the dangers of online gaming. However, we have also seen how online gaming environments can be very positive experiences—especially in terms of social interactions and the development of friendships. Through online gaming, we have also seen how cultural limitations in the social interactions of men and women offline can be overcome online. The creation of avatars in online games not only allows users to meet and chat, but also allows them to "gender-bend." Gaming environments do present challenges, they are also environments inhabited by online predators, and those who wish to bully or cause harm to others.

Reality or Not? How Enmeshed Are We?

In our first edition, we included a chapter on the ethics of undertaking research in cyberspace. Our aim in crafting that chapter was to consider how data is collected and whether or not researchers, at the time, had an understanding of the impact of their presence in an environment such as an online game could have. Ultimately, through a study of *Runescape*, we got a sense of how enmeshed our lives were long before COVID-19.

Setting the Scene

To successfully navigate a multiplayer online game, each player's route to success requires that one or more opponents are challenged and overcome. Sometimes this involves killing an opponent's avatar; sometimes it involves the destruction or theft of hard-fought-for commodities or valuables. Whatever method is used to move to the next level, someone will win, and someone will lose. Losers may find themselves having to begin the game all over again or be held back from progressing in the game for a predetermined period. Whatever the sanction, there is clearly a cost to failure.

The Dilemma

The only way in which you can both experience the full game and meet participants at various levels is to challenge and defeat those who stand in your way. Does killing an avatar or depriving a player of his or her hard-won status present you with an ethical dilemma? Has harm really been done? How do you know? For some players, this may be just a hazard of the game, but remember that for you, the researcher, losing means you cannot complete your study, and this may have implications in terms of future projects. Are you sure that the online environment you are researching does not hold significance beyond gaming for others too?

Take, for example, one young *Runescape* player's coping mechanism when she faced her own offline difficulties (Crowe & Bradford, 2006, p. 341):

> Last year my dad lost his job, he's ok now but we didn't have money so we couldn't go on holiday and I spent the six weeks playing Rune. I used to go down to Cathaby and hang out on the beach, when the sun came through my window it was nearly like being at the seaside … lol this is sooo stoopid I know but guess what … I used to go to the gnome village for cocktails in the evening, it was well good, I would meet up with my friends and we would all put the same beats on and pretend like we were at Ibiza or something.

9 Conclusion 173

Here, there is clearly an attempt to escape from reality, and through the fantasy world of *Runescape* enjoy the holiday that perhaps this young woman had hoped she would have with her family. Crowe and Bradford describe this young woman's strategy in terms of "a powerful imagination, creating a narrative of identity"—an identity that was not disembodied but, at a fundamental level, linked to her life offline (p. 341). In this instance, the separation of offline reality and virtual reality seems tenuous at best. Would you, for example, deny this player the pleasure of a virtual holiday in the pursuit of your own goals in the game? Another example of how online and offline worlds intersect can be found in Crowe's (2009) ethnographic study where he recounts how one player in *Runescape*—"Tigzrulz"—made an emotional investment in an online boyfriend which ultimately affected her offline:

> 1 nite he told me dat he luved me but den jest sed bye n every1 knos dat bye dont mean nuttin widout hugz n xxxs n den I knew … n I didnt do enefin fer dayz cos I wus cryin … ma sistaz just hugged me and we didn't do enefin. (p. 224)

Crowe argues that the feelings that "Tigzrulz" had for her virtual boyfriend were just as real to her as those for any offline boyfriend, and while she explained that her virtual relationships within the game were, "a way of testing out in a safe environment what she is not yet ready to partake in within the material realm," the hurt she felt did not go away when she logged off. So, what do you do when an online gamer tells you that the game is, "like my life but more, and better" (p. 221)? Do you cause that gamer discomfort in the name of research?

The above example offers an insight into the potential value that virtual reality and online gaming can have for mental health and well-being in terms of user investment, but that potential must also be measured against another—the potential to cause emotional harm (Reid et al., 2022; Wolfendale, 2007).

Where Do We Go from Here?

Throughout this book, and in the examples given above, we can see that the online world is a paradox: it has elements of clarity and elements of confusion. It leads us down paths of discovery and of disillusionment. It offers sage advice but also provides countless examples of uninformed and dangerous advice. As users, we need to be skilled in navigating the World Wide Web and in discerning the sound from the unsound. Never more was this needed than during the COVID-19 pandemic when we sought answers to what were, at times, insoluble questions. In 2016 we wrote that "there is no handbook or crib sheet to help us plot our path through the information superhighway." It was certainly the case that there was no crib sheet to help us through the overwhelming information we faced in the combat to rid ourselves of COVID-19.

We have learned so much about what is possible now that we have the World Wide Web, and we have learned to create virtual infrastructures to support our economy in times of crisis. We have found new ways of delivering medical and psychotherapeutic interventions through the application of artificial intelligence and virtual reality. We have found new ways of educating our students through communication tools such as Zoom, and of working effectively and remotely through applications such as Microsoft Teams. Our lives are enriched by the ability to access information when we need it, to buy products online when we need it (and have it delivered), and to talk to one another (face-to-face) regardless of where we are in the world.

So, what is the next step in our evolution? Perhaps Estonia leads the way (https://e-estonia.com). In 1991, after half a century of foreign rule, Estonia gained independence, but rather than follow the path of other countries, it initiated a bold plan to catch up with Western countries by building an IT infrastructure and making computer skills a priority in schools. In 1996, it launched its first e-bank, and by 2000, the Estonian Government held its first e-cabinet meeting. At the same time, Estonians were able to return their taxes online (98% of the population now do so), and it introduced mobile parking (allowing drivers to pay for their parking from their mobile/cell phones). In 2001, it introduced "X-Road," a national integration platform for data. By 2002, it had introduced e-identity cards and digital signatures—now used by 98% of the population. In 2005, it introduced i-voting, and by 2007, it was building a cybersecurity infrastructure to safeguard online data. In 2008, it introduced a nationwide system integrating data held by healthcare providers (e-Health) and by 2010, had introduced a paperless system of prescriptions (e-prescription). Prior to the pandemic, the Estonian government produced a green paper designed to better understand the nation's needs in terms of e-services, as well as creating the e-residency program to attract business and talent to the country. Today, in addition to an AI strategy for the government and the private sector, Estonia has introduced proactive childcare whereby services and benefits are automatically initiated when a child is born. It has also introduced remote verification of notaries, which means that only two legal procedures require citizens to appear in person—to get married and to obtain a divorce. Estonian society is truly an enmeshed society and one that is flourishing.

Conclusion

This edition of *Mental Health in the Digital Age* was commissioned to consider the evidence relating to the impact of COVID-19 and how our lives and indeed our mental health and well-being altered because of the global pandemic. We have demonstrated how our online world has changed since 2016 and recognize that despite monumental changes, some as a result of COVID-19, there remain inequalities. We have explored both the benefits (e.g., access to information, support services, treatment options, etc.) and pitfalls (e.g., widespread misinformation, cyberbullying, pernicious environments, etc.) that exist online, and have considered how much more our lives have become intertwined with technology. The digital world is constantly moving forward; developments in artificial intelligence, virtual reality, and quantum is changing the look, capacity, and ability of computers to process information and deal with complex issues. Who knows what the next eight years will bring?

References

Crowe, N. (2009). *Hanging with the 'Cathaby Shark Gurlz' and other Runescape stories: Young people, identity and community in a virtual world.* Unpublished PhD thesis. Brunel University London.

Crowe, N., & Bradford, S. (2006). Hanging out in 'Runescape': Identity, work and leisure in the virtual playground. *Children's Geographies, 4*(4), 331–346. https://doi.org/10.1080/14733280601005740

Ipsen, C., van Veldhoven, M., Kirchner, K., & Hansen, J. P. (2021). Six key advantages and disadvantages of working from home in Europe during COVID-19. *International Journal of Environmental Research and Public Health, 18*(4), 1826. https://doi.org/10.3390/ijerph18041826

Jurgenson, N. (2011). *Amber case: Cyborg anthropologist (a critique).* http://thesocietypages.org/cyborgology/2011/02/10/amber-case-cyborg-anthropologist-a-critique/.

Keyes, C. L. M. (2002). The mental health continuum: From languishing to flourishing in life. *Journal of Health and Social Behavior, 43*(2), 207–222.

Lufkin, B. (2020, December 16). How online gaming has become a social lifeline. *BBC: The Life Project.* https://www.bbc.com/worklife/article/20201215-how-online-gaming-has-become-a-social-lifeline

Mehta, S., & Maniar, A. (2023). Technology during COVID-19: Boon or a curse. *International Journal of Management, Public Policy, and Research, 2*(Special Issue), 40–44. https://doi.org/10.55829/ijmpr.v2iSpecialIssue.135

Reid, E., Mandryk, R. L., Beres, N. A., Klarkowski, M., & Frommel, J. (2022). Feeling good and in control: In-game tools to support targets of toxicity. *Proceedings of the ACM on Human-Computer Interaction, 6*(CHI PLAY), 235. https://doi.org/10.1145/3549498

Vargo, D., Zhu, L., Benwell, B., & Yan, Z. (2020). Digital technology use during VOID-19 pandemic: A rapid review. *Human Behavior and Emerging Technologies, 3*(1), 13–24. https://doi.org/10.1002/hbe2.242

Wolfendale, J. (2007). My avatar, my self: Virtual harm and attachment. *Ethics and Information Technology, 9*(1), 111–119. https://doi.org/10.1007/s10676-006-9125-z

References

Abdalla, S. M., Cohen, G. H., Tamrakar, S., Koya, S. F., & Galea, S. (2021). Media exposure and the risk of post-traumatic stress disorder following a mass traumatic event: An in-silico experiment. *Frontiers in Psychiatry, 12,* 674263. https://doi.org/10.3389/fpsyt.2021.674263

Abd-Alrazaq, A., Al-Jafar, E., Alajlani, M., Toro, C., Alhuwail, D., Ahmed, A., Reagu, S. M., Al-Shorbaji, N., & Househ, M. (2022). The effectiveness of serious games for alleviating depression: Systematic review and meta-analysis. *JMIR Serious Games, 10*(1), e32331. https://doi.org/10.2196/32331

Ahlse, J., Nilsson, F., & Sandström, N. (2020). *It's time to TikTok.* https://www.diva-portal.org/smash/get/diva2:1434091/FULLTEXT01.pdf

Ahmad, A., Chung, R., Eckenwiler, L., Ganguli-Mutri, A., Hunt, M., Richards, R., Saghai, Y., Schwartz, L., Scully, J. L., & Wild, V. (2020). What does it mean to be made vulnerable in the era of COVID-19? *The Lancet, 395*(10235), 1481–1482. https://doi.org/10.1016/S0140-6736(20)30979-X

Al-Alawi, M., McCall, R. K., Sultan, A., Balushi, N. A., Al-Mahrouqi, T., Ghailani, A. A., Sabti, H. A., Al-Maniri, A., Panchatcharam, S. M., & Sinawi, H. A. (2021). Efficacy of a six-week-long therapist-guided online therapy versus self-help internet-based therapy for COVID-19–induced anxiety and depression: Open-label, pragmatic, randomized controlled trial. *JMIR Mental Health, 8*(2), e26683. https://doi.org/10.2196/26683

© The Author(s), under exclusive license to Springer Nature Switzerland AG 2023
S. Bauman, I. Rivers, *Mental Health in the Digital Age,*
https://doi.org/10.1007/978-3-031-32122-1

178 References

Al-Jarf, R. (2022). Blogging about the Covid-19 pandemic in EFL writing courses. *Journal of Learning and Development Studies, 2*(1), 01–08. https://doi.org/10.32996/jlds.2022.2.1.1

All the latest cyberbullying statistics for 2023. (2023). https://www.broadband-search.net/blog/cyber-bullying-statistics

Alsunni, A. A., & Latif, R. (2021). Higher emotional investment in social media is related to anxiety and depression in university students. *Journal of Taibah University Medical Sciences, 16*(2), 247–252. https://doi.org/10.1016/j.jtumed.2020.11.004

Alvarez-Jimenez, M., Rice, S., D'Alfonso, S., Leicester, S., Bendall, S., Pryor, I., Russon, P., McEnery, C., Santesteban-Echarri, O., Costa, G. D., Gilbertson, T., Valentine, L., Solves, L., Ratheesh, A., McGorry, P. D., & Gleeson, J. (2020). A novel multimodal digital service (moderated online social therapy+) for help-seeking young people experiencing mental ill-health: Pilot evaluation within a national youth e-mental health service. *Journal of Medical Internet Research, 22*(8), e17155. https://doi.org/10.2196/17155

Amichai-Hamburger, Y., Kingsbury, M., & Schneider, B. H. (2013). Friendship: An old concept with a new meaning? *Computers in Human Behavior, 29*(1-2), 33–39. https://doi.org/10.1016/j.chb.2012.05.025

Anderson, C. A., & Dill, K. W. (2000). Video games and aggressive thoughts, feelings, and behaviour in the laboratory and in life. *Journal of Personality and Social Psychology, 78*(4), 772–790. https://doi.org/10.1037/0022-3514.78.4.772

Andersson, G. (2022). 17—Internet-based psychotherapies. In D. J. Stein, N. A. Fineberg, & S. R. Chamberlain (Eds.), *Mental health in a digital world* (pp. 377–394). Academic Press. https://doi.org/10.1016/B978-0-12-822201-0.00008-3

Anonymous. (2013, May 5). Cyberbullying in the workplace. *Secure NU.* http://www.northeastern.edu/securenu/?p=1995

Anthenunis, M. L., Valkenburg, P. M., & Peter, J. (2012). The quality of online, offline, and mixed-mode friendships among users of a social networking site. *Cyberpsychology: Journal of Psychosocial Research on Cyberspace, 6*(3), 6. https://doi.org/10.5817/CP2012-3-6

Asgari, M., & Kaufman, D. (2004, July). *Relationships among computer gamers, fantasy, and learning.* Paper presented at the 2nd International Conference on Imagination and Education, Vancouver, Canada.

Au, L., & Eyal, G. (2022). What advice is credible? Claiming lay expertise in a COVID-19 online community. *Qualitative Sociology, 45*(1), 31–61. https://doi.org/10.1007/s11133-021-09492-1

References 179

Austria, J. L. (2007). Developing evaluation criteria for podcasts. *Libri, 57*(4). https://doi.org/10.1515/LIBR.2007.179

Bacher-Hicks, A., Goodman, J., Green, J. G., & Holt, M. (2021). *The COVID-19 pandemic disrupted both school bullying and cyberbullying.* National Bureau of Economic Research (Working Paper 29590). https://www.nber.org/papers/w29590

Bailenson, J. N. (2021). Nonverbal overload: A theoretical argument for the causes of Zoom fatigue. *Technology, Mind, and Behavior, 2*(1). https://doi.org/10.1037/tmb0000030

Baird, K., & Connolly, J. (2023). Recruitment and entrapment pathways of minors into sex trafficking in Canada and the United States: A systematic review. *Trauma, Violence, & Abuse, 24*(1), 189–202. https://doi.org/10.1177/15248380211025241

Bakker, D., Kazantzis, N., Rickwood, D., & Rickard, N. (2018). A randomized controlled trial of three smartphone apps for enhancing public mental health. *Behaviour Research and Therapy, 109*, 75–83. https://doi.org/10.1016/j.brat.2018.08.003

Barman-Adhikari, A., & Rice, E. (2011). Sexual health information seeking online among runaway and homeless youth. *Journal of the Society for Socail Work Research, 2*(2), 88–103. https://doi.org/10.5243/jsswr.2011.5

Basch, C. H., Donelle, L., Fera, J., & Jaime, C. (2022). Deconstructing TikTok videos on mental health: Cross-sectional, descriptive content analysis. *JMIR Formative Research, 6*(5), e38340. https://doi.org/10.2196/38340

Bassi, M., Negri, L., Delle Fave, A., & Accardi, R. (2021). The relationship between post-traumatic stress and positive mental health symptoms among health workers during COVID-19 pandemic in Lombardy, Italy. *Journal of Affective Disorders, 280*, 1–6. https://doi.org/10.1016/j.jad.2020.11.065

Bates, S. (2017). Revenge porn and mental health: A qualitative analysis of the mental health effects of revenge porn on female survivors. *Feminist Criminology, 12*(1), 22–42. https://doi.org/10.1177/1557085116654565

Bauman, S. (2015). Cyberbullying and sexting: School mental health concerns. In R. Witte & S. Mosley-Howard (Eds.), *Mental health practice in today's schools: Current issues and interventions* (pp. 241–264). Springer.

Bauman, S., Toomey, R., & Walker, J. (2013). Relations among bullying, cyberbullying and suicide in high school students. *Journal of Adolescence, 36*(2), 341–360. https://doi.org/10.1016/j.adolescence.2012.12.001

BBC. (2021, October 13). Covid: Scientists targeted with abuse during pandemic. https://www.bbc.co.uk/news/health-58903268

180 **References**

Bean, A. M., Daniel, E. S., Jr., & Hays, S. A. (Eds.). (2020). *Integrating geek culture into therapeutic practice: The clinician's guide to geek therapy.* Leyline Publishing, Inc.

Bekalu, M. A., McCloud, R. F., & Viswanath, K. (2019). Association of social media use with social well-being, positive mental health, and self-rated health: disentangling routine use from emotional connection to use. *Health Education & Behavior, 46*(2_suppl), 69S–80S.

Bell, I. H., Nicholas, J., Alvarez-Jimenez, M., Thompson, A., & Valmaggia, L. (2020). Virtual reality as a clinical tool in mental health research and practice. *Dialogues in Clinical Neuroscience, 22*(2), 169–177. https://doi.org/10.31887/DCNS.2020.22.2/lvalmaggia

Bell, V. (2007). Online information, extreme communities, and internet therapy: Is the internet good for our mental health? *Journal of Mental Health, 16*, 445–457.

Benvenuti, M., Giovagnoli, S., Mazzoni, E., Cipressoo, P., Pedroni, E., & Riva, G. (2020). The releevance of online social relationships among the elderly: How using the web could enhance quality of life. *Frontiers in Psychology, 11*, 551862. https://doi.org/10.3389/fpsyg.2020.551862

Best, E., & Clark, C. (2020). *Children and young people's engagement with podcasts before and during lockdown* (p. 13). National Literacy Trust.

Bickman, L. (2020). Improving mental health services: A 50-year journey from randomized experiments to artificial intelligence and precision mental health. *Administration and Policy in Mental Health and Mental Health Services Research, 47*(5), 795–843. https://doi.org/10.1007/s10488-020-01065-8

Bonanno, R. A., & Hymel, S. (2013). Cyber bullying and internalizing difficulties: Above and beyond the impact of traditional forms of bullying. *Journal of Youth and Adolescence, 42*, 685–697. https://doi.org/10.1007/s10964-013-9937-1

Bonifazi, G., Cecchini, S., Corradini, E., Giuliani, L., Ursino, D., & Virgili, L. (2022). Investigating community evolutions in TikTok dangerous and non-dangerous challenges. *Journal of Information Science.* https://doi.org/10.1177/01655515221116519

Bonilla del Río, M., Castillo Abdul, B., García Ruiz, R., & Rodríguez Martín, A. (2022). Influencers with intellectual disability in digital society: An opportunity to advance social inclusion. *Media and Communication, 10*(1), 222–234. https://doi.org/10.17645/mac.v10i1.4763

Boukes, M., & Vliegenthart, R. (2017). News consumption and its unpleasant side effect: Studying the effect of hard and soft news exposure on mental well-being over time. *Journal of Media Psychology, 29*(3), 137–147. https://doi.org/10.1027/1864-1105/a000224

References · 181

Boyd, D., Ryan, J., & Leavitt, A. (2011). Pro-harm and the visibility of youth-generated problematic content. *I/S: A Journal of Law and Policy for the Information Society, 7,* 1–32.

Brewer, G., Centifanti, L., Castro Caicedo, J., Huxley, G., Peddie, C., Stratton, K., & Lyons, M. (2022). Experiences of mental distress during COVID-19: Thematic analysis of discussion forum posts for anxiety, depression and obsessive-compulsive disorder. *Illness, Crisis & Loss, 30*(4), 795–811. https://doi.org/10.1177/10541373211023951

Broadband Search (2023). Key Internet usage statistics in 2023 (including mobile). https://www.broadbandsearch.net/blog/internet-statistics

Cantor, J. (1998). Children's attraction to violent television programming. In J. Goldstein (Ed.), *Why we watch: The attraction of violent entertainment* (pp. 88–115). Oxford University Press.

CASAColumbia. (2011, August 24). *2011 National teen survey finds teens regularly using social networking likelier to smoke, drink, use drugs.* http://www.casacolumbia.org/newsroom/press-releases/2011-national-teen-survey-finds

Casares, D. R., & Binkley, E. E. (2021). Podcasts as an evolution of bibliotherapy. *Journal of Mental Health Counseling, 43*(1), 19–39. https://doi.org/10.17744/mehc.43.1.02

Cénat, J. M., Blais, M., Hébert, M., Lavoie, F., & Guerrier, M. (2015). Correlates of bullying in Quebec high school students: The vulnerability of sexual-minority youth. *Journal of Affective Disorders, 183*(September), 315–321. https://doi.org/10.1016/j.jad.2015.05.011

Chan, D. K.-S., & Cheng, G. H.-L. (2004). A comparison of offline and online friendship qualities at different stages of relationship development. *Journal of Social and Personal Relationships, 21*(3), 305–320. https://doi.org/10.1177/0265407504042834

Chan, S., Torous, J., Hinton, L., & Yellowlees, P. (2015). Towards a framework for evaluating mobile mental health apps. *Telemedicine and E-Health, 21*(12), 1038–1041. https://doi.org/10.1089/tmj.2015.0002

Cheded, M., & Skandalis, A. (2020). Touch and contact during COVID-19: Insights form queer digital spaces. *Feminist Frontiers, 28*(S2), 340–347. https://doi.org/10.1111/gwao.12697

Chirico, F., Ferrari, G., Nucera, G., Szarpak, L., Crescenzo, P., & Ilesanmi, O. (2021). Prevalence of anxiety, depression, burnout syndrome, and mental health disorders among healthcare workers during the COVID-19 pandemic: A rapid umbrella review of systematic reviews. *Journal of Health and Social Sciences, 6*(2), 209–220.

182 References

Cinelli, M., Quattrociocchi, W., Galeazzi, A., Valensise, C. M., Bugnoli, E., Schmidt, A. L., Zola, P., Zollo, F., & Scala, A. (2020). The COVID-19 social media infodemic. *Scientific Reports, 10*, 16598. https://doi.org/10.1038/s41598-020-73510-5

Clark, J. L., Algoe, S. B., & Green, M. C. (2018). Social networking sites and well-being: The role of social connectedness. *Current Directions in Psychological Science, 27*(1), 32–37. https://doi.org/10.1177/0963721417730833

Clinnin, K. (2022). Critical essay—playing with masculinity: Gender bending in second life. *Technoculture: An Online Journal of Technology and Society, 12.* https://tcjournal.org/vol12/

Colón, Y., & Stern, S. (2011). Online counseling groups. In R. Kraus, G. Stricker, & C. Speyer (Eds.), *Online counseling: A handbook for mental health professionals.* Academic Press/Elsevier.

Comer, J. S. & Dick, A. S. (2022, February 20). Disaster news can trigger post-traumatic stress in kids thousands of miles away. *The Washington Post.* https://www.washingtonpost.com/health/2022/02/20/children-disasters-mental-health/

Companion, M., & Sambrook, R. (2008). The influence of sex on character attribute preference. *Cyberpsychology & Behavior, 11*(6), 673–674. https://doi.org/10.1089/cpb.2007.0197

Cookingham, L. M., & Ryan, G. L. (2015). The Impact of social media on the sexual and social wellness of adolescents. *Journal of Pediatric and Adolescent Gynecology, 28*(1), 2–5. https://doi.org/10.1016/j.jpag.2014.03.001

Cosantino, G., Malgady, R. G., & Rogler, L. H. (1986). Cuento therapy: A culturally sensitive modality for Puerto Rican children. *Journal of Consulting Anad Clinical Psychology, 54*(5), 639–645.

Crowe, N. (2009). *Hanging with the 'Cathaby Shark Gurlz' and other Runescape stories: Young people, identity and community in a virtual world.* Unpublished PhD thesis. Brunel University London.

Crowe, N. (2012). "It's like my life but more, and better!" – Playing with the Cathaby Shark Girls: MMORPGs, young people and fantasy-based social play. *International Journal of Adolescence and Youth, 16*(2), 201–223. https://doi.org/10.1080/02673843.2011.9748055

Crowe, N., & Bradford, S. (2006). Hanging out in 'Runescape': Identity, work and leisure in the virtual playground. *Children's Geographies, 4*(4), 331–346. https://doi.org/10.1080/14733280601005740

Crowe, N and Watts, M (2014). 'When I click "ok" I become Sassy – I become a girl'. Young people and gender identity: Subverting the 'body' in massively multi-player online role-playing games. *International Journal of Adolescence and Youth, 19*(2), 217–231. https://doi.org/10.1080/0267384 3.2012.736868

D'Alfonso, S., Santesteban-Echarri, O., Rice, S., Wadley, G., Lederman, R., Miles, C., Gleeson, J., & Alvarez-Jimenez, M. (2017). Artificial intelligence-assisted online social therapy for youth mental health. *Frontiers in Psychology, 8*. https://www.frontiersin.org/articles/10.3389/fpsyg.2017.00796

D'Hotman, D., & Loh, E. (2020). AI enabled suicide prediction tools: A qualitative narrative review. *BMJ Health & Care Informatics, 27*(3), e100175. https://doi.org/10.1136/bmjhci-2020-100175

D'Mello, S. K. (2016). Chapter 5—Automated mental state detection for mental health care. In D. D. Luxton (Ed.), *Artificial intelligence in behavioral and mental health care* (pp. 117–136). Academic Press. https://doi.org/10.1016/ B978-0-12-420248-1.00005-2

Davis, H. E., McCorkell, L., Vogel, J. M., & Topol, E. J. (2023). Long COVID: Major findings, mechanisms and recommendations. *Nature Reviews Microbiology, 21*(March), 133–146. https://doi.org/10.1038/s41579-022-00846-2

de Araujo Reinert, C., & Kowacs, C. (2019). Patient-targeted "Googling:" When therapists search for information about their patients online. *Psychodynamic Psychiatry, 47*(1), 27–38. https://doi.org/10.1521/pdps.2019. 47.1.27

de Hoog, N., & Verboon, P. (2020). Is the news making us unhappy? The influence of daily news exposure on emotional states. *British Journal of Psychology (London, England), 111*(2), 157–173. https://doi.org/10.1111/bjop.12389

Dick, A. S., & Comer, J. S. (2022, February 7). *Disaster news on TV and social media can trigger post-traumatic stress in kids thousands of miles away—here's why some are more vulnerable.* The Conversation. http://theconversation.com/ disaster-news-on-tv-and-social-media-can-trigger-post-traumatic-stress-in-kids-thousands-of-miles-away-heres-why-some-are-more-vulnerable-173627

Döring, N. (2020). How is the COVID-19 pandemic affecting our sexualities? An overview of the current media narratives and research hypotheses. *Archives of Sexual Behavior, 49*, 2765–2778. https://doi.org/10.1007/s10508-020-01790-z

Dueweke, A. R., Wallace, M. M., Nicasio, A. V., Villalobos, B. T., & Rodriguez, J. H. (2020). Resources and recommendations for engaging children and adolescents in telemental health interventions during COVID-19 and beyond. *The Behavior Therapist, 43*(5), 171–176.

184 References

Dunn, R. A., & Guadagno, R. (2019). Who are you online? A study of gender, race, and gaming experience and context on avatar self-representation. *International Journal of Cyber Behavior, Psychology and Learning, 9*(3), 15–31. https://doi.org/10.4018/IJCBPL.2019070102

Economic and Social Research Council. (2012, November 2). *Cyberbullying in the workplace 'worse than conventional bullying.* http://www.esrc.ac.uk/news-and-events/press-releases/23829/cyberbullying-in-the-workplace-worse-than-conventional-bullying.aspx

Ellison, N., Steinfield, C., & Lampe, C. (2007). The benefits of Facebook "friends:" Social capital and college students' use of online social network sites. *Journal of Computer-Mediated Communication, 12*, 1143–1168. https://doi.org/10.1111/j.1083-6101.2007.00367.x

Emmelkamp, P. M. G., & Meyerbröker, K. (2021). Virtual reality therapy in mental health. *Annual Review of Clinical Psychology, 17*(1), 495–519. https://doi.org/10.1146/annurev-clinpsy-081219-115923

Fauville, G., Luo, M., Muller Queiroz, A. C., Bailenson, J. N., & Hancock, J. (2021). *Nonverbal mechanisms predict zoom fatigue and explain why women experience higher levels than men.* SSRN Scholarly Paper No. 3820035. https://doi.org/10.2139/ssrn.3820035

Feijt, M., de Kort, Y., Bongers, I., Bierbooms, J., Westerink, J., & IJsselsteijn, W. (2020). Mental health care goes online: Practitioners' experiences of providing mental health care during the COVID-19 pandemic. *Cyberpsychology, Behavior, and Social Networking, 23*(12), 860–864. https://doi.org/10.1089/cyber.2020.0370

Fineberg, N. A., Pellegrini, L., Wellsted, D., Hall, N., Corazza, O., Giorgetti, V., Cicconcelli, D., Theofanous, E., Sireau, N., Adam, D., Chamberlain, S. R., & Laws, K. R. (2021). Facing the "new normal": How adjusting to the easing of COVID-19 lockdown restrictions exposes mental health inequalities. *Journal of Psychiatric Research, 141*(September), 276–286. https://doi.org/10.1016/j.jpsychires.2021.07.001

Finfgeld, D. L. (2000). Therapeutic groups online: The good, the bad, and the unknown. *Issues in Mental Health Nursing, 21*(3), 241–255. https://doi.org/10.1080/016128400248068

Firth, J., Torous, J., Nichols, J., Carney, R., Rosenbaum, S., & Sarris, J. (2017). Can smartphone mental health interventions reduce symptoms of anxiety? A meta-analysis of randomized controlled trials | Elsevier Enhanced Reader. *Journal of Affective Disorders, 218*, 15–22. https://doi.org/10.1016/j.jad.2017.04.046

Fish, M. T., Russoniello, C. V., & O'Brien, K. (2018). Zombies vs. anxiety: An augmentation study of prescribed video game play compared to medication in reducing anxiety symptoms. *Simulation & Gaming, 49*(5), 553–566. https://doi.org/10.1177/1046878118773126

Fitzpatrick, N. (2022). No news is not good news: The implications of news fatigue and news avoidance in a pandemic world. In Z. Boutsioli, V. Bigelow, & O. Gkounta (Eds.), *Essays on COVID-19 research* (pp. 169–180). Athens Institute for Education and Research.

Fleming, T., Poppelaars, M., & Thabrew, H. (2023). The role of gamification in digital mental health. *World Psychiatry, 22*(1), 46–47. https://doi.org/10.1002/wps.21041

Fonseka, T. M., Bhat, V., & Kennedy, S. H. (2019). The utility of artificial intelligence in suicide risk prediction and the management of suicidal behaviors. *Australian & New Zealand Journal of Psychiatry, 53*(10), 954–964. https://doi.org/10.1177/0004867419864428

Fordham, B., Sugavanam, T., Edwards, K., Stallard, P., Howard, R., Nair, R. d., Copsey, B., Lee, H., Howick, J., Hemming, K., & Lamb, S. E. (2021). The evidence for cognitive behavioural therapy in any condition, population or context: A meta-review of systematic reviews and panoramic meta-analysis. *Psychological Medicine, 51*(1), 21–29. https://doi.org/10.1017/S003329 1720005292

Foster, C. B. (2013). *Mental health on YouTube: Exploring the potential of interactive media to change knowledge, attitudes and behaviors about mental health.* Ph.D., University of South Carolina. https://www.proquest.com/docview/1438102253/abstract/871EF7835D414FEFPQ/1

Fowler, G. A. (2023, March 14). Snap tried to make a safe AI. It chats with me about booze and sex. https://www.washingtonpost.com/technology/2023/03/14/snapchat-myai/

Fox, J., & Anderegg, C. (2014). Romantic relationship stages and social networking sites: Uncertainty reduction strategies and perceived relational norms on Facebook. *Cyberpsychology, Behavior, and Social Networking, 17*(11), 685–691. https://doi.org/10.1089/cyber.2014.0232

Fox, J., & Moreland, J. J. (2015). The dark side of social networking sites: An exploration of the relational and psychological stressors associated with Facebook use and affordances. *Computers in Human Behavior, 45*, 168–176. https://doi.org/10.1016/j.chb.2014.11.083

Fox, N., Ward, K., & O'Rourke, A. (2005). Pro-anorexia, weight-loss drugs and the internet: An 'anti-recovery' explanatory model of anorexia. *Sociology of Health & Illness, 27*, 944–971.

186   References

Franklin, J. C., Ribeiro, J. D., Fox, K. R., Bentley, K. H., Kleiman, E. M., Huang, X., Musacchio, K. M., Jaroszewski, A. C., Chang, B. P., & Nock, M. K. (2017). Risk factors for suicidal thoughts and behaviors: A meta-analysis of 50 years of research. *Psychological Bulletin, 143*(2), 187–232. https://doi.org/10.1037/bul0000084

Freeman, D., Reeve, S., Robinson, A., Ehlers, A., Clark, D., Spanlang, B., & Slater, M. (2017). Virtual reality in the assessment, understanding, and treatment of mental health disorders. *Psychological Medicine, 47*(14), 2393–2400. https://doi.org/10.1017/S003329171700040X

Freeman, G., & Maloney, D. (2021). Body, avatar, and me: The presentation and perception of self in social virtual reality. *Proceedings of the ACM on Human-Computer Interaction, 4*(CSCW3), 1–27. https://doi.org/10.1145/3432938

Fuchs, M. (2022, May 6). V.R. 'reminiscence therapy' lets seniors relive the past. *The New York Times*. https://www.nytimes.com/2022/05/06/well/mind/virtual-reality-therapy-seniors.html

Gamble, A. (2020). Artificial intelligence and mobile apps for mental healthcare: A social informatics perspective. *Aslib Journal of Information Management, 72*(4), 509–523. https://doi.org/10.1108/AJIM-11-2019-0316

Gamble, C. (2022). Rethinking the accessibility of digital mental health. *Counseling Today, 65*(1), 48–51.

Garfin, D. R., Silver, R. C., & Holman, E. A. (2020). The novel coronavirus (COVID-2019) outbreak: Amplification of public health consequences by media exposure. *Health Psychology, 39*(5), 355–357. https://doi.org/10.1037/hea0000875

Global Social Media Statistics. (2022). DataReportal—Global Digital Insights. https://datareportal.com/social-media-users

Goldman, B. (2017, August 21). Andrew Huberman on using virtual reality to cure fears, no matter what you see. *Stanford Medicine Magazine*. https://stanmed.stanford.edu/huberman-virtual-reality-curing-fear-anxiety/

González-Padilla, D. A., & Tortolero-Blanco, L. (2020). Social media influence in the COVID-19 pandemic. *International Brazilian Journal of Urology, 46*(S1). https://doi.org/10.1590/S1677-5538.IBJU.2020.S121

Gorini, A., Griez, E., Petrova, A., & Riva, G. (2010). Assessment of the emotional responses produced by exposure to real food, virtual food and photographs of food in patients affected by eating disorders. *Annals of General Psychiatry, 9*(1), 30. https://doi.org/10.1186/1744-859X-9-30

Gowen, L. K. (2013). Online mental health information seeking in young adults with mental health challenges. *Journal of Technology in Human Services, 31*(2), 97–111. https://doi.org/10.1080/15228835.2013.765533

Grace, E., Raghavendra, P., Newman, L., Wood, D., & Connell, T. (2014). Learning to use the Internet and online social media: What is the effectiveness of home-based intervention for youth with complex communication needs? *Child Language, Teaching & Therapy, 30*(2), 141–157. https://doi.org/10.1177/0265659013518565

Gradinger, P., Strohmeier, D., Schiller, E. M., Stefanek, E., & Spiel, C. (2012). Cyber-victimization and popularity in early adolescence: Stability and predictive associations. *European Journal of Developmental Psychology, 9*(2), 228–243. https://doi.org/10.1080/17405629.2011.643171

Graham, S., Depp, C., Lee, E. E., Nebeker, C., Tu, X., Kim, H.-C., & Jeste, D. V. (2019). Artificial intelligence for mental health and mental illnesses: An overview. *Current Psychiatry Reports, 21*(11), 116. https://doi.org/10.1007/s11920-019-1094-0

Greene, C. J., Morland, L. A., Macdonald, A., Frueh, B. C., Grubbs, K. M., & Rosen, C. S. (2010). How does tele-mental health affect group therapy process? Secondary analysis of a noninferiority trial. *Journal of Consulting and Clinical Psychology, 78*, 746–750. https://doi.org/10.1037/a0020158

Greenberg, N. (2020). Mental health of health-care workers in the COVID-19 era. *Nature Reviews Nephrology, 16*(8), 425–426. https://doi.org/10.1038/s41581-020-0314-5

Griffith, M (2011, April 27). *Can Twitter help save lives? A health care social media case study.* http://advancingyourhealth.org/highlights/2011/04/27/can-twitter-help-save-lives-a-health-care-social-media-case-study-part-i/

Guardian. (2021, 13 October). Scientists abused and threatened for discussing Covid, global survey finds. https://www.theguardian.com/world/2021/oct/13/scientists-abused-and-threatened-for-discussing-covid-global-survey-finds

Hayes, S. C., & Hofmann, S. G. (2018). *Process-based CBT: The science and core clinical competencies of cognitive behavioral therapy.* New Harbinger Publications.

Hayles, N. K. (1999). *How we became posthuman: Virtual bodies in cybernetics and informatics.* University of Chicago Press.

Hermida, A. (2016). Social media and the news. In T. Witschge, C. W. Anderson, D. Domingo, & A. Hermida (Eds.), *The SAGE handbook of digital journalism* (pp. 81–94). SAGE Publications. https://doi.org/10.4135/97814739 57909.n6

188   References

Hinduja, S., & Patchin, J. W. (2020). Bullying, cyberbullying, and sexual orientation/gender identity. *Cyberbullying Research Center (cyberbullying.org)*. https://cyberbullying.org/bullying-cyberbullying-lgbtq

Hollis, C., Morriss, R., Martin, J., Amani, S., Cotton, R., Denis, M., & Lewis, S. (2015). Technological innovations in mental healthcare: Harnessing the digital revolution. *British Journal of Psychiatry, 206*(4), 263–265. https://doi.org/10.1192/bjp.bp.113.142612

Holman, E. A., Garfin, D. R., Lubens, P., & Silver, R. C. (2020). Media exposure to collective trauma, mental health, and functioning: Does it matter what you see? *Clinical Psychological Science, 8*(1), 111–124. https://doi.org/10.1177/2167702619858300

Holmes, K., & Taube, D. O. (2016). Client discovery of psychotherapist personal information online. *Professional Psychology: Research and Practice, 47*(2), 147–154. https://doi.org/10.1037/pro0000065

Hooi, R., & Cho, H. (2013). Deception in avatar-mediated virtual environment. *Computers in Human Behavior, 29*(1), 276–284. https://doi.org/10.1016/j.chb.2012.09.004

Houston, T. K., Cooper, L. A., Vu, H. T., Kahn, J., Toser, J., & Ford, D. E. (2001). Screening the public for depression through the Internet. *Psychiatric Services, 52*(3), 362–367.

Houston, T. K., Cooper, L. A., & Ford, D. E. (2002). Internet support groups for depression: A 1-year prospective cohort study. *American Journal of Psychiatry, 159*(12), 2062–2068.

How Many Gamers Are There? (New 2023 Statistics). (2022, October 7). Exploding topics. https://explodingtopics.com/blog/number-of-gamers

Hsiung, R. C. (2000). The best of both worlds: An online self-help group hosted by a mental health professional. *CyberPsychology & Behavior, 3*, 935–950.

Hudlicka, E. (2016). Chapter 4—Virtual affective agents and therapeutic games. In D. D. Luxton (Ed.), *Artificial intelligence in behavioral and mental health care* (pp. 81–115). Academic Press. https://doi.org/10.1016/B978-0-12-420248-1.00004-0

Hughes, A. L., & Palen, L. (2009). Twitter adoption and use in mass convergence and emergency events. *International Journal of Emergency Management, 6*(3-4), 248–260. https://doi.org/10.1504/IJEM.2009.031564

Hull, T. D., & Mahan, K. (2017). A study of asynchronous mobile-enabled SMS text psychotherapy. *Telemedicine and E-Health, 23*(3), 240–247. https://doi.org/10.1089/tmj.2016.0114

International Telecommuniations Union. (2022). *Global connectivity report 2022* (p. 186). International Telecommuncations Union.

Ipsen, C., van Veldhoven, M., Kirchner, K., & Hansen, J. P. (2021). Six key advantages and disadvantages of working from home in Europe during COVID-19. *International Journal of Environmental Research and Public Health, 18*(4), 1826. https://doi.org/10.3390/ijerph18041826

Is Bing too belligerent? Microsoft looks to tame AI chatbot. (2023, February 16). AP NEWS. https://apnews.com/article/technology-science-microsoft-corp-business-software-fb49e5d625bf37be0527e5173116bef3

Jain, O., Gupta, M., Satam, S., & Panda, S. (2020). Has the COVID-19 pandemic affected the susceptibility to cyberbullying in India? *Computers in Human Behavior Reports, 2*(August–December), 100029. https://doi.org/10.1016/j.chbr.2020.100029

Johnston, J. (2010, January 6). Don't be a cyberchondriac: Use the internet to self-screen. Not self-diagnose. https://www.psychologytoday.com/us/blog/the-human-equation/201001/dont-be-cyberchondriac-use-the-internet-self-screen-not-self-diagnose

Jones, R., Mougouei, D., & Evans, S. L. (2021). Understanding the emotional response to COVID-19 information in news and social media: A mental health perspective. *Human Behaviour and Emerging Technologies, 3*(5), 831–842. https://doi.org/10.1002/hbe2.304

Jurgenson, N. (2011). *Amber case: Cyborg anthropologist (a critique).* http://the-societypages.org/cyborgology/2011/02/10/amber-case-cyborg-anthropologist-a-critique/

Kaluzeviciute, G. (2020). Social media and its impact on therapeutic relationships. *British Journal of Psychotherapy, 36*(2), 303–320. https://doi.org/10.1111/bjp.12545

Kar, S. K., Kabir, R., Menon, V., Arafat, S. M. Y., Prakash, A. J., & Saxena, S. K. (2021). Artificial intelligence in mental healthcare during COVID-19 pandemic. In S. Nandan Mohanty, S. K. Saxena, S. Satpathy, & J. M. Chatterjee (Eds.), *Applications of artificial intelligence in COVID-19* (pp. 327–343). Springer. https://doi.org/10.1007/978-981-15-7317-0_17

Kay, A. (2013, June 8). At work: Cyberbullies graduate to workplace. *USA Today.* http://www.usatoday.com/story/money/columnist/kay/2013/06/08/at-work-office-cyberbullies/2398671/

Keib, K., Espina, C., Lee, Y.-I., Wojdynski, B. W., Choi, D., & Bang, H. (2018). Picture this: The influence of emotionally valenced images, on attention, selection, and sharing of social media news. *Media Psychology, 21*(2), 202–221. https://doi.org/10.1080/15213269.2017.1378108

190   References

Kellerman, J. K., Hamilton, J. L., Selby, E. A., & Kleiman, E. M. (2022). The mental health impact of daily news exposure during the COVID-19 pandemic: Ecological momentary assessment study. *JMIR Mental Health, 9*(5), e36966. https://doi.org/10.2196/36966

Kelley, P. G., Brewer, R., Mayer, Y., Cranor, L. F., & Sadeh, N. (2011). An investigation into Facebook friend grouping. In *Human-computer interaction—INTERACT 2011: 13th IFIP TC 13 international conference, Lisbon, Portugal: Proceedings, Part III* (pp. 216–233). Springer.

Kemp, B. (2022, February 9). Digital 2022: The United States of America. https://datareportal.com/reports/digital-2022-united-states-of-america

Kessler, R. C., Chiu, W. T., Hwang, I. H., Puac-Polanco, V., Sampson, N. A., Ziobrowski, H. N., & Zaslavsky, A. M. (2022). Changes in prevalence of mental illness among US adults during compared with before the COVID-19 pandemic. *Psychiatric Clinics, 45*(1), 1–28.

Keyes, C. L. M. (2002). The mental health continuum: From languishing to flourishing in life. *Journal of Health and Social Behavior, 43*(2), 207–222.

Keyes, C. L. M. (2007). Promoting and protecting mental health as flourishing: A complementary strategy for improving national mental health. *American Psychologist, 62*(2), 95–108. https://doi.org/10.1037/0003-066X.62.2.95

King, S. A., & Moreggi, D. (1998). Internet therapy and self-help groups—the pros and the cons. In J. Gackenbach (Ed.), *Psychology and the internet: Intrapersonal, interpersonal, and transpersonal implications* (pp. 77–109). Academic Press.

Ko, H. S., & Kuo, F. Y. (2009). Can blogging enhance subjective well-being through self-disclosure? *Cyberpsychology & Behavior, 12*(1), 75–79. https://doi.org/10.1089/cpb.2008.016

Kowal, M., Conroy, E., Ramsbottom, N., Smithies, T., Toth, A., & Campbell, M. (2021). Gaming your mental health: A narrative review on mitigating symptoms of depression and anxiety using commercial video games. *JMIR Serious Games, 9*(2), e26575. https://doi.org/10.2196/26575

Kühn, S., Berna, F., Lüdtke, T., Gallinat, J., & Moritz, S. (2018). Fighting depression: Action video game play may reduce rumination and increase subjective and objective cognition in depressed patients. *Frontiers in Psychology, 9*, 129. https://doi.org/10.3389/fpsyg.2018.00129

Lamers, S. M. A. (2012). *Positive mental health: Measurement, relevance and implications*. PhD, University of Twente. https://doi.org/10.3990/1.9789036533706

References 191

Lastauskas, P. (2022). Lockdown, employment adjustment, and financial frictions. *Small Business Economics, 58*(2), 919–942. https://doi.org/10.1007/s11187-021-00496-3

Leung, F. F., Zhang, J. Z., Gu, F. F., & Palmatier, R. W. (2022) Does influence marketing really pay off? *Harvard Business Review.* https://hbr.org/2022/11/does-influencer-marketing-really-pay-off

Li, A. (2013). *Teen brags on Facebook after alleged bullying victim commits suicide.* http://mashable.com/2013/10/15/bullying-teen-brags-facebook/

Limaye, R. J., Sauer, M., Ali, J., Bernstein, J., Walh, B., Barnhill, A., & Labrique, A. (2020). Building trust while influencing online COVID-19 content in the social media world. *The Lancet, 2*(6), E277–E278. https://doi.org/10.1016/S2589-7500(20)30084-4

Litwiller, B. J., & Brausch, A. M. (2013). Cyber bullying and physical bullying in adolescent suicide: The role of violent behavior and substance use. *Journal of Youth and Adolescence, 42*(5), 675–684. https://doi.org/10.1007/s10964-013-9925-5

Livingstone, S., Kirwil, L., Ponte, C., & Statksrud, E. (2013). *In their own words: What bothers children online.* http://www.lse.ac.uk/media@lse/research/EUKidsOnline/EU%20Kids%20III/Reports/Intheirownwords020213.pdf

Lo, J., Panchal, N., & Miller, B. P. (2022, March 15). Telehealth has played an outsized role meeting mental health needs during the COVID-19 pandemic. *KFF.* https://www.kff.org/coronavirus-covid-19/issue-brief/telehealth-has-played-an-outsized-role-meeting-mental-health-needs-during-the-covid-19-pandemic/

Lobe, B., Livingstone, S., Ólafsson, K., & Voleb, H. (2011). *Cross-national comparisons of risks and safety on the Internet: Initial analysis from the EU Kids online survey of European children.* London School of Economics & Political Science.

Lovejoy, C. A. (2019). Technology and mental health: The role of artificial intelligence. *European Psychiatry, 55,* 1–3. https://doi.org/10.1016/j.eurpsy.2018.08.004

Lufkin, B. (2020, 16 December). How online gaming has become a social lifeline. *BBC: The Life Project.* https://www.bbc.com/worklife/article/20201215-how-online-gaming-has-become-a-social-lifeline

Mahoney, A., Li, I., Haskelberg, H., Millard, M., & Newby, J. M. (2021). The uptake and effectiveness of online cognitive behaviour therapy for symptoms of anxiety and depression during COVID-19. *Journal of Affective Disorders, 292,* 197–203. https://doi.org/10.1016/j.jad.2021.05.116

192 **References**

Manicavasagar, V., Horswood, D., Burckhardt, R., Lum, A., Hadzi-Pavlovic, D., & Parker, G. (2014). Feasibility and effectiveness of a web-based positive psychology program for youth mental health: Randomized controlled trial. *Journal of Medical Internet Research, 16*(6), e140. https://doi.org/10.2196/jmir.3176

Marciano, L., Ostroumova, M., Schulz, P. J., & Camerini, A.-L. (2022). Digital media use and adolescents' mental health during the Covid-19 pandemic: A systematic review and meta-analysis. *Frontiers in Public Health, 9*. https://www.frontiersin.org/articles/10.3389/fpubh.2021.793868

Matsa, K. E. (2022, October 21). More Americans are getting news on TikTok, bucking the trend on other social media sites. *Pew Research Center*. https://www.pewresearch.org/fact-tank/2022/10/21/more-americans-are-getting-news-on-tiktok-bucking-the-trend-on-other-social-media-sites/

Mattoon, E. R. (2021, April 10). TikTok therapy: Hopkins professor addresses mental health on social media. The Johns Hopkins News-Letter. https://www.jhunewsletter.com/article/2021/04/tiktok-therapy-hopkinsprofessor addressesmental-health-on-social-media

Meel, P., & Vishwakarma, D. K. (2020). Fake news, rumor, information pollution in social media and web: A contemporary survey of state-of-the-arts, challenges and opportunities. *Expert Systems with Applications, 153*, 112986. https://doi.org/10.1016/j.eswa.2019.112986

Mehta, S., & Maniar, A. (2023). Technology during COVID-19: Boon or a curse. *International Journal of Management, Public Policy, and Research, 2*(Special Issue), 40–44. https://doi.org/10.55829/ijmpr.v2iSpecialIssue.135

Miodus and Jimenez. (2021). TikTok Therapy: An Exploratory Study on Popular TikTok Mental Health Content. TMS Proceedings 2021. https://doi.org/10.1037/tms0000137

Morahan-Martin, J., & Anderson, C. D. (2000). Information and misinformation online: Recommendations for facilitating accurate mental health information retrieval and evaluation. *CyberPsychology & Behavior, 3*(5), 731–746. https://doi.org/10.1089/10949310050191737

Moreno, C., Wykes, T., Galderisi, S., Nordentoft, M., Crossley, N., Jones, N., Cannon, M., Correll, C. U., Byrne, L., Carr, S., Chen, E. Y. H., Gorwood, P., Johnson, S., Kärkkäinen, H., Krystal, J. H., Lee, J., Lieberman, J., López-Jaramillo, C., Männikkö, M., et al. (2020). How mental health care should change as a consequence of the COVID-19 pandemic. *The Lancet Psychiatry, 7*(9), 813–824. https://doi.org/10.1016/S2215-0366(20)30307-2

Moreno, M. A., & Joliff, A. F. (2022). Depression and anxiety in the context of digital media. In J. Nesi, E. H. Telzer, & M. J. Prinstein (Eds.), *Handbook of adolescent digital media use and mental health* (pp. 217–362). Cambridge University Press.

Morton, T., Genova, A., Neild, B., Wilson, N., Haslam, C., Dell'Atti, A., Sansonetti, S., & Di Furia, L. (2015). *AGES 2.0: Activating and guiding the engagement of seniors through social media: Final report.* http://www.ages2.eu/sites/default/files/page/Ages-final-report-EN.pdf

Naeem, S. B., Bhatti, R., & Khan, A. (2021). An exploration of how fake news is taking over social media and putting public health at risk. *Health Information & Libraries Journal, 38*(2), 143–149. https://doi.org/10.1111/hir.12320

Naslund, J. A., & Aschbrenner, K. A. (2021). Technology use and interest in digital apps for mental health promotion and lifestyle intervention among young adults with serious mental illness | Elsevier Enhanced Reader. *Journal of Affective Disorders Reports, 6,* 100227. https://doi.org/10.1016/j.jadr.2021.100227

Niederhoffer, K. G., & Pennebaker, J. W. (2002). Sharing one's story. In C. R. Snyder & S. J. Lopez (Eds.), *Handbook of positive psychology* (pp. 573–583). Oxford University Press.

Norris, K. O. (2004). Gender stereotypes, aggression, and computer games: An online survey of women. *Cyberpsychology & Behavior, 7*(6), 714–727. https://doi.org/10.1089/cpb.2004.7.714

Nutley, S. K., Falise, A. M., Hendeson, R., Apostolou, V., Mathews, C. A., & Striley, C. W. (2020). The impact of COVID-19 on disordered eating behavior: A qualitative analysis of social media users' response to the global pandemic. *JMIR Mental Health.* https://preprints.jmir.org/preprint/26011

O'Keeffe and Clarke-Pearson. (2011). Clinical report. The impact of social media on children, adolescents end families. *American Academy of Pedriatics, 127*(4), 799–805.

Oksanen, A., Oksa, R., Savela, N., Mantere, E., Savolainen, L., & Kaakinen, M. (2021). COVID-19 crisis and digital stressors at work: A longitudinal study on the Finnish working population. *Computers in Human Behavior, 122,* 106853. https://doi.org/10.1016/j.chb.2021.106853

Papageorgiou, A., Fisher, C., & Cross, D. (2022). "Why don't I look like her?" How adolescent girls view social media and its connection to body image. *BMC Womens Health, 22*(1), 261. https://doi.org/10.1186/s12905-022-01845-4

194   References

Park, C. S. (2019). Does too much news on social media discourage news seeking? Mediating role of news efficacy between perceived news overload and news avoidance on social media. *Social Media + Society, 5*(3), 205630511987295. https://doi.org/10.1177/2056305119872956

Parks, M. R., & Floyd, K. (1996). Making friends in cyberspace. *Journal of Communication, 46*(1), 80–97. https://doi.org/10.1111/j.1460-2466.1996.tb01462.x

Parks, A. C., Williams, A. L., Tugade, M. M., Hokes, K. E., Honomichl, R. D., & Zilca, R. D. (2018). Testing a scalable web and smartphone based intervention to improve depression, anxiety, and resilience: A randomized controlled trial. *International Journal of Wellbeing, 8*(2), 22–67. https://doi.org/10.5502/ijw.v8i2.745

Parry, S. L., Carr, N. A., Staniford, L. J., & Walker, L. (2022). Rebuilding the workplace to promote young workers' mental health. *International Journal of Workplace Health Management, 15*(3), 307–319. https://doi.org/10.1108/IJWHM-10-2021-0188

Patchin, J., & Hinduja, S. (2010). Bullying, cyberbullying, and suicide. *Archives of Suicide Research, 14*(3), 206–211. https://doi.org/10.1080/13811118.2010.494133

Penninx, B. W. J. H., Benros, M. E., Klein, R. S., & Vinkers, C. H. (2022). How COVID-19 shaped mental health: From infection to pandemic effects. *Nature Medicine, 28*(10), 10. https://doi.org/10.1038/s41591-022-02028-2

Perren, S., Dooley, J., Shaw, T., & Cross, D. (2010). Bullying in schools and cyberspace: Associations with depressive symptoms in Swiss and Australian adolescents. *Child and Adolescent Psychiatry and Mental Health, 4*(1), 28. https://doi.org/10.1186/1753-2000-4-28

Petrosyan, A. (2022a, October 18). Internet usage in the United Kingdom (UK) – Statistics & Facts. https://www.statista.com/topics/3246/internet-usage-in-the-uk/#dossierContents__outerWrapper.

Petrosyan, A. (2022b, July 7). Percentage of teenagers in the United States who have been cyber bullied as of April 2018, by age and frequency. https://www.statista.com/statistics/207508/teenagers-personal-experiences-of-bullying-on-social-media-websites/

Petrosyan, A. (2023, February 24). Number of internet and social media users worldwide as of January 2023. https://www.statista.com/statistics/617136/digital-population-worldwide/

Philio, J. (2012, February 27). The danger of self-diagnosis. https://jolenephilo.com/a-self-diagnosis-crisis/

Phillips, L. (2022, March 25). The rise of counselors on social media. *Counseling Today*. https://ct.counseling.org/2022/03/

Pierce, M., Hope, H., Ford, T., Hatch, S., Hotopf, M., John, A., Kontopantelis, E., Webb, R., Wessely, S., McManus, S., & Abel, K. M. (2020). *Mental health before and during the COVID-19 pandemic: A longitudinal probability sample survey of the UK population. 7*, 11.

Piquero, A. R., Jennings, W. G., Jemison, E., Kaukinen, C., & Knaul, F. M. (2021). Domestic violence during the COVID-19 pandemic—Evidence from a systematic review and meta-analysis. *Journal of Criminal Justice, 74*, 101806. https://doi.org/10.1016/j.jcrimjus.2021.101806

Poletti, B., Tagini, S., Brugnera, A., Parolin, L., Pievani, L., Ferrucci, R., Compare, A., & Silani, V. (2021). Telepsychotherapy: A leaflet for psychotherapists in the age of COVID-19. A review of the evidence. *Counselling Psychology Quarterly, 34*(3–4), 352–367. https://doi.org/10.1080/0951507 0.2020.1769557

Porter, K. R., McCarthy, B. J., Freels, S., Kim, Y., & Davis, F. G. (2010). Prevalence estimates for primary brain tumors in the United States by age, gender, behavior, and histology. *Neuro-oncology, 12*(6), 520–527.

Przybylski, A. K., Mishkin, A., Shotbolt, V., & Linington, S. (2014). *A shared responsibility: Building children's online resilience*. Oxford Internet Institute. https://parentzone.org.uk/sites/default/files/2021-12/PZ_Building_Online_Resilience_2014.pdf

Purves, D. G., & Dutton, J. (2013). An exploration of the therapeutic process while using computerised cognitive behaviour therapy. *Counselling and Psychotherapy Research, 13*(4), 308–316. https://doi.org/10.1080/1473314 5.2012.761259

Raghavendra, P., Grace, E., Newman, L., & Wood, D. (2013). 'They think I'm really cool and nice' the impact of Internet support on the social networks and loneliness of young people with disabilities. *Telecommunications Journal of Australia, 63*(2), 2. http://www.swinburne.edu.au/lib/ir/onlinejournals/tja/

Rauschenberg, C., Schick, A., Hirjak, D., Seidler, A., Paetzold, I., Apfelbacher, C., et al. (2021). Evidence synthesis of digital interventions to mitigate the negative impact of the COVID-19 pandemic on public mental health: Rapid meta-review. *Journal of Medical Internet Research, 23*(3), e23365.

Reid, E., Mandryk, R. L., Beres, N. A., Klarkowski, M., & Frommel, J. (2022). Feeling good and in control: In-game tools to support targets of toxicity. *Proceedings of the ACM on Human-Computer Interaction, 6*(CHI PLAY), 235. https://doi.org/10.1145/3549498

196   References

Reworking work. (n.d.). https://www.Apa.Org. Retrieved March 17, 2023, from https://www.apa.org/monitor/2022/01/special-reworking-work

Rice, E., & Barman-Adhikari, A. (2014). Internet and social media use as a resource among homeless youth. *Journal of Computer Mediated Communication, 19*(1), 232–247. https://doi.org/10.1111/jcc4.12038

Rice, R. (2022). *Video games in psychotherapy* (1st ed.). Routledge. https://doi.org/10.4324/9781003222132

Riva, G., & Serino, S. (2020). Virtual reality in the assessment, understanding and treatment of mental health disorders. *Journal of Clinical Medicine, 9*(11), 11. https://doi.org/10.3390/jcm9113434

Rivers, I. (2012, June). *Homophobic bullying and inclusion in an age of technology.* Keynote address presented at the National Center Against Bullying (NCAB) Bi-Annual Conference entitled 'Social media, bullying and vulnerability: Connect, respect, protect', Melbourne, Australia.

Rivers, I. (2013). Cyberbullying and cyberaggression: Sexualised and gendered experiences explored. In I. Rivers & N. Duncan (Eds.), *Bullying: Experiences and discourses of sexuality and gender* (pp. 19–30). Routledge.

Rivers, I., Daly, J., & Stevenson, L. (2023). Homophobic and transphobic online harassment: Young people in Scotland during the COVID-19 pandemic. In H. A. Cowie & C.-A. Myers (Eds.), *Cyberbullying and online harms: Preventions and interventions form community to campus*. Routledge.

Rivers, I., & Noret, N. (2010). 'I h8 u': Findings from a five-year study of text and email bullying. *British Journal of Educational Research, 36*(4), 643–671. https://doi.org/10.1080/01411920903071918

Rivers, I., & Noret, N. (2010). 'I h8 u': Findings form a five-year study of text and email bullying. *British Educational Research Journal, 36*(4), 643–671. https://doi.org/10.1080/01411920903071918

Rocha, Y. M., de Moura, G. A., Desidério, G. A., de Oliveira, C. H., Lourenço, F. D., & de Figueiredo Nicolete, L. D. (2021). The impact of fake news on social media and its influence on health during the COVID-19 pandemic: A systematic review. *Journal of Public Health.* https://doi.org/10.1007/s10389-021-01658-z

Rodriguez-Cayro, K. (2018, June 28). Here's how to tell if you have headline stress disorder—and how to protect yourself from it. *Bustle.* https://www.bustle.com/p/what-is-headline-stress-disorder-heres-how-to-protect-yourself-from-anxiety-about-the-news-cycle-9611772

Royal Society for Public Health & Young Health Movement. (2017). Status Of Mind social media and young people's mental health and wellbeing. Retrieved from https://www.rsph.org.uk/uploads/assets/uploaded/62be270a-a55f-4719-ad668c2ec7a74c2a.pdf

Ruwaard, J. J. (2013). *The efficacy and effectiveness of online CBT*. Universiteit van Amsterdam [Host].

Saura, J. R., & Punzo, J. G. (2020). Defining types of "fakers" in social media. *Marketing and Management of Innovations, 11*(4), 231–236. https://doi.org/10.21272/mmi.2020.4-18

Schmitt, J. B., Debbelt, C. A., & Schneider, F. M. (2018). Too much information? Predictors of information overload in the context of online news exposure. *Information, Communication & Society, 21*(8), 1151–1167. https://doi.org/10.1080/1369118X.2017.1305427

Scottish Government. (2020). Coronavirus (COVID-19): Mental health—transition and recovery plan. *Scottish Government*. https://www.gov.scot/publications/mental-health-scotlands-transition-recovery/

Sepulveda-Escobar, P., & Morrison, A. (2020). Online teaching placement during the COVID-19 pandemic in Chile: Challenges and opportunities. *European Journal of Teacher Education, 43*(4), 587–607. https://doi.org/10.1080/02619768.2020.1820981

Sfoggia, A., Kowacs, C., Gastaud, M. B., Laskoski, P. B., Bassols, A. M., Severo, C. T., Machado, D., Krieger, D. V., Torres, M. B., & Teche, S. P. (2014). Therapeutic relationship on the web: To face or not to face? *Trends in Psychiatry and Psychotherapy, 36*, 3–10.

Shelton, A. K., & Skalski, P. (2014). Blinded by the light: Illuminating the dark side of social network use through content analysis. *Computers in Human Behavior, 33*, 339–348. https://doi.org/10.1016/j.chb.2013.08.017

Sherman, L. E., & Greenfield, P. M. (2013). Forging friendship, soliciting support. A mixed-method examination of message boards for pregnant teens and teen mothers. *Computers in Human Behavior, 29*(1), 75–85. https://doi.org/10.1016/j.chb.2012.07.018

Shimura, A., Yokoi, K., Ishibashi, Y., Akatsuka, Y., & Inoue, T. (2021). Remote work decreases psychological and physical stress responses, but full-remote work increases presenteeism. *Frontiers in Psychology, 12*. https://www.frontiersin.org/articles/10.3389/fpsyg.2021.730969

Shore, J. H., Yellowlees, P., Caudill, R., Johnston, B., Turvey, C., Mishkind, M., Krupinski, E., Myers, K., Shore, P., Kaftarian, E., & Hilty, D. (2018). Best practices in videoconferencing-based telemental health April 2018. *Telemedicine and E-Health, 24*(11), 827–832. https://doi.org/10.1089/tmj.2018.0237

Shu, K., Bhattacharjee, A., Alatawi, F., Nazer, T. H., Ding, K., Karami, M., & Liu, H. (2020). Combating disinformation in a social media age. *WIREs Data Mining and Knowledge Discovery, 10*(6). https://doi.org/10.1002/widm.1385

198 References

Sigursteinsdottir, H., & Karlsdottir, F. B. (2022). Does social support matter in the workplace? Social support, job satisfaction, bullying and harassment in the workplace during COVID-19. *International Journal of Environmental Research and Public Health, 19*(8), 4724. https://doi.org/10.3390/ijerph19084724

Sinclair, K. O., Bauman, S., Poteat, V. P., Koenig, B., & Russell, S. T. (2012). The association between cyber and bias-based harassment and academic, substance use and mental health problems. *Journal of Adolescent Health, 50*(5), 521–523. https://doi.org/10.1016/j.jadohealth.2011.09.009

Slater, M., & Sanchez-Vives, M. V. (2016). Enhancing our lives with immersive virtual reality. *Frontiers in Robotics and AI, 3*. https://doi.org/10.3389/frobt.2016.00074

Smart, K., Smith, L., Harvey, K., & Waite, P. (2021). The acceptability of a therapist-assisted internet-delivered cognitive behaviour therapy program for the treatment of anxiety disorders in adolescents: A qualitative study. *European Child & Adolescent Psychiatry*. https://doi.org/10.1007/s00787-021-01903-6

Söderström, S. (2009). Offline social ties and online use of computers: A study of disabled youth and their use of ICT advances. *New Media & Society, 11*(5), 709–727. https://doi.org/10.1177/1461444809105347

Somani, R., Muntaner, C., Smith, P., Hillan, E. M., & Velonis, A. J. (2022). Increased workplace bullying against nurses during COVID-19: A health and safety issue. *Journal of Nursing Education and Practice, 12*(9), 47–53. https://doi.org/10.5430/jnep.v12n9p47

Sourander, A., Klomek, A. B., Ikonen, M., Lindroos, J., Luntamo, T., Koskelainen, M., et al. (2010). Psychosocial risk factors associated with cyberbullying among adolescents. *Archives of General Psychiatry, 67*(7), 720–728. https://doi.org/10.1001/archgenpsychiatry.2010.79

Spencer, L., & Pahl, R. E. (2006). *Rethinking friendship: Hidden solidarities today*. Princeton University Press.

Statista (2023). Cyber bulling – Statistics & Facts. https://www.statista.com/topics/1809/cyber-bullying/

Stawarz, K., Preist, C., & Coyle, D. (2019). Use of smartphone apps, social media, and web-based resources to support mental health and well-being: Online survey. *JMIR Mental Health, 6*(7), e12546. https://doi.org/10.2196/12546

Stephens, M. (1988). *A history of news: From the drum to the satellite*. Viking. http://archive.org/details/historyofnewsfro00step

Stosny, S. (2017, February 6). *Most people get their news online – but many are switching off altogether: Here's why*. https://www.washingtonpost.com/news/inspired-life/wp/2017/02/06/suffering-from-headline-stress-disordersince-trumps-win-youre-definitely-not-alone/

Strauss, J., Zhang, J., Jarrett, M. L., Patterson, B., & Van Ameringen, M. (2022). 18—Apps for mental health. In D. J. Stein, N. A. Fineberg, & S. R. Chamberlain (Eds.), *Mental health in a digital world* (pp. 395–433). Academic Press. https://doi.org/10.1016/B978-0-12-822201-0.00006-X

Streckfuss, R. (1998). News before newpapers. *Journalism and Mass Communication Quarterly, 75*(1), 84–97. http://www.proquest.com/docview/216922768/abstract/266E17E1B59D4A02PQ/12

Suler, J. (2004). The online disinhibition effect. *Cyberpsychology & Behavior, 7*(3), 321–326. https://doi.org/10.1089/1094931041291295

Sweeney, G. M., Donovan, C. L., March, S., & Forbes, Y. (2019). Logging into therapy: Adolescent perceptions of online therapies for mental health problems. *Internet Interventions, 15*, 93–99. https://doi.org/10.1016/j.invent.2016.12.001

Szkody, E., Stearns, M., Stanhope, L., & McKinney, C. (2021). Stress-buffering role of social support during COVID-19. *Family Process, 60*(3), 1002–1015. https://doi.org/10.1111/famp.12618

Tate, D. F., & Zabinski, M. F. (2004). Computer and Internet applications for psychological treatment: Update for clinicians. *Journal of Clinical Psychology, 60*, 209–220.

Telnor Group. (2013). Building digital resilience. http://www.telenor.com/wp-content/uploads/2013/04/Telenor-report-Building-Digital-Resilience.pdf

Thomas, A. B. (2002). *Internet chat room participation and the coming out experiences of young gay men: A qualitative study*. Unpublished PhD thesis. The University of Texas at Austin.

Top Countries & Markets by Game Revenues | Biggest Games Markets. (n.d.). *Newzoo*. Retrieved January 24, 2023, from https://newzoo.com/insights/rankings/top-10-countries-by-game-revenues

Tsuno, K., & Tabuchi, T. (2022). Risk factors for workplace bullying, severe psychological distress and suicidal ideation during the COVID-19 pandemic among the general working population in Japan: A large-scale cross-sectional study. *BMJOpen, 12*, e059860. https://doi.org/10.1136/bmjopen-2021-059860

Turkle, S. (1995a). *Life on the screen: Identity in the age of the internet*. Simon & Schuster.

200 References

Turkle, S. (1995b). Rethinking identity through virtual community. In L. Hershman Leeson (Ed.), *Clicking in: Hotlinks to a digital culture* (pp. 116–122). Bay Press.

Uhls, Y. T., Ellison, N. B., & Subrahmanyam, K. (2017). Benefits and costs of social media in adolescence. *Pediatrics, 140*(Supplement_2), S67–S70. https://doi.org/10.1542/peds.2016-1758E

Vaillancourt, T., Brittain, H., Krygsman, A., Farrell, A. H., Landon, S., & Pepler, D. (2021). School bullying before and during COVID-19: Results from a population-based randomized design. *Aggressive Behavior, 47*(5), 557–569. https://doi.org/10.1002/ab.21986

Valkenburg, P. M., & Peter, J. (2009). Social consequences of the Internet for adolescents. *Current Directions in Psychological Science, 18*(1), 1–5. https://doi.org/10.1111/j.1467-8721.2009.01595.x

Valkenburg, P. M., Peter, J., & Schouten, A. P. (2006). Friend networking sites and their relationship to adolescents' well-being and social self-esteem. *CyberPsychology & Behavior, 9*, 584–590. https://doi.org/10.1089/cpb.2006.9.584

Vargo, D., Zhu, L., Benwell, B., & Yan, Z. (2020). Digital technology use during VOID-19 pandemic: A rapid review. *Human Behavior and Emerging Technologies, 3*(1), 13–24. https://doi.org/10.1002/hbe2.242

Von Holtz, L. A. H., Frasso, R., Golinkoff, J. M., Lozano, A. J., Hanlon, A., & Dowshen, N. (2018). Internet and social media access among youth experiencing homelessness: Mixed methods study. *Journal of Medical Internet Research, 20*(5), e184. https://doi.org/10.2196/jmir.9306

Vosoughi, S., Roy, D., & Aral, S. (2018). The spread of true and false news online. *Science, 359*(6380), 1146–1151. https://doi.org/10.1126/science.aap9559

Walton, M., Murray, E., & Christian, M. D. (2020). Mental health care for medical staff and affiliated healthcare workers during the COVID-19 pandemic. *European Heart Journal. Acute Cardiovascular Care, 9*(3), 241–247. https://doi.org/10.1177/2048872620922795

Wang, B., Liu, Y., Qian, J., & Parker, S. K. (2021). Achieving effective remote working during the COVID-19 pandemic: A work design perspective. *Applied Psychology, 70*(1), 16–59. https://doi.org/10.1111/apps.12290

Wang, J., Iannotti, R. J., & Nansel, T. R. (2009). School bullying among U.S. adolescents: Physical, verbal, relational, and cyber. *Journal of Adolescent Health, 45*(4), 368–375. https://doi.org/10.1016/j.jadohealth.2009.03.021

Washburn, M., & Parrish, D. E. (2013). DBT self-help application for mobile devices. *Journal of Technology in Human Services, 31*(2), 175–183. https://doi.org/10.1080/15228835.2013.775904

Weaver, A., Zhang, A., Xiang, X., Felsman, P., Fischer, D. J., & Himle, A. A. (2023). Entertain me well: An entertaining, tailorable online platform delivering CBT for depression. *Cognitive & Behavioral Practice, 30*(1), 96–115. https://doi.org/10.1016/j.cbpra.2021.09.003

White, R. W., & Horvitz, E. (2009). Cyberchondria: Studies of the escalation of medical concerns in web search. *ACM Transactions on Information Systems (TOIS), 27*(4), 1–37.

WHO Coronavirus (COVID-19) Dashboard. (2023). World Health Organization. https://covid19.who.int/

Williams, A. (2015, January 22). *How to protect your teen's online privacy.* Family Online Safety Institute. https://www.fosi.org/good-digital-parenting/helping-parents-protect-teen-privacy-online-/

Wolfendale, J. (2007). My avatar, my self: Virtual harm and attachment. *Ethics and Information Technology, 9*(1), 111–119. https://doi.org/10.1007/s10676-006-9125-z

World Economic Forum. (2022, September 12). *European Sting.* https://europeansting.com/2022/09/12/most-people-get-their-news-online-but-many-are-switching-off-altogether-heres-why/

Yalom, I. D., & Leszcz, M. (2020). *Theory and practice of group psychotherapy* (5th ed). New York: Basic Books.

Yang, Y., Zeng, D., & Yang, F. (2022). Internet use and subjective well-being of the elderly: An analysis of the mediating effect based on social capital. *International Journal of Environmental Research and Public Health, 19*, 12087. https://doi.org/10.3390/ijerph191912087

Yau, J. C., & Reich, S. M. (2018). Are the qualities of adolescents offline friendships present in digital interactions? *Adolescent Research Review, 3*(3), 339–355. https://doi.org/10.1007/s40894-017-0059-y

Yee, N. (2007). *WoW gender bending.* http://www.nickyee.com/daedalus/archives/001369.php

Yee, N., Bailenson, J. N., & Ducheneaut, N. (2009). The Proteus effect: Implications of transformed digital self-representation in online and offline behaviour. *Communication Research, 36*(2), 285–312. https://doi.org/10.1177/0093650208330254

Young, R. M. (1996a) *NETDYNAM: Some parameters of virtual reality.* http://human-nature.com/rmyoung/papers/paper17h.html

202 References

Young, R. M. (1996b). *Psychoanalysis and/of the internet.* http://human-nature.com/free-associations/psaint.html

Zayapragassarazan, Z. (2020). *COVID-19: Strategies for engaging remote learners in medical education.* https://files.eric.ed.gov/fulltext/ED604479.pdf

Zhang, X., Gao, Q., Khoo, C. S. G., & Wu, A. (2013). Categories of friends on social networking sites: An exploratory study. In *Proceedings of the 5th international conference on Asia-Pacific library and information education and practice* (pp. 244–259). University of Khon Kaen.

Index

A

Academy of Pediatrics, 116
Adolescents, 11, 19, 34–35, 69–71, 85, 116–117, 141
Alcoholics Anonymous, 44
Alzheimer's, 37, 136
Anxiety, 17, 20, 21, 27, 30, 31, 34, 37, 40, 47, 61, 64, 78, 89, 91, 93, 94, 109, 114, 116, 117, 119–121, 123, 130, 136, 139, 141, 170
Applications (apps), 3, 7, 10, 16–18, 20, 23, 29, 32, 59, 60, 88, 101, 103, 112, 113, 127, 128, 130–135, 138–140, 167, 168, 174
Artificial intelligence (AI), 4, 127–142, 168, 170, 174, 175
Avatars, 4, 89, 134, 135, 149, 152, 154, 157, 158, 171, 172

B

Bite Back, 11
Blogs, 3, 10, 37, 51, 141, 160, 161
BlueJeans, 120
Blues Begone, 154, 155

C

Center for Epidemiological Studies-Depression (CES-D), 36
Chatbot, 128, 130–134, 168
ChatGPT, 128, 132
Chatrooms, 41, 69, 72, 100, 101, 159, 160
Children, 19, 28, 34–35, 52, 74, 85, 86, 88, 90–92, 98–101, 116, 128, 139, 141, 175
Cognitive Behavioral Therapy (CBT), 17, 32–34, 53, 130, 131, 139, 140, 154, 156, 157

© The Author(s), under exclusive license to Springer Nature Switzerland AG 2023
S. Bauman, I. Rivers, *Mental Health in the Digital Age*,
https://doi.org/10.1007/978-3-031-32122-1

204　　Index

Cognitive load, 121, 122
Commercial games, 140–141
Computer Fraud and Abuse Act, 63
Connectedness, 59–79
Coronavirus Baby Boom, 77
Counselors, 19, 21, 29, 33
COVID-19, 2, 3, 5, 8, 23, 27–29,
　　31, 59, 65, 76–79, 85–103,
　　109, 111, 114, 115, 117, 119,
　　122, 147–151, 153, 154, 161,
　　162, 167–171, 174, 175
COVID-19 Together, 154, 157
Co-viewing, 98, 99
Crowd funding, 66
Cyberbullying, 2, 4, 5, 21,
　　85–103, 175
Cyberchondria, 36

D

Deep learning (DL), 129
Depression, 11, 17, 20, 21, 27, 30,
　　32, 33, 36, 42, 43, 61, 63, 78,
　　89, 91, 93, 94, 97, 116, 117,
　　119–121, 123, 129, 133, 139,
　　141, 154–156
Dialectical behavior therapy
　　(DBT), 131
Digital
　　aggression, 4, 85–103
　　sources of information, 8, 23
　　universe, 7
　　world, 7, 19, 51, 75, 86,
　　　98, 99, 175
Direct messages (DMs), 60
Disinformation, 8, 62, 115, 119
Distributed self, 149
DSM-V, 129

E

Easy PC, 75
e-estonia, 77
e-estonia.com, 77, 174
Elderly citizens, 72, 75–76, 169
Enmeshed self, 152–153, 170–171
Entertain Me Well (EMW),
　　156, 157
EUKids online, 92, 100

F

Facebook, 3, 18, 59, 64, 68–70, 76,
　　77, 99, 109, 112, 114, 134
Fake news, 62, 117, 119–123
Fakers (social media), 62–66
Flourishing, 1, 2, 168–169, 175
Forms of friendships, 64
Friendships (online), 3, 61–65, 78

G

Gay, lesbian, bisexual, trans, queer/
　　questioning plus (GLBTQ+),
　　71, 95–96
Gender, 18, 40, 115, 161, 171
General Health Questionnaire
　　(GHQ-12), 32
Google, 7, 13, 15, 51, 110, 131, 134
　　Google Meet, 4, 45
Goto Meeting, 120

H

Headline stress disorder, 117
Headspace, 17, 139
Hybrid, 102, 123, 157, 162, 167
Hypergaze, 121

Index

I

ICD-11, 129
Image-based sexual abuse, 88
Influencers, 12, 20, 21, 60, 62, 75
Infodemic, 119
Information overload, 109–123
Instagram, 3, 18, 20, 60, 77, 95
International Telecommunications
    Union, 8, 21
Internet
    connectivity, 4, 7, 169
    Internet Relay Chat (IRC), 72
    support groups, 38–46

L

Languishing, 1, 2, 168–169
Library, 7, 73, 78, 169
Life on the Screen, 87
Lockdown, 14, 77, 93–97, 102, 119,
    148, 150, 151, 157, 170, 171
Long COVID, 157–159
Low-income, 8

M

Machine learning (ML), 63, 129
Massive Multi-player Online Role
    Playing Games (MMORPGs),
    157, 158
Mediation, 98–99
Meier, Megan, 63, 89, 93, 159
Mental health
    diagnosis, 9–10
    Mental Health Continuum
        Short Form, 2
    mental health professionals, 3, 4,
        8, 10, 15, 18, 19, 22, 23, 30,
        37, 40, 51, 53, 54, 123,
        129, 142
    virtual mental health, 29
Mentoring, 103
Microsoft Teams, 4, 41, 76, 120, 174
Misinformation, 2, 5, 8, 115, 119, 175
Mood
    MoodKit, 17
    MoodMission, 17
Multi-user domains (MUDs), 87
My AI, 132
MyStory, 11

N

National Alliance for the Mental Ill
    (NAMI), 13
National Health Service (NHS),
    UK, 29, 133
Natural language processing
    (NLP), 129
News fatigue, 110, 115
NHS Digital Apps Library, 133

O

Online games, 99, 127–142,
    159, 170–172
Online news, 112–114, 117
Online self, 5, 148–149

P

Pandemic, 2, 4, 8, 10, 23, 27,
    29–31, 59, 76–78, 94–98,
    101, 102, 111, 114, 115, 119,
    147, 148, 154, 157, 167, 168,
    170, 174, 175

206   Index

Parkinson's disease, 136
Parkland High School, 118
Patient-targeting googling (PTG), 51
Peer relationships, 19
Pew Research Center, 112
Platforms, 3, 7, 10, 13, 17–21,
    31–33, 35, 39, 41, 44, 51,
    59–63, 67–69, 71, 73–75, 77,
    78, 89, 91, 94, 95, 114, 120,
    122, 134, 148, 150, 151, 153,
    156, 160, 167, 168, 175
Podcasts, 10, 14–16, 21, 23,
    113, 114
Positive psychology, 10, 11
Posttraumatic stress disorder
    (PTSD), 2, 27, 30, 37, 43, 89,
    116, 118, 129, 130, 133, 137
Pro sites
    pro-anorexia, 48
    pro-bulimia, 48
PsychCentral, 11
Psychologists, 20, 21, 131

Q

Quantum, 175

R

REBT-based games, 139
Reminiscence therapy, 137
Resilience, 1, 8, 98–103
Restriction, 2, 3, 8, 23, 28–31, 77,
    98, 99, 119, 122
Revenge porn, 88
Risk
    conduct-related risk, 90–92
    contact-related risk, 90, 91

content-related risk, 90–91
risky behavior, 69–71
Role Playing Games (RPGs), 141
Runescape, 158, 171–173

S

Sadness, 93
Scottish Government, 101
Second Life, 149
Self-diagnosis, 3, 36–38
Self-esteem, 19, 20, 38, 69, 70, 75
Serious games, 138–140
Sexual minorities, *see* Gay, lesbian,
    bisexual, trans, queer/
    questioning plus (GLBTQ+)
Sexual orientation, *see* Gay, lesbian,
    bisexual, trans, queer/
    questioning plus (GLBTQ+)
Skype, 41, 45, 76, 120
Slack, 120
Smartphone, 4, 7, 16, 20, 23, 31,
    32, 60, 73, 101
Snapchat, 3, 60
Social anxiety, 93, 136
Social media, 3–5, 7, 13, 18–23, 51,
    52, 59–79, 89, 93, 95, 99,
    101, 103, 109, 111, 113–119,
    129, 133, 134, 148, 150–154,
    160–161, 168
Solipsistic introjection, 150–152
SPARKS, 140
Suicide
    suicidal behaviors, 27, 133
    prevention, 133–134
Supervised machine learning
    (SML), 129
Synchronous chat, 45

T

Talkspace.com, 32
TED Talks, 10, 153
Tele-mental health, 29–35
Telenor group, 86
Text messages, 10, 117, 169
Therachat, 131
TikTok, 3, 18–20, 22, 60, 68, 70, 114
Toxic groups (online), 47–50
Trolls, 22, 44, 100
Tweet-ups, 65
Twitter, 3, 18, 60, 66–68, 77, 119, 148

U

Unsupervised machine learning
(UML), 129

V

Verywellmind.com, 10
Veterans, 43
Virtual impingement, 50
Virtual Reality (VR), 4, 87,
127–142, 149, 170, 173–175

W

Webinars, 10
Website manner, 29

Websites, 3, 10–13, 20, 23, 29,
35, 38, 44, 51, 73,
91, 99, 111–114,
139–141, 160
WhatsApp, 3, 18, 60
Woebot, 131
Working Alliance Inventory
(WAI), 32
Workplace, 29, 93, 94, 96–97,
102, 138
World Health Organization
(WHO), 1, 111
Wysa, 131

Y

Young people/youth
disabled, 72, 74
gay, lesbian, bisexual, trans, queer/
questioning plus
(GLBTQ+), 95
homeless, 72–74
YouTube, 3, 10, 13, 18,
19, 91, 134

Z

Zoom, 4, 41, 42, 45, 46, 76,
120–122, 174
fatigue, 109–123

Printed in the United States
by Baker & Taylor Publisher Services